William Michael Rossetti, Dante Gabriel Rossetti

Dante and his Circle

With the Italian Poets Preceding him

William Michael Rossetti, Dante Gabriel Rossetti

Dante and his Circle
With the Italian Poets Preceding him

ISBN/EAN: 9783744769129

Printed in Europe, USA, Canada, Australia, Japan

Cover: Foto ©ninafisch / pixelio.de

More available books at **www.hansebooks.com**

DANTE AND HIS CIRCLE

WITH THE ITALIAN POETS PRECEDING HIM

(1100—1200—1300)

A COLLECTION OF LYRICS

TRANSLATED IN THE ORIGINAL METRES BY

DANTE GABRIEL ROSSETTI

PART I.
DANTE'S VITA NUOVA, ETC.
POETS OF DANTE'S CIRCLE

PART II.
POETS CHIEFLY BEFORE DANTE

A NEW EDITION
WITH PREFACE BY
WILLIAM M. ROSSETTI

ELLIS AND ELVEY
LONDON
1892

PRINTED BY
HAZELL, WATSON, AND VINEY, LD.,
LONDON AND AYLESBURY.

PREFACE

TO THE PRESENT EDITION.

D ANTE GABRIEL ROSSETTI published in 1861 his book *The Early Italian Poets*, which is the first form of the present book named *Dante and his Circle*. Ever since its first publication this series of translations has occupied, I think, a somewhat peculiar position; partly as being the only form in which a large portion of the poems here treated are available for English readers; and partly because the Italian compositions have so special a character of their own, and the translator has entered so keenly into their spirit, and has reinforced this with so manifest a poetic tone and savour proper to himself, that the versions have taken rank as a sort of cross between translated and original work. They have been accepted as bringing the English reader as close to the mediæval Italians as he is ever likely to be brought; and also as introducing him to the tone and quality of Rossetti's own mind and hand in poetic production. While they serve as a kind of epilogue to the Italian *trecento*, they serve likewise as a kind of prologue to Rossetti's personality among English poets. If he had not undertaken the translations, and had not given them the development which they here assume, some substantial traits in his own poetry would be less intelligibly marked and less securely recognisable.

In the *Collected Works of Dante Gabriel Rossetti*, published under my editorship in two volumes at the end of 1886, *Dante and his Circle* occupies the greater part of the second volume. The original poems occupy in like manner the greater part of the first volume. These latter were reprinted in a separate form in 1890 ; and it is now thought that there may perhaps be room for a similar separate form of *Dante and his Circle*. Any person who may possess these two works in this state of reissue will be entitled to say that he owns the great bulk of the writings upon which the literary reputation of Rossetti depends; though it is a fact that the *Collected Works* comprise in addition a considerable variety of other writings, chiefly in prose, which require to be taken into account by any such readers as are disposed for an accurate or complete study of him.

In my Preface to the *Collected Works* I have given a few details, which I shall here slightly amplify, regarding *Dante and his Circle*. Our father, Gabriele Rossetti, was a native of Vasto, in the Abruzzi. Being exiled from his own country in consequence of having taken a part in the liberal movement which led to the short-lived Neapolitan constitution of 1820-21, he settled in London towards 1824; and at once immersed himself in Dantesque studies. Of these the principal results were four books : the *Inferno* of Dante, with a *Comento Analitico*, 1826; *Sullo Spirito Antipapale che produsse la Riforma*, 1832 ; *Il Mistero dell' Amor Platonico del Medio Evo*, 1840 ; and *La Beatrice di Dante*, 1842. In all these works the dominant conception is that Dante, and other writers his contemporaries or successors, were religious and political reformers, leagued together in a secret society having some substantial analogy to free-masonry; and that their writings have an esoteric signi-ficance and value highly different and divergent from their exoteric meaning. Whether he was right or wrong in this view I shall in no wise debate; but will affirm that he was at any rate ingenious, subtle, and laboriously diligent. Dante Gabriel Rossetti, who was born in London in May 1828, and who from his earliest years spoke Italian with our father just as he spoke English with other people, was thus breathing a Dantesque intellectual atmosphere as soon as his perceptions began to expand to any matters of the mind. Never-theless he did not, in the years of childhood or of early boyhood, take any particular interest in Dante—this may have begun towards the year 1843, soon after he had left school, and commenced study as a painter : neither did he at any time show the least tendency to-wards adopting, or even towards scrutinising, the alle-gorical, non-natural, or abstruse interpretations which our father put upon Dante and the Italian Mediæval and Renaissance writers. To the younger Rossetti the interest of Dante was the interest of his poetry and his sentiment : he was quite inclined to take it on trust that Dante truly meant what he plainly—or sometimes what he not very plainly, yet still apparently and osten-sibly—said. Having once rallied with ardent zest to the great Florentine, he pursued the study of that line of poetic literature, as represented by Cavalcanti, Cino da Pistoja, and other writers who figure in the present volume; and from reading he soon went on to translating. To the best of my recollection, the great majority of these translations must have been executed in the years 1846 to 1848 ; some of them may be even a little earlier, others probably as late as 1850, but I should say very few belong to any date subsequent to that. He found his materials partly at home, and partly in the library of the British Museum, which he haunted with much assiduity for the purpose. After completing his version of the *Vita Nuova*—which was probably neither the first nor the last of the translations—he projected bringing it out with etched illustrations from designs of his own ; for meanwhile he was producing, in his profession as a painter, several water-colour and other illustrations of the kind. This project, however, fell through, from want of time and lack of opportunity or encouragement ; and finally, early in 1861, the volume of *The Early Italian Poets* was published without any illustrations by Messrs. Smith & Elder—Mr. Ruskin, with his usual liberality, coming forward to advance or guarantee the requisite funds. As to the relation between *The Early Italian Poets*, issued in 1861, and *Dante and his Circle*, issued by Messrs. Ellis & White in 1874, the Prefaces written by my brother may be consulted for any necessary details. The only other scheme of Italian translation which he ever seriously entertained applied to the poems of Michelangelo Buonarroti. Towards 1873 he re-studied these poems, and was greatly bent upon turning them into English : but after all he did not carry out, nor I think did he ever begin, this work.

WM. M. ROSSETTI.

LONDON, *February* 1892.

DANTE AND HIS CIRCLE:

WITH THE ITALIAN POETS PRECEDING HIM.

(1100—1200—1300.)

A COLLECTION OF LYRICS.

TRANSLATED IN THE ORIGINAL METRES.

PART I.
DANTE'S VITA NUOVA, etc.
POETS OF DANTE'S CIRCLE.

PART II.
POETS CHIEFLY BEFORE DANTE.

TO MY MOTHER

I DEDICATE THIS NEW EDITION

OF A BOOK PRIZED BY HER LOVE.

Advertisement to the Edition of 1874.

In re-entitling and re-arranging this book (originally published in 1861 as *The Early Italian Poets,*) my object has been to make more evident at a first glance its important relation to Dante. The *Vita Nuova,* together with the many among Dante's lyrics and those of his contemporaries which elucidate their personal intercourse, are here assembled, and brought to my best ability into clear connection, in a manner not elsewhere attempted even by Italian or German editors.

Preface to the First Edition
(1861).

———————————

I NEED not dilate here on the characteristics of the first epoch of Italian Poetry; since the extent of my translated selections is sufficient to afford a complete view of it. Its great beauties may often remain unapproached in the versions here attempted; but, at the same time, its imperfections are not all to be charged to the translator. Among these I may refer to its limited range of subject and continual obscurity, as well as to its monotony in the use of rhymes or frequent substitution of assonances. But to compensate for much that is incomplete and inexperienced, these poems possess, in their degree, beauties of a kind which can never again exist in art; and offer, besides, a treasure of grace and variety in the formation of their metres. Nothing but a strong impression, first of their poetic value, and next of the biographical interest of some of them (chiefly of those in my first division), would have inclined me to bestow the time and trouble which have resulted in this collection.

Much has been said, and in many respects justly, against the value of metrical translation. But I think it would be admitted that the tributary art might find a not illegitimate use in the case of poems which come down to us in such a form as do these early Italian ones. Struggling originally with corrupt dialect and imperfect expression, and hardly kept alive through centuries of neglect, they have reached that last and worst state in which the *coup-de-grâce* has almost been dealt them by clumsy transcription and pedantic super-structure. At this stage the task of talking much more about them in any language is hardly to be entered upon ; and a translation (involving as it does the necessity of settling many points without discussion,) remains perhaps the most direct form of commentary.

The life-blood of rhythmical translation is this commandment,—that a good poem shall not be turned into a bad one. The only true motive for putting poetry into a fresh language must be to endow a fresh nation, as far as possible, with one more possession of beauty. Poetry not being an exact science, literality of rendering is altogether secondary to this chief law. I say *literality*,—not fidelity, which is by no means the same thing. When literality can be combined with what is thus the primary condition of success, the translator is fortunate, and must strive his utmost to unite them ; when such object can only be attained by paraphrase, that is his only path.

Any merit possessed by these translations is derived from an effort to follow this principle ; and, in some degree, from the fact that such painstaking in arrangement and descriptive heading as is often indispensable to old and especially to "occasional" poetry, has here been bestowed on these poets for the first time.

That there are many defects in this collection, or that the above merit is its defect, or that it has no merits but only defects, are discoveries so sure to be made if necessary (or perhaps here and there in any case), that I may safely leave them in other hands. The series has probably a wider scope than some readers might look for, and includes now and then (though I believe in rare instances) matter which may not meet with universal approval; and whose introduction, needed as it is by the literary aim of my work, is I know inconsistent with the principles of pretty bookmaking. My wish has been to give a full and truthful view of early Italian poetry; not to make it appear to consist only of certain elements to the exclusion of others equally belonging to it.

Of the difficulties I have had to encounter,—the causes of imperfections for which I have no other excuse,—it is the reader's best privilege to remain ignorant; but I may perhaps be pardoned for briefly referring to such among these as concern the exigencies of translation. The task of the translator (and with all humility be it spoken) is one of some self-denial. Often would he avail himself of any special grace of his own idiom and epoch, if only his will belonged to him: often would some cadence serve him but for his author's structure—some structure but for his author's cadence: often the beautiful turn of a stanza must be weakened to adopt some rhyme which will tally, and he sees the poet revelling in abundance of language where himself is scantily supplied. Now he would slight the matter for the music, and now the music for the matter ; but no,—he must deal to each alike. Some-times too a flaw in the work galls him, and he would fain remove it, doing for the poet that which his age denied him ; but no,—it is not in the bond. His path is like that of Aladdin through the enchanted vaults : many are the precious fruits and flowers which he must pass by unheeded in search for the lamp alone ; happy if at last, when brought to light, it does not prove that his old lamp has been exchanged for a new one, —glittering indeed to the eye, but scarcely of the same virtue nor with the same genius at its summons.

In relinquishing this work (which, small as it is, is the only contribution I expect to make to our English knowledge of old Italy), I feel, as it were, divided from my youth. The first associations I have are connected with my father's devoted studies, which, from his own point of view, have done so much towards the general investigation of Dante's writings. Thus, in those early days, all around me partook of the influence of the great Florentine ; till, from viewing it as a natural element, I also, growing older, was drawn within the circle. I trust that from this the reader may place more confidence in a work not carelessly undertaken, though produced in the spare-time of other pursuits more closely followed. He should perhaps be told that it has occupied the leisure moments of not a few years ; thus affording, often at long intervals, every opportunity for consideration and revision ; and that on the score of care, at least, he has no need to mistrust it. Nevertheless, I know there is no great stir to be made by launching afresh, on high-seas busy with new traffic, the ships which have been long outstripped and the ensigns which are grown strange.

It may be well to conclude this short preface with a list of the works which have chiefly contributed to the materials of the present volume. An array of modern editions hardly looks so imposing as might a reference to Allacci, Crescimbeni, etc. ; but these older collections would be found less accessible, and all they contain has been reprinted.

I. Poeti del primo secolo della Lingua Italiana. 2 vol. (Firenze. 1816.)

II. Raccolta di Rime antiche Toscane. 4 vol. (Palermo. 1817.)

III. Manuale della Letteratura del primo Secolo, del Prof. V. Nannucci. 3 vol. (Firenze. 1843.)

IV. Poesie Italiane inedite di Dugento Autori : raccolte da Francesco Trucchi. 4 vol. (Prato. 1846.)

V. Opere Minori di Dante. Edizione di P. I. Fra-ticelli. (Firenze. 1843, etc.)

VI. Rime di Guido Cavalcanti; raccolte da A. Cicciaporci. (Firenze. 1813.)

VII. Vita e Poesie di Messer Cino da Pistoia. Edizione di S. Ciampi. (Pisa. 1813.)

VIII. Documenti d'Amore ; di Francesco da Barbe-rino. Annotati da F. Ubaldini. (Roma. 1640.)

IX. Del Reggimento e dei Costumi delle Donne; di Francesco da Barberino. (Roma. 1815.)

X. Il Dittamondo di Fazio degli Uberti. (Milano. 1826.)

CONTENTS.

PART I. DANTE AND HIS CIRCLE.

CONTENTS.

APPENDIX TO PART I.

PART II.   POETS CHIEFLY BEFORE DANTE.

INDEX OF FIRST LINES.

(*ENGLISH AND ITALIAN.*)

DANTE AND HIS CIRCLE.

INTRODUCTION TO PART I.

IN the first division of this volume are included all the poems I could find which seemed to have value as being personal to the circle of Dante's friends, and as illustrating their intercourse with each other. Those who know the Italian collections from which I have drawn these pieces (many of them most obscure) will perceive how much which is in fact elucidation is here attempted to be embodied in themselves, as to their rendering, arrangement, and heading : since the Italian editors have never yet paid any of them, except of course those by Dante, any such attention ; but have printed and reprinted them in a jumbled and dishearten-ing form, by which they can serve little purpose except as *testi di lingua*—dead stock by whose help the makers of dictionaries may smother the language with decayed words. Appearing now I believe for the first time in print, though in a new idiom, from their once living writers to such living readers as they may find, they require some preliminary notice.

The *Vita Nuova* (the Autobiography or Autopsycho-logy of Dante's youth till about his twenty-seventh year) is already well known to many in the original, or by means of essays and of English versions partial or entire. It is, therefore, and on all accounts, unnecessary to say

much more of the work here than it says for itself.
Wedded to its exquisite and intimate beauties are per-
sonal peculiarities which excite wonder and conjecture,
best replied to in the words which Beatrice herself is
made to utter in the *Commedia:* " Questi *fu tal* nella sua
vita nuova."* Thus then young Dante *was*. All that
seemed possible to be done here for the work was to
translate it in as free and clear a form as was consistent
with fidelity to its meaning ; to ease it, as far as possible,
from notes and encumbrances ; and to accompany it for
the first time with those poems from Dante's own lyrical
series which have reference to its events, as well as with
such native commentary (so to speak) as might be
afforded by the writings of those with whom its author
was at that time in familiar intercourse. Not chiefly to
Dante, then, of whom so much is known to all or may
readily be found written, but to the various other mem-
bers of his circle, these few pages should be devoted.

It may be noted here, however, how necessary a
knowledge of the *Vita Nuova* is to the full comprehen-
sion of the part borne by Beatrice in the *Commedia*.
Moreover, it is only from the perusal of its earliest and
then undivulged self-communings that we can divine the
whole bitterness of wrong to such a soul as Dante's, its
poignant sense of abandonment, or its deep and jealous
refuge in memory. Above all, it is here that we find the
first manifestations of that wisdom of obedience, that
natural breath of duty, which afterwards, in the *Com-
media*, lifted up a mighty voice for warning and testi-
mony. Throughout the *Vita Nuova* there is a strain like
the first falling murmur which reaches the ear in some
remote meadow, and prepares us to look upon the sea.

Boccaccio, in his Life of Dante, tells us that the great
poet, in later life, was ashamed of this work of his
youth. Such a statement hardly seems reconcilable with
the allusions to it made or implied in the *Commedia ;*

---

* Purgatorio, C. xxx.

but it is true that the *Vita Nuova* is a book which only youth could have produced, and which must chiefly remain sacred to the young; to each of whom the figure of Beatrice, less lifelike than lovelike, will seem the friend of his own heart. Nor is this, perhaps, its least praise. To tax its author with effeminacy on account of the extreme sensitiveness evinced by this narrative of his love, would be manifestly unjust, when we find that, though love alone is the theme of the *Vita Nuova*, war already ranked among its author's experiences at the period to which it relates. In the year 1289, the one preceding the death of Beatrice, Dante served with the foremost cavalry in the great battle of Campaldino, on the eleventh of June, when the Florentines defeated the people of Arezzo. In the autumn of the next year, 1290, when for him, by the death of Beatrice, the city as he says " sat solitary," such refuge as he might find from his grief was sought in action and danger : for we learn from the *Commedia* (Hell, C. xxi.) that he served in the war then waged by Florence upon Pisa, and was present at the surrender of Caprona. He says, using the reminiscence to give life to a description, in his great way :—

' I've seen the troops out of Caprona go
    On terms, affrighted thus, when on the spot
They found themselves with foemen compass'd so."
                (CAYLEY'S *Translation.*)

A word should be said here of the title of Dante's autobiography. The adjective *Nuovo, nuova,* or *Novello, novella,* literally *New,* is often used by Dante and other early writers in the sense of *young.* This has induced some editors of the *Vita Nuova* to explain the title as meaning *Early Life.* I should be glad on some accounts to adopt this supposition, as everything is a gain which increases clearness to the modern reader; but on consideration I think the more mystical interpretation of the words, as *New Life* (in reference to that revulsion of his being which Dante so minutely describes as

having occurred simultaneously with his first sight of
Beatrice), appears the primary one, and therefore the
most necessary to be given in a translation. The pro-
bability may be that both were meant, but this I cannot
convey.*

---

* I must hazard here (to relieve the first page of my translation
from a long note) a suggestion as to the meaning of the most
puzzling passage in the whole *Vita Nuova*,—that sentence just at
the outset which says, "La gloriosa donna della mia mente, la
quale fù chiamata da molti Beatrice, i quali non sapeano che si
chiamare." On this passage all the commentators seem helpless,
turning it about and sometimes adopting alterations not to be
found in any ancient manuscript of the work. The words mean
literally, "The glorious lady of my mind who was called Beatrice
by many who knew not how she was called." This presents the
obvious difficulty that the lady's name really *was* Beatrice, and
that Dante throughout uses that name himself. In the text of my
version I have adopted, as a rendering, the one of the various
compromises which seemed to give the most beauty to the mean-
ing. But it occurs to me that a less irrational escape out of the
difficulty than any I have seen suggested may possibly be found by
linking this passage with the close of the sonnet at page 69 of the
Vita Nuova, beginning, "I felt a spirit of Love begin to stir," in the
last line of which sonnet Love is made to assert that the name of
Beatrice is *Love*. Dante appears to have dwelt on this fancy with
some pleasure, from what is said in an earlier sonnet (page 38)
about "Love in his proper form" (by which Beatrice seems to be
meant) bending over a dead lady. And it is in connection with
the sonnet where the name of Beatrice is said to be Love, that
Dante, as if to show us that the Love he speaks of is only his own
emotion, enters into an argument as to Love being merely an acci-
dent in substance,—in other words, "Amore e il cor gentil son una
cosa." This conjecture may be pronounced extravagant; but the
Vita Nuova, when examined, proves so full of intricate and fan-
tastic analogies, even in the mere arrangement of its parts (much
more than appears on any but the closest scrutiny), that it seems
admissible to suggest even a whimsical solution of a difficulty
which remains unconquered. Or to have recourse to the much
more welcome means of solution afforded by simple inherent
beauty: may not the meaning be merely that any person looking
on so noble and lovely a creation, without knowledge of her name,
must have spontaneously called her Beatrice,—*i.e.*, the giver of
blessing? This would be analogous by antithesis to the transla-
tion I have adopted in my text.

Among the poets of Dante's circle, the first in order, the first in power, and the one whom Dante has styled his "first friend," is GUIDO CAVALCANTI, born about 1250, and thus Dante's senior by some fifteen years. It is therefore probable that there is some inaccuracy about the statement, often repeated, that he was Dante's fellow-pupil under Brunetto Latini; though it seems certain that they both studied, probably Guido before Dante, with the same teacher. The Cavalcanti family was among the most ancient in Florence; and its importance may be judged by the fact that in 1280, on the occasion of one of the various missions sent from Rome with the view of pacifying the Florentine factions, the name of "Guido the son of Messer Cavalcante de' Cavalcanti" appears as one of the sureties offered by the city for the quarter of San Piero Scheraggio. His father must have been notoriously a sceptic in matters of religion, since we find him placed by Dante in the sixth circle of Hell, in one of the fiery tombs of the unbelievers. That Guido shared this heresy was the popular belief, as is plain from an anecdote in Boccaccio which I shall give; and some corroboration of such reports, at any rate as applied to Guido's youth, seems capable of being gathered from an extremely obscure poem, which I have translated on that account (at page 156) as clearly as I found possible. It must be admitted, however, that there is to the full as much devotional as sceptical tendency implied here and there in his writings; while the presence of either is very rare. We may also set against such a charge the fact that Dino Compagni refers, as will be seen, to his having undertaken a religious pilgrimage. But indeed he seems to have been in all things of that fitful and vehement nature which would impress others always strongly, but often in opposite ways. Self-reliant pride gave its colour to all his moods; making his exploits as a soldier frequently abortive through the head-strong ardour of partisanship, and causing the perversity of a logician to prevail in much of his amorous poetry

The writings of his contemporaries, as well as his own, tend to show him rash in war, fickle in love, and presumptuous in belief; but also, by the same concurrent testimony, he was distinguished by great personal beauty, high accomplishments of all kinds, and daring nobility of soul.   Not unworthy, for all the weakness of his strength, to have been the object of Dante's early emulation, the first friend of his youth, and his precursor and fellow-labourer in the creation of Italian Poetry.

In the year 1267, when Guido cannot have been much more than seventeen years of age, a last attempt was made in Florence to reconcile the Guelfs and Ghibellines. With this view several alliances were formed between the leading families of the two factions; and among others, the Guelf Cavalcante de' Cavalcanti wedded his son Guido to a daughter of the Ghibelline Farinata degli Uberti.   The peace was of short duration; the utter expulsion of the Ghibellines (through French intervention solicited by the Guelfs) following almost immediately. In the subdivision, which afterwards took place, of the victorious Guelfs into so-called " Blacks " and "Whites," Guido embraced the White party, which tended strongly to Ghibellinism, and whose chief was Vieri de' Cerchi, while Corso Donati headed the opposite faction.   Whether his wife was still living at the time when the events of the *Vita Nuova* occurred is probably not ascertainable ; but about that time Dante tells us that Guido was enamoured of a lady named *Giovanna* or Joan, and whose Christian name is absolutely all that we know of her. However, on the occasion of his pilgrimage to Thoulouse, recorded by Dino Compagni, he seems to have conceived a fresh passion for a lady of that city named Mandetta, who first attracted him by a striking resemblance to his Florentine mistress.   Thoulouse had become a place of pilgrimage from its laying claim to the possession of the body, or part of the body, of St. James the Greater ; though the same supposed distinction had already made the shrine of Compostella in Galicia one of the most famous throughout all Christendom.   That this devout journey of Guido's had other results besides a new love will be seen by the passage from Compagni's Chronicle. He says :—

"A young and noble knight named Guido, son of Messer Cavalcante Cavalcanti,—full of courage and courtesy, but disdainful, solitary, and devoted to study,—was a foe to Messer Corso (Donati), and had many times cast about to do him hurt. Messer Corso feared him exceedingly, as knowing him to be of a great spirit, and sought to assassinate him on a pilgrimage which Guido made to the shrine of St. James; but he might not compass it. Wherefore, having returned to Florence and being made aware of this, Guido incited many youths against Messer Corso, and these · promised to stand by him. Who being one day on horseback with certain of the house of the Cerchi, and having a javelin in his hand, spurred his horse against Messer Corso, thinking to be followed by the Cerchi that so their companies might engage each other; and he running in on his horse cast the javelin, which missed its aim. And with Messer Corso were Simon, his son, a strong and daring youth, and Cecchino de' Bardi, who with many others pursued Guido with drawn swords; but not overtaking him they threw stones after him, and also others were thrown at him from the windows, whereby he was wounded in the hand. And by this matter hate was increased. And Messer Corso spoke great scorn of Messer Vieri, calling him the Ass of the Gate; because, albeit a very handsome man, he was but of blunt wit and no great speaker. And therefore Messer Corso would say often, 'To-day the Ass of the Gate has brayed,'·and so greatly disparage him; and Guido he called *Cavicchia.** And thus it was spread abroad of the *jongleurs;* and especially one named Scampolino reported worse things than were said, that so the Cerchi might be provoked to engage the Donati."

---

* A nickname chiefly chosen, no doubt, for its resemblance to *Cavalcanti.* The word *cavicchia, cavicchio,* or *caviglia,* means a wooden peg or pin. A passage in Boccaccio says, "He had tied his ass to a strong wooden pin" (*caviglia*). Thus Guido, from his mental superiority, might be said to be the Pin to which the Ass, Messer Vieri, was tethered at the Gate, (that is, the gate of San Pietro, near which he lived). However, it seems quite as likely that the nickname was founded on a popular phrase by which one who fails in any undertaking is said "to run his rear on a peg" (*dare del culo in un cavicchio*). The haughty Corso Donati

The praise which Compagni, his contemporary, awards to Guido at the commencement of the foregoing extract, receives additional value when viewed in connection with the sonnet addressed to him by the same writer (see page 141), where we find that he could tell him of his faults.

Such scenes as the one related above had become common things in Florence, which kept on its course from bad to worse till Pope Boniface VIII. resolved on sending a legate to propose certain amendments in its scheme of government by *Priori*, or representatives of the various arts and companies. These proposals, however, were so ill received, that the legate, who arrived in Florence in the month of June 1300, departed shortly afterwards greatly incensed, leaving the city under a papal interdict. In the ill-considered tumults which ensued we again hear of Guido Cavalcanti.

"It happened" (says Giovanni Villani in his History of Florence) "that in the month of December (1300) Messer Corso Donati with his followers, and also those of the house of the Cerchi and their followers, going armed to the funeral of a lady of the Frescobaldi family, this party defying that by their looks would have assailed the one the other; whereby all those who were at the funeral having risen up tumultuously and fled each to his house, the whole city got under arms, both factions assembling in great numbers, at their respective houses. Messer Gentile de' Cerchi, Guido Cavalcanti, Baldinuccio and Corso Adimari, Baschiero della Tosa and Naldo Gherardini, with their comrades and adherents on horse and on foot, hastened to St. Peter's Gate to the house of the Donati. Not finding them there they went on to San Pier Maggiore, where Messer Corso was with his friends and followers; by whom they were encountered and put to flight, with many wounds and with much shame to the party of the Cerchi and to their adherents."

By this time we may conjecture as probable that Dante, in the arduous position which he then filled as chief of the nine *Priori* on whom the Government of

himself went by the name of *Malefammi* or "Do-me-harm." For an account of his death in 1307, which proved in keeping with his turbulent life, see Dino Compagni's *Chronicle*, or the *Pecorone* of Giovanni Fiorentin (Gior. xxiv. Nov. 2).

Florence devolved, had resigned for far other cares the sweet intercourse of thought and poetry which he once held with that first friend of his who had now become so factious a citizen. Yet it is impossible to say how much of the old feeling may still have survived in Dante's mind when, at the close of the year 1300 or beginning of 1301, it became his duty, as a faithful magistrate of the republic, to add his voice to those of his colleagues in pronouncing a sentence of banishment on the heads of both the Black and White factions, Guido Cavalcanti being included among the latter. The Florentines had been at last provoked almost to demand this course from their governors, by the discovery of a conspiracy, at the head of which was Corso Donati (while among its leading members was Simone de' Bardi, once the husband of Beatrice Portinari), for the purpose of inducing the Pope to subject the republic to a French peace-maker (*Paciere*), and so shamefully free it from its intestine broils. It appears therefore that the immediate cause of the exile to which both sides were subjected lay entirely with the "Black" party, the leaders of which were banished to the Castello della Pieve in the wild district of Massa Traberia, while those of the "White" faction were sent to Sarzana, probably (for more than one place bears the name) in the Genovesato. "But this party" (writes Villani) "remained a less time in exile, being recalled on account of the unhealthiness of the place, which made that Guido Cavalcanti returned with a sickness, whereof he died. And of him was a great loss; seeing that he was a man, as in philosophy, so in many things deeply versed; but therewithal too fastidious and prone to take offence."* His death apparently took place in 1301.

When the discords of Florence ceased, for Guido, in death, Dante also had seen their native city for the last

---

* "Troppo tenero e stizzoso." I judge that "tenero" here is rather to be interpreted as above than as meaning "impressionable" in love affairs, but cannot be certain.

time. Before Guido's return he had undertaken that
embassy to Rome which bore him the bitter fruit of un-
just and perpetual exile : and it will be remembered that
a chief accusation against him was that of favour shown
to the White party on the banishment of the factions.

Besides the various affectionate allusions to Guido in
the *Vita Nuova*, Dante has unmistakably referred to
him in at least two passages of the *Commedia*. One of
these references is to be found in those famous lines of
the Purgatory (C. xi.) where he awards him the palm of
poetry over Guido Guinicelli (though also of the latter he
speaks elsewhere with high praise), and implies at the
same time, it would seem, a consciousness of his own
supremacy over both.

> "Against all painters Cimabue thought
>   To keep the field.   Now Giotto has the cry,
> And so the fame o' the first wanes nigh to nought.
>   Thus one from other Guido took the high
> Glory of language; and perhaps is born
>   He who from both shall bear it by-and-bye."

The other mention of Guido is in that pathetic passage
of the Hell (C. x.) where Dante meets among the lost
souls Cavalcante de' Cavalcanti :—

> "All roundabout he looked, as though he had
>   Desire to see if one was with me else.
>   But after his surmise was all extinct,
> He weeping said : 'If through this dungeon blind
>   Thou goest by loftiness of intellect,—
>   Where is my son, and wherefore not with thee?'
> And I to him : 'Of myself come I not :
>   He who there waiteth leads me thoro' here,
>   Whom haply in disdain your Guido had.'*
>   *   *   *   *
> Raised upright of a sudden, cried he : 'How
>   Didst say *He had?*   Is he not living still?

---

* Virgil, Dante's guide through Hell. Any prejudice which
Guido entertained against Virgil depended, no doubt, only on his
strong desire to see the Latin language give place, in poetry and
literature, to a perfected Italian idiom.

> Doth not the sweet light strike upon his eyes?'
> When he perceived a certain hesitance
> Which I was making ere I should reply,
> He fell supine, and forth appeared no more."

Dante, however, conveys his answer afterwards to the spirit of Guido's father, through another of the condemned also related to Guido, Farinata degli Uberti, with whom he has been speaking meanwhile :—

> "Then I, as in compunction for my fault,
> Said : 'Now then shall ye tell that fallen one
> His son is still united with the quick.
> And, if I erst was dumb to the response,
> I did it, make him know, because I thought
> Yet on the error you have solved for me.' "
> (W. M. ROSSETTI's Translation.)

The date which Dante fixes for his vision is Good Friday of the year 1300. A year later, his answer must have been different. The love and friendship of his *Vita Nuova* had then both left him. For ten years Beatrice Portinari had been dead, or (as Dante says in the *Convito*) "lived in heaven with the angels and on earth with his soul." And now, distant and probably estranged from him, Guido Cavalcanti was gone too.

Among the Tales of Franco Sacchetti, and in the Decameron of Boccaccio, are two anecdotes relating to Guido. Sacchetti tells us how, one day that he was intent on a game at chess, Guido (who is described as "one who perhaps had not his equal in Florence") was disturbed by a child playing about, and threatened punishment if the noise continued. The child, however, managed slily to nail Guido's coat to the chair on which he sat, and so had the laugh against him when he rose soon afterwards to fulfil his threat. This may serve as an amusing instance of Guido's hasty temper, but is rather a disappointment after its magniloquent heading, which sets forth how "Guido Cavalcanti, being a man of great valour and a philosopher, is defeated by the cunning of a child."

The ninth Tale of the sixth Day of the Decameron relates a repartee of Guido's, which has all the profound platitude of mediæval wit. As the anecdote, however, is interesting on other grounds, I translate it here.

"You must know that in past times there were in our city certain goodly and praiseworthy customs no one of which is now left, thanks to avarice, which has so increased with riches that it has driven them all away. Among the which was one whereby the gentlemen of the outskirts were wont to assemble together in divers places throughout Florence, and to limit their fellowships to a certain number, having heed to compose them of such as could fitly discharge the expense. Of whom to-day one, and to-morrow another, and so all in turn, laid tables each on his own day for all the fellowship. And in such wise often they did honour to strangers of worship and also to citizens. They all dressed alike at least once in the year, and the most notable among them rode together through the city; also at seasons they held passages of arms, and specially on the principal feast-days, or whenever any news of victory or other glad tidings had reached the city. And among these fellowships was one headed by Messer Betto Brunelleschi, into the which Messer Betto and his companions had often intrigued to draw Guido di Messer Cavalcante de' Cavalcanti; and this not without cause, seeing that not only he was one of the best logicians that the world held, and a surpassing natural philosopher (for the which things the fellowship cared little), but also he exceeded in beauty and courtesy, and was of great gifts as a speaker; and everything that it pleased him to do, and that best became a gentleman, he did better than any other; and was exceeding rich and knew well to solicit with honourable words whomsoever he deemed worthy. But Messer Betto had never been able to succeed in enlisting him; and he and his companions believed that this was through Guido's much pondering which divided him from other men. Also because he held somewhat of the opinion of the Epicureans, it was said among the vulgar sort that his speculations were only to cast about whether he might find that there was no God. Now on a certain day Guido having left Or San Michele, and held along the Corso degli Adimari as far as San Giovanni (which oftentimes was his walk); and coming to the great marble tombs which now are in the Church of Santa Reparata, but were then with many others in San Giovanni; he being between the porphyry columns which are there among those tombs, and the gate of San Giovanni which was locked;—it so chanced that Messer Betto and his fellowship came riding up by the Piazza di Santa Reparata, and seeing Guido among the sepulchres, said, 'Let us go and engage him.' Whereupon, spurring their horses in the fashion of a pleasant assault, they were on him almost before he was aware, ånd began to say to him, 'Thou, Guido, wilt none of our fellowship; but lo now! when thou shalt have found that there is no God, what wilt thou have done?' To whom Guido, seeing himself hemmed in among them, readily replied, 'Gentlemen, ye are at home here, and may say what ye please to me.' Wherewith, setting his hand on one of those high tombs, being very light of his person, he took a leap and was over on the other side; and so having freed himself from them, went his way. And they all remained bewildered, looking on one another; and began to say that he was but a shallow-witted fellow, and that the answer he had made was as though one should say nothing; seeing that where they were, they had not more to do than other citizens, and Guido not less than they. To whom Messer Betto turned and said thus: 'Ye yourselves are shallow-witted if ye have not understood him. He has civilly and in a few words said to us the most uncivil thing in the world; for if ye look well to it, these tombs are the homes of the dead, seeing that in them the dead are set to dwell; and here he says that we are at home; giving us to know that we and all other simple unlettered men, in comparison of him and the learned, are even as dead men; wherefore, being here, we are at home.' Thereupon each of them understood what Guido had meant, and was ashamed; nor ever again did they set themselves to engage him. Also from that day forth they held Messer Betto to be a subtle and understanding knight."

In the above story mention is made of Guido Cavalcanti's wealth, and there seems no doubt that at that time the family was very rich and powerful. On this account I am disposed to question whether the Canzone at page 154 (where the author speaks of his poverty) can really be Guido's work, though I have included it as being interesting if rightly attributed to him; and it is possible that, when exiled, he may have suffered for the time in purse as well as person. About three years after his death, on the 10th June, 1304, the Black party plotted together and set fire to the quarter of Florence chiefly ·held by their adversaries. In this conflagration the houses and possessions of the Cavalcanti were almost entirely destroyed; the flames in that neighbourhood (as Dino Compagni records) gaining rapidly in consequence of the great number of waxen images in the Virgin's shrine at Or San Michele; one of which, no doubt, was the very image resembling his lady to which Guido refers in a sonnet (see page 121). After this, their enemies succeeded in finally expelling from Florence the Cavalcanti family,* greatly impoverished by this monstrous fire, in which nearly two thousand houses were consumed.

Guido appears, by various evidence, to have written, besides his poems, a treatise on Philosophy and another on Oratory, but his poems only have survived to our day. As a poet, he has more individual life of his own than belongs to any of his predecessors; by far the best of his pieces being those which relate to himself, his loves and hates. The best known, however, and perhaps the one for whose sake the rest have been preserved, is the metaphysical canzone on the Nature of Love, beginning "Donna mi priega," and intended, it is said, as an answer to a sonnet by Guido Orlandi, written as though coming from a lady, and beginning, "Onde si muove e donde nasce Amore?" On this canzone of Guido's there are known to exist no fewer than eight commentaries, some of them very elaborate, and written by prominent learned men of the middle ages and *renaissance;* the earliest being that by Egidio Colonna, a beatified churchman who died in 1316; while most of the too numerous Academic writers on Italian literature speak of this performance with great admiration as Guido's crowning work. A love-song which acts as such a fly-catcher for priests and pedants looks very suspi-

---

* With them were expelled the still more powerful Gherardini, also great sufferers by the conflagration; who, on being driven from their own country, became the founders of the ancient Geraldine family in Ireland. The Cavalcanti reappear now and then in later European history; and especially we hear of a second Guido Cavalcanti, who also cultivated poetry, and travelled to collect books for the Ambrosian Library; and who, in 1563, visited England as Ambassador to the court of Elizabeth from Charles IX. of France.

cious ; and accordingly, on examination, it proves to be
a poem beside the purpose of poetry, filled with meta-
physical jargon, and perhaps the very worst of Guido's
productions. Its having been written by a man whose
life and works include so much that is impulsive and
real, is easily accounted for by scholastic pride in those
early days of learning. I have not translated it, as being
of little true interest ; but was pleased lately, neverthe-
less, to meet with a remarkably complete translation of
it by the Rev. Charles T. Brooks, of Cambridge, United
States.* The stiffness and cold conceits which prevail
in this poem may be found disfiguring much of what
Guido Cavalcanti has left, while much besides is blunt,
obscure, and abrupt: nevertheless, if it need hardly be
said how far he falls short of Dante in variety and per-
sonal directness, it may be admitted that he worked
worthily at his side, and perhaps before him, in adding
those qualities to Italian poetry. That Guido's poems
dwelt in the mind of Dante is evident by his having
appropriated lines from them (as well as from those of
Guinicelli) with little alteration, more than once, in the
Commedia.

Towards the close of his life, Dante, in his Latin
treatise *De Vulgari Eloquio*, again speaks of himself as
the friend of a poet,—this time of CINO DA PISTOIA. In
an early passage of that work he says that "those who
have most sweetly and subtly written poems in modern
Italian are Cino da Pistoia and a friend of his." This
friend we afterwards find to be Dante himself; as among
the various poetical examples quoted are several by
Cino followed in three instances by lines from Dante's

---

* This translation occurs in the Appendix to an Essay on the
Vita Nuova of Dante, including extracts, by my friend Mr. Charles
E. Norton, of Cambridge, U.S.,—a work of high delicacy and ap-
preciation, which originally appeared by portions in the *Atlantic
Monthly*, but has since been augmented by the author and pri-
vately printed in a volume which is a beautiful specimen of
American typography.

own lyrics, the author of the latter being again described merely as "Amicus ejus." In immediate proximity to these, or coupled in two instances with examples from Dante alone, are various quotations taken from Guido Cavalcanti ; but in none of these cases is anything said to connect Dante with him who was once " the first of his friends."* As commonly between old and new, the change of Guido's friendship for Cino's seems doubtful gain. Cino's poetry, like his career, is for the most part smoother than that of Guido, and in some instances it rises into truth and warmth of expression : but it conveys no idea of such powers, for life or for work, as seem to have distinguished the " Cavicchia" of Messer Corso Donati. However, his one talent (reversing the parable) appears generally to be made the most of, while Guido's two or three remain uncertain through the· manner of their use.

Cino's Canzone addressed to Dante on the death of Beatrice, as well as his answer to the first sonnet of the *Vita Nuova,* indicate that the two poets must have become

---

* It is also noticeable that in this treatise Dante speaks of Guido Guinicelli on one occasion as *Guido Maximus*, thus seeming to contradict the preference of Cavalcanti which is usually supposed to be implied in the passage I have quoted from the Purgatory. It has been sometimes surmised (perhaps for this reason) that the two Guidos there spoken of may be Guittone d'Arezzo and Guido Guinicelli, the latter being said to surpass the former, of whom Dante elsewhere in the Purgatory has expressed a low opinion. But I should think it doubtful whether the name Guittone, which (if not a nickname, as some say) is substantially the same as Guido, could be so absolutely identified with ·it : at that rate Cino da Pistoia even might be classed as one Guido, his full name, Guittoncino, being the diminutive of Guittone. I believe it more probable that Guinicelli and Cavalcanti were then really meant, and that Dante afterwards either altered his opinion, or may (conjecturably) have chosen to imply a change of preference in order to gratify Cino da Pistoia, whom he so markedly distinguishes as his friend throughout the treatise, and between whom and Cavalcanti some jealousy appears to have existed, as we may gather from one of Cino's sonnets (at page 175) ; nor is Guido mentioned anywhere with praise by Cino, as other poets are.

acquainted in youth, though there is no earlier mention of Cino in Dante's writings than those which occur in his treatise on the Vulgar Tongue. It might perhaps be inferred with some plausibility that their acquaintance was revived after an interruption by the sonnet and answer at pages 110-111, and that they afterwards corresponded as friends till the period of Dante's death, when Cino wrote his elegy. Of the two sonnets in which Cino expresses disapprobation of what he thinks the partial judgments of Dante's *Commedia*, the first seems written before the great poet's death, but I should think that the second dated after that event, as the *Paradise*, to which it refers, cannot have become fully known in its author's lifetime. Another sonnet sent to Dante elicited a Latin epistle in reply, where we find Cino addressed as "frater carissime." Among Cino's lyrical poems are a few more written in correspondence with Dante, which I have not translated as being of little personal interest.

Guittoncino de' Sinibuldi (for such was Cino's full name) was born in Pistoia, of a distinguished family, in the year 1270. He devoted himself early to the study of law, and in 1307 was Assessor of Civil Causes in his native city. In this year, and in Pistoia, first cradle of the "Black" and "White" factions, their endless contest again sprang into activity ; the "Blacks" and Guelfs of Florence and Lucca driving out the "Whites" and Ghibellines, who had ruled in the city since 1300. With their accession to power came many iniquitous laws in favour of their own party ; so that Cino, as a lawyer of Ghibelline opinions, soon found it necessary or advisable to leave Pistoia, for it seems uncertain whether his removal was voluntary or by proscription. He directed his course towards Lombardy, on whose confines the chief of the "White" party, in Pistoia, Filippo Vergiolesi, still held the fortress of Pitecchio. Hither Vergiolesi had retreated with his family and adherents when resistance in the city became no longer possible ; and it may be supposed that Cino came to join him, not

2

on account of political sympathy alone; as Selvaggia
Vergiolesi, his daughter, is the lady celebrated through-
out the poet's compositions.   Three years later, the
Vergiolesi and their followers, finding Pitecchio unten-
able, fortified themselves on the Monte della Sambuca,
a lofty peak on the Apennines; which again they were
finally obliged to abandon, yielding it to the Guelfs of
Pistoia at the price of eleven thousand *lire*.   Meanwhile
the bleak air of the Sambuca had proved fatal to the
lady Selvaggia, who remained buried there, or, as Cino
expresses it in one of his poems,

"Cast out upon the steep path of the mountains,
  Where Death had shut her in between hard stones."

Over her cheerless tomb Cino bent and mourned, as
he has told us, when, after a prolonged absence spent
partly in France, he returned through Tuscany on his
way to Rome.   He had not been with Selvaggia's family
at the time of her death; and it is probable that, on his
return to the Sambuca, the fortress was already sur-
rendered, and her grave almost the only record left
there of the Vergiolesi.

Cino's journey to Rome was on account of his having
received a high office under Louis of Savoy, who pre-
ceded the Emperor Henry VII. when he went thither to
be crowned in 1310.   In another three years the last
blow was dealt to the hopes of the exiled and persecuted
Ghibellines, by the death of the Emperor, caused almost
surely by poison.   This death Cino has lamented in a
canzone.   It probably determined him to abandon a
cause which seemed dead, and return, when possible, to
his native city.   This he succeeded in doing before 1319,
as in that year we find him deputed, together with six
other citizens, by the Government of Pistoia to take
possession of a stronghold recently yielded to them.
He had now been for some time married to Margherita
degli Ughi, of a very noble Pistoiese family, who bore
him a son named Mino, and four daughters, Diamante,

Beatrice, Giovanna, and Lombarduccia. Indeed, this marriage must have taken place before the death of Selvaggia in 1310, as in 1325-26 his son Mino was one of those by whose aid from within the Ghibelline Castruccio Antelminelli obtained possession of Pistoia, which he held in spite of revolts till his death some two or three years afterwards, when it again reverted to the Guelfs.

After returning to Pistoia, Cino's whole life was devoted to the attainment of legal and literary fame. In these pursuits he reaped the highest honours, and taught at the universities of Siena, Perugia, and Florence ; having for his disciples men who afterwards became celebrated, among whom rumour has placed Petrarch, though on examination this seems very doubtful. A sonnet by Petrarch exists, however, commencing "Piangete donne e con voi pianga Amore," written as a lament on Cino's death, and bestowing the highest praise on him. He and his Selvaggia are also coupled with Dante and Beatrice in the same poet's *Trionfi d' Amore* (cap. 4).

Though established again in Pistoia, Cino resided there but little till about the time of his death, which occurred in 1336-7. His monument, where he is represented as a professor among his disciples, still exists in the Cathedral of Pistoia, and is a mediæval work of great interest. Messer Cino de' Sinibuldi was a prosperous man, of whom we have ample records, from the details of his examinations as a student, to the inventory of his effects after death, and the curious items of his funeral expenses. Of his claims as a poet it may be said that he filled creditably the interval which elapsed between the death of Dante and the full blaze of Petrarch's success. Most of his poems in honour of Selvaggia are full of an elaborate and mechanical tone of complaint which hardly reads like the expression of a real love; nevertheless there are some, and especially the sonnet on her tomb (at page 172), which display feeling and power. The finest, as well as the most interesting, of all his pieces, is the very beautiful canzone in which he attempts to console Dante for the death of Beatrice. Though I have found much fewer among Cino's poems than among Guido's which seem to call for translation, the collection of the former is a larger one. Cino produced legal writings also, of which the chief one that has survived is a Commentary on the Statutes of Pistoia, said to have great merit, and whose production in the short space of two years was accounted an extraordinary achievement.

Having now spoken of the chief poets of this division, it remains to notice the others of whom less is known.

Dante da Maiano (Dante being, as with Alighieri, the short of Durante, and Maiano in the neighbourhood of Fiesole) had attained some reputation as a poet before the career of his great namesake began; his Sicilian lady Nina (herself, it is said, a poetess, and not personally known to him) going by the then unequivocal title of " La Nina di Dante." This priority may also be inferred from the contemptuous answer sent by him to Dante Alighieri's dream sonnet in the *Vita Nuova* (see page 178). All the writers on early Italian poetry seem to agree in specially censuring this poet's rhymes as coarse and trivial in manner; nevertheless, they are sometimes distinguished by a careless force not to be despised, and even by snatches of real beauty. Of Dante da Maiano's life no record whatever has come down to us.

Most literary circles have their prodigal, or what in modern phrase might be called their " scamp"; and among our Danteans, this place is indisputably filled by Cecco Angiolieri, of Siena. Nearly all his sonnets (and no other pieces by him have been preserved) relate either to an unnatural hatred of his father, or to an infatuated love for the daughter of a shoemaker, a certain married Becchina. It would appear that Cecco was probably enamoured of her before her marriage as well as afterwards, and we may surmise that his rancour against his father may have been partly dependent, in the first

instance, on the disagreements arising from such a con-
nection. However, from an amusing and lifelike story
in the Decameron (Gior. ix. Nov. 4) we learn that on one
occasion Cecco's father paid him six months' allowance in
advance, in order that he might proceed to the Marca
d'Ancona, and join the suite of a Papal Legate who was
his patron ; which looks, after all, as if the father had
some care of his graceless son. The story goes on to ·
relate how Cecco (whom Boccaccio describes as a hand-
some and well-bred man) was induced to take with him
as his servant a fellow-gamester with whom he had
formed an intimacy purely on account of the hatred
which each of the two bore his own father, though in
other respects they had little in common. The result
was that this fellow, during the journey, while Cecco was
asleep at Buonconvento, took all his money and lost it at
the gaming table, and afterwards managed by an adroit
trick to get possession of his horse and clothes, leaving
him nothing but his shirt. Cecco then, ashamed to return
to Siena, made his way, in a borrowed suit and mounted
on his servant's sorry hack, to Corsignano, where he had
relations ; and there he stayed till his father once more
(surely much to his credit) made him a remittance of
money. Boccaccio seems to say in conclusion that Cecco
ultimately had his revenge on the thief.

In reading many both of Cecco's love-sonnets and
hate-sonnets, it is impossible not to feel some pity for
the indications they contain of self-sought poverty, un-
happiness, and natural bent to ruin. Altogether they
have too much curious individuality to allow of their
being omitted here : especially as they afford the earliest
prominent example of a naturalism without afterthought
in the whole of Italian poetry. Their humour is some-
times strong, if not well chosen ; their passion always
forcible from its evident reality : nor indeed are several
among them devoid of a certain delicacy. This quality
is also to be discerned in other pieces which I have not
included as having less personal interest ; but it must

be confessed that for the most part the sentiments expressed in Cecco's poetry are either impious or licentious. Most of the sonnets of his which are in print are here given; * the selections concluding with an extraordinary one in which he proposes a sort of murderous crusade against all those who hate their fathers. This I have placed last (exclusive of the Sonnet to Dante in exile) in order to give the writer the benefit of the possibility that it was written last, and really expressed a still rather blood-thirsty contrition; belonging at best, I fear, to the content of self-indulgence when he came to enjoy his father's inheritance.   But most likely it is to be received as an expression of impudence alone, unless perhaps of hypocrisy.·

Cecco Angiolieri seems to have had poetical intercourse with Dante early as well as later in life; but even from the little that remains, we may gather that Dante soon put an end to any intimacy which may have existed between them.   That Cecco already poetized at the time to which the *Vita Nuova* relates, is evident from a date given in one of his sonnets,—the 20th June 1291, and from his sonnet raising objections to the one at the close of Dante's autobiography.   When the latter was written he was probably on good terms with the young Alighieri; but within no great while afterwards they had discovered that they could not agree, as is shown by a sonnet in which Cecco can find no words bad enough for Dante, who has remonstrated with him about Becchina.†   Much

---

* It may be mentioned (as proving how much of the poetry of this period still remains in MS.) that Ubaldini, in his Glossary to Barberino, published in 1640, cites as grammatical examples no fewer than twenty-three short fragments from Cecco Angiolieri, one of which alone is to be found among the sonnets which I have seen, and which I believe are the only ones in print. Ubaldini quotes them from the Strozzi MSS.

† Of this sonnet I have seen two printed versions, in both of which the text is so corrupt as to make them very contradictory in important points; but I believe that by comparing the two I have given its meaning correctly. (See page 192.)

later, as we may judge, he again addresses Dante in an insulting tone, apparently while the latter was living in exile at the court of Can Grande della Scala. No other reason can well be assigned for saying that he had " turned Lombard"; while some of the insolent allusions seem also to point to the time when Dante learnt by experience "how bitter is another's bread and how steep the stairs of his house."

Why Cecco in this sonnet should describe himself as having become a Roman, is more puzzling. Boccaccio certainly speaks of his luckless journey to join a Papal legate, but does not tell us whether fresh clothes and the wisdom of experience served him in the end to become so far identified with the Church of Rome. However, from the sonnet on his father's death he appears (though the allusion is desperately obscure) to have been then living at an abbey; and also, from the one mentioned above, we may infer that he himself, as well as Dante, was forced to sit at the tables of others : coincidences which almost seem to afford a glimpse of the phenomenal fact that the bosom of the Church was indeed for a time the refuge of this shorn lamb. If so, we may further conjecture that the wonderful crusade-sonnet was an *amende honorable* then imposed on him, accompanied probably with more fleshly penance.

Though nothing indicates the time of Cecco Angiolieri's death, I will venture to surmise that he outlived the writing and revision of Dante's *Inferno,* if only by the token that he is not found lodged in one of its meaner circles. It is easy to feel sure that no sympathy can ever have existed for long between Dante and a man like Cecco ; however arrogantly the latter, in his verses, might attempt to establish a likeness and even an equality. We may accept the testimony of so reverent a biographer as Boccaccio, that the Dante of later years was far other than the silent and awe-struck lover of the *Vita Nuova ;* but he was still (as he proudly called him-self) "the singer of Rectitude," and his that "indignant soul" which made blessed the mother who had borne him.*

Leaving to his fate (whatever that may have been) the Scamp of Dante's Circle, I must risk the charge of a confirmed taste for slang by describing GUIDO ORLANDI as its Bore. No other word could present him so fully. Very few pieces of his exist besides the five I have given. In one of these, † he rails against his political adversaries; in three, ‡ falls foul of his brother poets; and in the remaining one, § seems somewhat appeased (I think) by a judicious morsel of flattery. I have already referred to a sonnet of his which is said to have led to the composition of Guido Cavalcanti's Canzone on the Nature of Love. He has another sonnet beginning, " Per troppa sottiglianza il fil si rompe," ‖ in which he is certainly enjoying a fling at somebody, and I suspect at Cavalcanti in rejoinder to the very poem which he himself had instigated. If so, this stamps him a master-critic of the deepest initiation. Of his life nothing is recorded; but no wish perhaps need be felt to know much of him, as one would probably have dropped his acquaintance. We may be obliged to him, however, for his character of Guido Cavalcanti (at page 137), which is boldly and vividly drawn.

Next follow three poets of whom I have given one specimen apiece. By BERNARDO DA BOLOGNA (page 139) no other is known to exist, nor can anything be learnt of his career. GIANNI ALFANI was a noble and distinguished Florentine, a much graver man, it would seem, than one could judge from this sonnet of his (page 138), which belongs rather to the school of Sir Pandarus of Troy.

DINO COMPAGNI, the chronicler of Florence, is repre-

---

* " Alma sdegnosa,
Benedetta colei che in te s' incinse ! "
                                        (*Inferno*, C. VIII.)

† Page 206.   ‡ Pages 122, 137, 180.   § Page 143.
‖ This sonnet, as printed, has a gap in the middle ; let us hope (in so immaculate a censor) from unfitness for publication.

sented here by a sonnet addressed to Guido Cavalcanti,*
which is all the more interesting, as the same writer's
historical work furnishes so much of the little known
about Guido. Dino, though one of the noblest citizens
of Florence, was devoted to the popular cause, and held
successively various high offices in the state. The date
of his birth is not fixed, but he must have been at least
thirty in 1289, as he was one of the *Priori* in that
year, a post which could not be held by a younger man.
He died at Florence in 1323. Dino has rather lately
assumed for the modern reader a much more important
position than he occupied before among the early Italian
poets. I allude to the valuable discovery, in the Ma-
gliabecchian Library at Florence, of a poem by him
in *nona rima*, containing 309 stanzas. It is entitled
" L'Intelligenza," and is of an allegorical nature inter-
spersed with historical and legendary abstracts. †

I have placed LAPO GIANNI in this my first division on
account of the sonnet by Dante (page 126), in which he
seems undoubtedly to be the Lapo referred to. It has
been supposed by some that Lapo degli Uberti (father of
Fazio, and brother-in-law of Guido Cavalcanti) is meant ;
but this is hardly possible. Dante and Guido seem to
have been in familiar intercourse with the Lapo of the
sonnet at the time when it and others were written ;
whereas no Uberti can have been in Florence after the
year 1267, when the Ghibellines were expelled ; the
Uberti family (as I have mentioned elsewhere) being the
one of all others which was most jealously kept afar and
excluded from every amnesty. The only information
which I can find respecting Lapo Gianni is the statement

---

* Crescimbeni (*Ist. d. Volg. Poes.*) gives this sonnet from a
MS., where it is headed "To Guido Guinicelli " ; but he surmises,
and I have no doubt correctly, that Cavalcanti is really the person
addressed in it.

† See *Documents inédits pour servir à l'histoire littéraire de l'Italie,
&c., par A. F. Ozanam* (*Paris*, 1850), where the poem is printed
entire.

that he was a notary by profession.   I have also seen it somewhere asserted (though where I cannot recollect, and am sure no authority was given), that he was a cousin of Dante.   We may equally infer him to have been the Lapo mentioned by Dante in his treatise on the Vulgar Tongue, as being one of the few who up to that time had written verses in pure Italian.

DINO FRESCOBALDI's claim to the place given him here will not be disputed when it is remembered that by his pious care the seven first cantos of Dante's *Hell* were restored to him in exile, after the Casa Alighieri in Florence had been given up to pillage ; by which restoration Dante was enabled to resume his work. This sounds strange when we reflect that a world without Dante would be a poorer planet.   Meanwhile, beyond this great fact of Dino's life, which perhaps hardly occupied a day of it, there is no news to be gleaned of him.

GIOTTO falls by right into Dante's circle, as one great man comes naturally to know another.   But he is said actually to have lived in great intimacy with Dante, who was about twelve years older than himself ; Giotto having been born in or near the year 1276, at Vespignano, fourteen miles from Florence.   He died in 1336, fifteen years after Dante.   On the authority of Benvenuto da Imola (an early commentator on the *Commedia*), of Vasari, and others, it is said that Dante visited Giotto while he was painting at Padua ; that the great poet furnished the great painter with the conceptions of a series of subjects from the Apocalypse, which he painted at Naples ; and that Giotto, finally, passed some time with Dante in the exile's last refuge at Ravenna.   There is a tradition that Dante also studied drawing with Giotto's master Cimabue ; and that he practised it in some degree is evident from the passage in the *Vita Nuova*, where he speaks of his drawing an angel.   The reader will not need to be reminded of Giotto's portrait of the youthful Dante, painted in the Bargello at Florence, then the chapel of the Podestà. This is the author of the *Vita Nuova.* That other portrait shown us in the posthumous mask,—a face dead in exile after the death of hope,—should front the first page of the Sacred Poem to which heaven and earth had set their hands, but which might never bring him back to Florence, though it had made him haggard for many years.*

Giotto's Canzone on the doctrine of voluntary poverty, —the only poem we have of his,—is a protest against a perversion of gospel teaching which had gained ground in his day to the extent of becoming a popular frenzy. People went literally mad upon it; and to the reaction against this madness may also be assigned (at any rate partly) Cavalcanti's poem on Poverty, which, as we have seen, is otherwise not easily explained, if authentic. Giotto's canzone is all the more curious when we remember his noble fresco at Assisi, of Saint Francis wedded to Poverty.† It would really almost seem as if the poem had been written as a sort of safety-valve for the painter's true feelings, during the composition of the picture. At any rate, it affords another proof of the strong common sense and turn for humour which all accounts attribute to Giotto.

I have next introduced, as not inappropriate to the series of poems connected with Dante, SIMONE DALL' ANTELLA's fine sonnet relating to the last enterprises of Henry of Luxembourg, and to his then approaching end, —that deathblow to the Ghibelline hopes which Dante so deeply shared. This one sonnet is all we know of its author, besides his name.

GIOVANNI QUIRINO is another name which stands

---

* " Se mai continga che il poema sacro
    Al quale ha posto mano e cielo e terra,
    Sì che m' ha fatto per più anni macro,
    Vinca la crudeltà che fuor mi serra," etc.
                        (*Parad. C.* xxv.)
† See Dante's reverential treatment of this subject. (*Parad.* C. xi.)

forlorn of any personal history. Fraticelli (in his well-known and valuable edition of Dante's Minor Works) says that there lived about 1250 a bishop of that name, belonging to a Venetian family. It is true that the tone of the sonnet which I give (and which is the only one attributed to this author) seems foreign at least to the confessions of bishops. It might seem credibly thus ascribed, however, from the fact that Dante's sonnet probably dates from Ravenna, and that his correspondent writes from some distance; while the poet might well have formed a friendship with a Venetian bishop at the court of Verona.

For me Quirino's sonnet has great value; as Dante's answer* to it enables me to wind up this series with the name of its great chief; and, indeed, with what would almost seem to have been his last utterance in poetry, at that supreme juncture when he

"Slaked in his heart the fervour of desire,"

as at last he neared the very home

"Of Love which sways the sun and all the stars."†

I am sorry to see that this necessary introduction to my first division is longer than I could have wished. Among the severely-edited books which had to be consulted in forming this collection, I have often suffered keenly from the buttonholders of learned Italy, who will not let one go on one's way; and have contracted a horror of those editions where the text, hampered with numerals for reference, struggles through a few lines at the top of the page only to stick fast at the bottom in a

* In the case of the above two sonnets, and of all others interchanged between two poets, I have thought it best to place them together among the poems of one or the other correspondent, wherever they seemed to have most biographical value; and the same with several epistolary sonnets which have no answer.

† The last line of the *Paradise* (CAYLEY's *Translation*).

slough of verbal analysis.   It would seem unpardonable to make a book which should be even as these; and I have thus found myself led on to what I fear forms, by its length, an awkward *intermezzo* to the volume, in the hope of saying at once the most of what was to say; that so the reader may not find himself perpetually worried with footnotes during the consideration of something which may require a little peace.   The glare of too many tapers is apt to render the altar-picture confused and inharmonious, even when their smoke does not obscure or deface it.

DANTE ALIGHIERI.

THE NEW LIFE.

(LA VITA NUOVA.)

IN that part of the book of my memory before the which is little that can be read, there is a rubric, saying, *Incipit Vita Nova.** Under such rubric I find written many things; and among them the words which I purpose to copy into this little book; if not all of them, at the least their substance.

Nine times already since my birth had the heaven of light returned to the selfsame point almost, as concerns its own revolution, when first the glorious Lady of my mind was made manifest to mine eyes; even she who was called Beatrice by many who knew not wherefore.† She had already been in this life for so long as that, within her time, the starry heaven had moved towards the Eastern quarter one of the twelve parts of a degree; so that she appeared to me at the beginning of her ninth year almost, and I saw her almost at the end of

---

* " Here beginneth the new life."

† In reference to the meaning of the name, "She who confers blessing." We learn from Boccaccio that this first meeting took place at a May Feast, given in the year 1274 by Folco Portinari, father of Beatrice, who ranked among the principal citizens of Florence : to which feast Dante accompanied his father, Alighiero Alighieri,

my ninth year. Her dress, on that day, was of a most noble colour, a subdued and goodly crimson, girdled and adorned in such sort as best suited with her very tender age. At that moment, I say most truly that the spirit of life, which hath its dwelling in the secretest chamber of the heart, began to tremble so violently that the least pulses of my body shook therewith; and in trembling it said these words: *Ecce deus fortior me, qui veniens dominabitur mihi.** At that moment the animate spirit, which dwelleth in the lofty chamber whither all the senses carry their perceptions, was filled with wonder, and speaking more especially unto the spirits of the eyes, said these words: *Apparuit jam beatitudo vestra.†* At that moment the natural spirit, which dwelleth there where our nourishment is administered, began to weep, and in weeping said these words: *Heu miser! quia frequenter impeditus ero deinceps.‡*

I say that, from that time forward, Love quite governed my soul; which was immediately espoused to him, and with so safe and undisputed a lordship (by virtue of strong imagination) that I had nothing left for it but to do all his bidding continually. He oftentimes commanded me to seek if I might see this youngest of the Angels: wherefore I in my boyhood often went in search of her, and found her so noble and praiseworthy that certainly of her might have been said those words of the poet Homer, "She seemed not to be the daughter of a mortal man, but of God."§ And albeit her image, that was with me always, was an exultation of Love to subdue me, it was yet of so perfect a quality

---

* "Here is a deity stronger than I; who, coming, shall rule over me."

† "Your beatitude hath now been made manifest unto you."

‡ "Woe is me! for that often I shall be disturbed from this time forth!"

§

Οὐδὲ ἐῴκει

'Ανδρός γε θνητοῦ παῖς ἔμμεναι, ἀλλὰ θεοῖο.

(*Iliad*, XXIV. 258.)

that it never allowed me to be overruled by Love with-
out the faithful counsel of reason, whensoever such
counsel was useful to be heard.   But seeing that were
I to dwell overmuch on the passions and doings of such
early youth, my words might be counted something
fabulous, I will therefore put them aside; and passing
many things that may be conceived by the pattern of
these, I will come to such as are writ in my memory
with a better distinctness.

After the lapse of so many days that nine years
exactly were completed since the above-written appear-
ance of this most gracious being, on the last of those
days it happened that the same wonderful lady ap-
peared to me dressed all in pure white, between two
gentle ladies elder than she.   And passing through a
street, she turned her eyes thither where I stood sorely
abashed : and by her unspeakable courtesy, which is
now guerdoned in the Great Cycle, she saluted me with
so virtuous a bearing that I seemed then and there to
behold the very limits of blessedness.   The hour of her
most sweet salutation was exactly the ninth of that day ;
and because it was the first time that any words from
her reached mine ears, I came into such sweetness that
I parted thence as one intoxicated.   And betaking me
to the loneliness of mine own room, I fell to thinking of
this most courteous lady, thinking of whom I was over-
taken by a pleasant slumber, wherein a marvellous vision
was presented for me : for there appeared to be in my
room a mist of the colour of fire, within the which I dis-
cerned the figure of a lord of terrible aspect to such as
should gaze upon him, but who seemed therewithal to
rejoice inwardly that it was a marvel to see.   Speaking
he said many things, among the which I could under-
stand but few ; and of these, this : *Ego dominus tuus.**
In his arms it seemed to me that a person was sleeping,
covered only with a blood-coloured cloth ; upon whom

---

* "I am thy master."

looking very attentively, I knew that it was the lady of the salutation who had deigned the day before to salute me. And he who held her held also in his hand a thing that was burning in flames; and he said to me, *Vide cor tuum.** But when he had remained with me a little while, I thought that he set himself to awaken her that slept; after the which he made her to eat that thing which flamed in his hand; and she ate as one fearing. Then, having waited again a space, all his joy was turned into most bitter weeping; and as he wept he gathered the lady into his arms, and it seemed to me that he went with her up towards heaven : whereby such a great anguish came upon me that my light slumber could not endure through it, but was suddenly broken. And immediately having considered, I knew that the hour wherein this vision had been made manifest to me was the fourth hour (which is to say, the first of the nine last hours) of the night.

Then, musing on what I had seen, I proposed to relate the same to many poets who were famous in that day : and for that I had myself in some sort the art of discoursing with rhyme, I resolved on making a sonnet, in the which, having saluted all such as are subject unto Love, and entreated them to expound my vision, I should write unto them those things which I had seen in my sleep. And the sonnet I made was this :—

To every heart which the sweet pain doth move,
    And unto which these words may now be brought
    For true interpretation and kind thought,
Be greeting in our Lord's name, which is Love.
Of those long hours wherein the stars, above,
    Wake and keep watch, the third was almost nought,
    When Love was shown me with such terrors fraught
As may not carelessly be spoken of.

---

* "Behold thy heart."

He seemed like one who is full of joy, and had
  My heart within his hand, and on his arm
  My lady, with a mantle round her, slept;
Whom (having wakened her) anon he made
  To eat that heart; she ate, as fearing harm.
  Then he went out; and as he went, he wept.

*This sonnet is divided into two parts. In the first part
I give greeting, and ask an answer; in the second, I signify
what thing has to be answered to. The second part com-
mences here: "Of those long hours."*

To this sonnet I received many answers, conveying
many different opinions; of the which one was sent by
him whom I now call the first among my friends, and
it began thus, "Unto my thinking thou beheld'st all
worth."* And indeed, it was when he learned that I was
he who had sent those rhymes to him, that our friendship
commenced. But the true meaning of that vision was
not then perceived by any one, though it be now evident.
to the least skilful.

From that night forth, the natural functions of my
body began to be vexed and impeded, for I was given
up wholly to thinking of this most gracious creature:
whereby in short space I became so weak and so reduced
that it was irksome to many of my friends to look
upon me; while others, being moved by spite, went
about to discover what it was my wish should be con-
cealed. Wherefore I (perceiving the drift of their
unkindly questions), by Love's will, who directed me
according to the counsels of reason, told them how it
was Love himself who had thus dealt with me: and I
said so, because the thing was so plainly to be discerned
in my countenance that there was no longer any means
of concealing it. But when they went on to ask, "And

---

* The friend of whom Dante here speaks was Guido Cavalcanti.
For his answer, and those of Cino da Pistoia and Dante da Maiano,
see their poems further on.

by whose help hath Love done this ?" I looked in their faces smiling, and spake no word in return.

Now it fell on a day, that this most gracious creature was sitting where words were to be heard of the Queen of Glory;* and I was in a place whence mine eyes could behold their beatitude : and betwixt her and me, in a direct line, there sat another lady of a pleasant favour; who looked round at me many times, marvelling at my continued gaze which seemed to have *her* for its object. And many perceived that she thus looked; so that departing thence, I heard it whispered after me, " Look you to what a pass *such a lady* hath brought him "; and in saying this they named her who had been midway between the most gentle Beatrice and mine eyes. Therefore I was reassured, and knew that for that day my secret had not become manifest. Then immediately it came into my mind that I might make use of this lady as a screen to the truth : and so well did I play my part that the most of those who had hitherto watched and wondered at me, now imagined they had found me out. By her means I kept my secret concealed till some years were gone over; and for my better security, I even made divers rhymes in her honour; whereof I shall here write only as much as concerneth the most gentle Beatrice, which is but a very little. Moreover, about the same time while this lady was a screen for so much love on my part, I took the resolution to set down the name of this most gracious creature accompanied with many other women's names, and especially with hers whom I spake of. And to this end I put together the names of sixty the most beautiful ladies in that city where God had placed mine own lady; and these names I introduced in an epistle in the form of a *sirvent*, which it is not my intention to tran-scribe here. Neither should I have said anything of this matter, did I not wish to take note of a certain

---

* *I.e.* in a church.

strange thing, to wit : that having written the list, I found my lady's name would not stand otherwise than ninth in order among the names of these ladies.

Now it so chanced with her by whose means I had thus long time concealed my desire, that it behoved her to leave the city I speak of, and to journey afar : wherefore I, being sorely perplexed at the loss of so excellent a defence, had more trouble than even I could before have supposed.   And thinking that if I spoke not somewhat mournfully of her departure, my former counterfeiting would be the more quickly perceived, I determined that I would make a grievous sonnet * thereof ; the which I will write here, because it hath certain words in it whereof my lady was the immediate cause, as will be plain to him that understands.   And the sonnet was this :—

ALL ye that pass along Love's trodden way,
Pause ye awhile and say
    If there be any grief like unto mine :
I pray you that you hearken a short space
Patiently, if my case
    Be not a piteous marvel and a sign.

Love (never, certes, for my worthless part,
But of his own great heart,)
    Vouchsafed to me a life so calm and sweet
That oft I heard folk question as I went
What such great gladness meant :—
    They spoke of it behind me in the street.

---

* It will be observed that this poem is not what we now call a sonnet.   Its structure, however, is analogous to that of the sonnet, being two sextetts followed by two quatrains, instead of two quatrains followed by two triplets.   Dante applies the term sonnet to both these forms of composition, and to no other.

But now that fearless bearing is all gone
   Which with Love's hoarded wealth was given me ;
   Till I am grown to be   .
So poor that I have dread to think thereon.

And thus it is that I, being like as one
   Who is ashamed and hides his poverty,
   Without seem full of glee,
And let my heart within travail and moan.

*This poem has two principal parts ; for, in the first,
I mean to call the Faithful of Love in those words of
Jeremias the Prophet,* " O vos omnes qui transitis per
viam, attendite et videte si est dolor sicut dolor meus,"
*and to pray them to stay and hear me. In the second I tell
where Love had placed me, with a meaning other than that
which the last part of the poem shows, and I say what I
have lost. The second part begins here, " Love, (never,
certes.")*

A certain while after the departure of that lady, it
pleased the Master of the Angels to call into His glory a
damsel, young and of a gentle presence, who had been
very lovely in the city I speak of : and I saw her body
lying without its soul among many ladies, who held a
pitiful weeping. Whereupon, remembering that I had
seen her in the company of excellent Beatrice, I could
not hinder myself from a few tears ; and weeping, I
conceived to say somewhat of her death, in guerdon of
having seen her somewhile with my lady ; which thing I
spake of in the latter end of the verses that I writ in this
matter, as he will discern who understands. And I
wrote two sonnets, which are these :—

I.

Weep, Lovers, sith Love's very self doth weep,
   And sith the cause for weeping is so great ;

When now so many dames, of such estate
In worth, show with their eyes a grief so deep
For Death the churl has laid his leaden sleep
  Upon a damsel who was fair of late,
  Defacing all our earth should celebrate,—
Yea all save virtue, which the soul doth keep.
Now hearken how much Love did honour her.
  I myself saw him in his proper form
    Bending above the motionless sweet dead,
And often gazing into Heaven; for there
  The soul now sits which when her life was warm
    Dwelt with the joyful beauty that is fled.

*This first sonnet is divided into three parts. In the first,
I call and beseech the Faithful of Love to weep; and I say
that their Lord weeps, and that they, hearing the reason
why he weeps, shall be more minded to listen to me. In the
second, I relate this reason. In the third, I speak of honour
done by Love to this Lady. The second part begins here,
"When now so many dames"; the third here, "Now
hearken."*

II.

DEATH, alway cruel, Pity's foe in chief,
Mother who brought forth grief,
  Merciless judgment and without appeal!
  Since thou alone hast made my heart to feel
  This sadness and unweal,
My tongue upbraideth thee without relief.

And now (for I must rid thy name of ruth)
Behoves me speak the truth
  Touching thy cruelty and wickedness:
  Not that they be not known; but ne'ertheless
  I would give hate more stress
With them that feed on love in very sooth.

Out of this world thou hast driven courtesy,
   And virtue, dearly prized in womanhood ;
   And out of youth's gay mood
The lovely lightness is quite gone through thee.

Whom now I mourn, no man shall learn from me
   Save by the measure of these praises given.
   Whoso deserves not Heaven
May never hope to have her company.*

This poem is divided into four parts. In the first I address Death by certain proper names of hers. In the second, speaking to her, I tell the reason why I am moved to denounce her. In the third, I rail against her. In the fourth, I turn to speak to a person undefined, although defined in my own conception. The second part commences here, "Since thou alone"; the third here, "And now (for I must)"; the fourth here, "Whoso deserves not."

Some days after the death of this lady, I had occasion to leave the city I speak of, and to go thitherwards where she abode who had formerly been my protection ; albeit the end of my journey reached not altogether so far. And notwithstanding that I was visibly in the company of many, the journey was so irksome that I had scarcely sighing enough to ease my heart's heaviness ; seeing that as I went, I left my beatitude behind me. Wherefore it came to pass that he who ruled me by virtue of

---

* The commentators assert that the last two lines here do not allude to the dead lady, but to Beatrice. This would make the poem very clumsy in construction ; yet there must be some covert allusion to Beatrice, as Dante himself intimates. The only form in which I can trace it consists in the implied assertion that such person as *had* enjoyed the dead lady's society was worthy of heaven, and that person was Beatrice. Or indeed the allusion to Beatrice might be in the first poem, where he says that Love "*in forma vera*" (that is, Beatrice,) mourned over the corpse : as he afterwards says of Beatrice, "*Quella ha nome Amor.*" Most probably *both* allusions are intended,

my most gentle lady was made visible to my mind, in
the light habit of a traveller, coarsely fashioned. He
appeared to me troubled, and looked always on the
ground; saving only that sometimes his eyes were
turned towards a river which was clear and rapid, and
which flowed along the path I was taking. And then
I thought that Love called me and said to me these
words : "I come from that lady who was so long thy
surety; for the matter of whose return, I know that it
may not be. Wherefore I have taken that heart which
I made thee leave with her, and do bear it unto another
lady, who, as she was, shall be thy surety;" (and when
he named her I knew her well.) "And of these words
I have spoken if thou shouldst speak any again, let it be
in such sort as that none shall perceive thereby that thy
love was feigned for her, which thou must now feign
for another." And when he had spoken thus, all my
imagining was gone suddenly, for it seemed to me that
Love became a part of myself : so that, changed as it
were in mine aspect, I rode on full of thought the whole
of that day, and with heavy sighing. And the day being
over, I wrote this sonnet :—

A DAY agone, as I rode sullenly
    Upon a certain path that liked me not,
    I met Love midway while the air was hot,
Clothed lightly as a wayfarer might be.
And for the cheer he showed, he seemed to me
    As one who hath lost lordship he had got;
    Advancing tow'rds me full of sorrowful thought,
Bowing his forehead so that none should see.
Then as I went, he called me by my name,
    Saying : "I journey since the morn was dim
        Thence where I made thy heart to be : which now
I needs must bear unto another dame."
    Wherewith so much passed into me of him
        That he was gone, and I discerned not how.

This sonnet has three parts. In the first part, I tell how I met Love, and of his aspect. In the second, I tell what he said to me, although not in full, through the fear I had of discovering my secret. In the third, I say how he disappeared. The second part commences here, " Then as I went"; the third here, " Wherewith so much."

On my return, I set myself to seek out that lady whom my master had named to me while I journeyed sighing. And because I would be brief, I will now narrate that in a short while I made her my surety, in such sort that the matter was spoken of by many in terms scarcely courteous ; through the which I had oftenwhiles many troublesome hours. And by this it happened (to wit : by this false and evil rumour which seemed to misfame me of vice) that she who was the destroyer of all evil and the queen of all good, coming where I was, denied me her most sweet salutation, in the which alone was my blessedness.

And here it is fitting for me to depart a little from this present matter, that it may be rightly understood of what surpassing virtue her salutation was to me. To the which end I say that when she appeared in any place, it seemed to me, by the hope of her excellent salutation, that there was no man mine enemy any longer ; and such warmth of charity came upon me that most certainly in that moment I would have pardoned whosoever had done me an injury ; and if one should then have questioned me concerning any matter, I could only have said unto him "Love," with a countenance clothed in humbleness. And what time she made ready to salute me, the spirit of Love, destroying all other perceptions, thrust forth the feeble spirits of my eyes, saying, "Do homage unto your mistress," and putting itself in their place to obey : so that he who would, might then have beheld Love, beholding the lids of my eyes shake. And when this most gentle lady gave her salutation, Love, so far from being a medium beclouding mine intolerable beatitude, then bred in me such an overpowering sweetness that my body, being all subjected thereto, remained many times helpless and passive. Whereby it is made manifest that in her salutation alone was there any beatitude for me, which then very often went beyond my endurance.

And now, resuming my discourse, I will go on to relate that when, for the first time, this beatitude was denied me, I became possessed with such grief that, parting myself from others, I went into a lonely place to bathe the ground with most bitter tears : and when, by this heat of weeping, I was somewhat relieved, I betook myself to my chamber, where I could lament unheard. And there, having prayed to the Lady of all Mercies, and having said also, "O Love, aid thou thy servant," I went suddenly asleep like a beaten sobbing child. And in my sleep, towards the middle of it, I seemed to see in the room, seated at my side, a youth in very white raiment, who kept his eyes fixed on me in deep thought. And when he had gazed some time, I thought that he sighed and called to me in these words : " *Fili mi, tempus est ut prætermittantur simulata nostra.*"* And thereupon I seemed to know him; for the voice was the same wherewith he had spoken at other times in my sleep. Then looking at him, I perceived that he was weeping piteously, and that he seemed to be waiting for me to speak. Wherefore, taking heart, I began thus : "Why weepest thou, Master of all honour?" And he made answer to me : " *Ego tanquam centrum circuli, cui simili modo se habent circumferentiæ partes : tu autem non sic.*" †

* " My son, it is time for us to lay aside our counterfeiting."

† "I am as the centre of a circle, to the which all parts of the circumference bear an equal relation : but with thee it is not thus." This phrase seems to have remained as obscure to commentators as Dante found it at the moment. No one, as far as I know, has even fairly tried to find a meaning for it. To me the following appears a not unlikely one. Love is weeping on Dante's account, and not on his own. He says, "I am the centre of a circle (*Amor che muove il sole e l' altre stelle*) : therefore all lovable objects, whether in heaven or earth, or any part of the circle's circum-

And thinking upon his words, they seemed to me
obscure; so that again compelling myself unto speech, I
asked of him : "What thing is this, Master, that thou
hast spoken thus darkly?" To the which he made
answer in the vulgar tongue : "Demand no more than
may be useful to thee." Whereupon I began to discourse
with him concerning her salutation which she had denied
me; and when I had questioned him of the cause, he
said these words : "Our Beatrice hath heard from certain
persons, that the lady whom I named to thee while thou
journeyedst full of sighs is sorely disquieted by thy
solicitations : and therefore this most gracious creature,
who is the enemy of all disquiet, being fearful of such
disquiet, refused to salute thee. For the which reason
(albeit, in very sooth, thy secret must needs have become
known to her by familiar observation) it is my will that
thou compose certain things in rhyme, in the which thou
shalt set forth how strong a mastership I have obtained
over thee, through her; and how thou wast hers even
from thy childhood. Also do thou call upon him that
knoweth these things to bear witness to them, bidding
him to speak with her thereof; the which I, who am he,
will do willingly. And thus she shall be made to know
thy desire; knowing which, she shall know likewise that
they were deceived who spake of thee to her. And so
write these things, that they shall seem rather to be
spoken by a third person; and not directly by thee to
her, which is scarce fitting. After the which, send them,
not without me, where she may chance to hear them;
but have them fitted with a pleasant music, into the
which I will pass whensoever it needeth." With this
speech he was away, and my sleep was broken up.

Whereupon, remembering me, I knew that I had

---

ference, are equally near to me. Not so thou, who wilt one day
lose Beatrice when she goes to heaven." The phrase would thus
contain an intimation of the death of Beatrice, accounting for
Dante being next told not to inquire the meaning of the speech,—
"Demand no more than may be useful to thee."

:

beheld this vision during the ninth hour of the day;
and I resolved that I would make a ditty, before I left
my chamber, according to the words my master had
spoken.   And this is the ditty that I made :—

Song, 'tis my will that thou do seek out Love,
    And go with him where my dear lady is ;
    That so my cause, the which thy harmonies
Do plead, his better speech may clearly prove.

Thou goest, my Song, in such a courteous kind,
    That even companionless
    Thou mayst rely on thyself anywhere.
And yet, an thou wouldst get thee a safe mind,
    First unto Love address
    Thy steps ; whose aid, mayhap, 'twere ill to spare,
    Seeing that she to whom thou mak'st thy prayer
Is, as I think, ill-minded unto me,
And that if Love do not companion thee,
    Thou'lt have perchance small cheer to tell me of.

With a sweet accent, when thou com'st to her,
    Begin thou in these words,
    First having craved a gracious audience :
" He who hath sent me as his messenger,
    Lady, thus much records,
    An thou but suffer him, in his defence.
    Love, who comes with me, by thine influence
Can make this man do as it liketh him :
Wherefore, if this fault *is* or doth but *seem*
    Do thou conceive : for his heart cannot move."

Say to her also : " Lady, his poor heart
    Is so confirmed in faith
    That all its thoughts are but of serving thee :

'Twas early thine, and could not swerve apart."
　Then, if she wavereth,
　　Bid her ask Love, who knows if these things be.
　　And in the end, beg of her modestly
To pardon so much boldness : saying too :—
" If thou declare his death to be thy due,
　The thing shall come to pass, as doth behove."

Then pray thou of the Master of all ruth,
　Before thou leave her there,
　　That he befriend my cause and plead it well.
" In guerdon of my sweet rhymes and my truth "
　(Entreat him) " stay with her ;
　　Let not the hope of thy poor servant fail ;
　　And if with her thy pleading should prevail,
Let her look on him and give peace to him."
Gentle my Song, if good to thee it seem,
　Do this : so worship shall be thine and love.

This ditty is divided into three parts. In the first, I tell it whither to go, and I encourage it, that it may go the more confidently, and I tell it whose company to join if it would go with confidence and without any danger. In the second, I say that which it behoves the ditty to set forth. In the third, I give it leave to start when it pleases, recommending its course to the arms of Fortune. The second part begins here, " With a sweet accent"; the third here, " Gentle my Song." Some might contradict me, and say that they understand not whom I address in the second person, seeing that the ditty is merely the very words I am speaking. And therefore I say that this doubt I intend to solve and clear up in this little book itself, at a more difficult passage, and then let him understand who now doubts, or would now contradict as aforesaid.

After this vision I have recorded, and having written those words which Love had dictated to me, I began to be harassed with many and divers thoughts, by each of

which I was sorely tempted ; and in especial, there were
four among them that left me no rest. The first was
this : "Certainly the lordship of Love is good ; seeing
that it diverts the mind from all mean things." The
second was this : "Certainly the lordship of Love is
evil ; seeing that the more homage his servants pay to
him, the more grievous and painful are the torments
wherewith he torments them." The third was this :
"The name of Love is so sweet in the hearing that it
would not seem possible for its effects to be other than
sweet ; seeing that the name must needs be like unto
the thing named : as it is written : *Nomina sunt con-
sequentia rerum.*"* And the fourth was this : "The
lady whom Love hath chosen out to govern thee is not
as other ladies, whose hearts are easily moved."

And by each one of these thoughts I was so sorely
assailed that I was like unto him who doubteth which
path to take, and wishing to go, goeth not. And if I
bethought myself to seek out some point at the which all
these paths might be found to meet, I discerned but one
way, and that irked me ; to wit, to call upon Pity, and
to commend myself unto her. And it was then that,
feeling a desire to write somewhat thereof in rhyme, I
wrote this sonnet :—

ALL my thoughts always speak to me of Love,
　　Yet have between themselves such difference
　　That while one bids me bow with mind and sense,
A second saith, "Go to : look thou above" ;
The third one, hoping, yields me joy enough ;
　　And with the last come tears, I scarce know whence :
　　All of them craving pity in sore suspense,
Trembling with fears that the heart knoweth of.
And thus, being all unsure which path to take,
　　Wishing to speak I know not what to say,
　　And lose myself in amorous wanderings :

---

* "Names are the consequents of things."

Until, (my peace with all of them to make,)
Unto mine enemy I needs must pray,
My Lady Pity, for the help she brings.

This sonnet may be divided into four parts. In the first, I say and propound that all my thoughts are concerning Love. In the second, I say that they are diverse, and I relate their diversity. In the third, I say wherein they all seem to agree. In the fourth, I say that, wishing to speak of Love, I know not from which of these thoughts to take my argument; and that if I would take it from all, I shall have to call upon mine enemy, my Lady Pity. "Lady," I say, as in a scornful mode of speech. The second begins here, "Yet have between themselves"; the third, "All of them craving"; the fourth, "And thus."

After this battling with many thoughts, it chanced on a day that my most gracious lady was with a gathering of ladies in a certain place; to the which I was conducted by a friend of mine; he thinking to do me a great pleasure by showing me the beauty of so many women. Then I, hardly knowing whereunto he conducted me, but trusting in him (who yet was leading his friend to the last verge of life), made question: "To what end are we come among these ladies?" and he answered: "To the end that they may be worthily served." And they were assembled around a gentlewoman who was given in marriage on that day; the custom of the city being that these should bear her company when she sat down for the first time at table in the house of her husband. Therefore I, as was my friend's pleasure, resolved to stay with him and do honour to those ladies.

But as soon as I had thus resolved, I began to feel a faintness and a throbbing at my left side, which soon took possession of my whole body. Whereupon I remember that I covertly leaned my back unto a painting that ran round the walls of that house; and being fearful lest my trembling should be discerned of them, I lifted mine eyes to look on those ladies, and then first perceived among them the excellent Beatrice.   And when I perceived her, all my senses were overpowered by the great lordship that Love obtained, finding himself so near unto that most gracious being, until nothing but the spirits of sight remained to me ; and even these remained driven out of their own instruments because Love entered in that honoured place of theirs, that so he might the better behold her.   And although I was other than at first, I grieved for the spirits so expelled, which kept up a sore lament, saying : " If he had not in this wise thrust us forth, we also should behold the marvel of this lady."   By this, many of her friends, having discerned my confusion, began to wonder ; and together with herself, kept whispering of me and mocking me.   Whereupon my friend, who knew not what to conceive, took me by the hands, and drawing me forth from among them, required to know what ailed me.   Then, having first held me at quiet for a space until my perceptions were come back to me, I made answer to my friend : " Of a surety I have now set my feet on that point of life, beyond the which he must not pass who would return." *

Afterwards, leaving him, I went back to the room where I had wept before ; and again weeping and ashamed, said : " If this lady but knew of my condition, I do not think that she would thus mock at me ; nay, I am sure that she must needs feel some pity."   And in my weeping I bethought me to write certain words, in the which, speaking to her, I should signify the occasion

---

* It is difficult not to connect Dante's agony at this wedding-feast, with our knowledge that in her twenty-first year Beatrice was wedded to Simone de' Bardi.   That she herself was the bride on this occasion might seem out of the question, from the fact of its not being in any way so stated : but on the other hand, Dante's silence throughout the *Vita Nuova* as regards her marriage (which must have brought deep sorrow even to his ideal love) is so startling, that we might almost be led to conceive in this passage the only intimation of it which he thought fit to give.

of my disfigurement, telling her also how I knew that she had no knowledge thereof; which, if it were known, I was certain must move others to pity. And then, because I hoped that peradventure it might come into her hearing, I wrote this sonnet :—

EVEN as the others mock, thou mockest me;
  Not dreaming, noble lady, whence it is
  That I am taken with strange semblances,
Seeing thy face which is so fair to see :
For else, compassion would not suffer thee
  To grieve my heart with such harsh scoffs as these.
  Lo! Love, when thou art present, sits at ease,
And bears his mastership so mightily
That all my troubled senses he thrusts out,
  Sorely tormenting some, and slaying some,
    Till none but he is left and has free range
    To gaze on thee. This makes my face to change
Into another's ; while I stand all dumb,
And hear my senses clamour in their rout.

This sonnet I divide not into parts, because a division is only made to open the meaning of the thing divided : and this, as it is sufficiently manifest through the reasons given, has no need of division. True it is that, amid the words whereby is shown the occasion of this sonnet, dubious words are to be found ; namely, when I say that Love fills all my spirits, but that the visual remain in life, only outside of their own instruments. And this difficulty it is impossible for any to solve who is not in equal guise liege unto Love ; and, to those who are so, that is manifest which would clear up the dubious words. And therefore it were not well for me to expound this difficulty, inasmuch as my speaking would be either fruitless or else superfluous.

A while after this strange disfigurement, I became possessed with a strong conception which left me but very seldom, and then to return quickly. And it was this : " Seeing that thou comest into such scorn by the companionship of this lady, wherefore seekest thou to behold her ? If she should ask thee this thing, what answer couldst thou make unto her ? yea, even though thou wert master of all thy faculties, and in no way hindered from answering." Unto the which, another very humble thought said in reply: "If I were master of all my faculties, and in no way hindered from answering, I would tell her that no sooner do I image to myself her marvellous beauty than I am possessed with the desire to behold her, the which is of so great strength that it kills and destroys in my memory all those things which might oppose it ; and it is therefore that the great anguish I have endured thereby is yet not enough to restrain me from seeking to behold her." And then, because of these thoughts, I resolved to write somewhat, wherein, having pleaded mine excuse, I should tell her of what I felt in her presence. Whereupon I wrote this sonnet :—

THE thoughts are broken in my memory,
　　Thou lovely Joy, whene'er I see thy face ;
　　When thou art near me, Love fills up the space,
Often repeating, " If death irk thee, fly."
My face shows my heart's colour, verily,
　　Which, fainting, seeks for any leaning-place ;
　　Till, in the drunken terror of disgrace,
The very stones seem to be shrieking, "Die !"
It were a grievous sin, if one should not
　　Strive then to comfort my bewildered mind
　　　　(Though merely with a simple pitying)
For the great anguish which thy scorn has wrought
　　In the dead sight o' the eyes grown nearly blind,
　　　　Which look for death as for a blessed thing.

This sonnet is divided into two parts. In the first, I tell the cause why I abstain not from coming to this lady.

*In the second, I tell what befalls me through coming to her ;
and this part begins here, " When thou art near." And
also this second part divides into five distinct statements:
For, in the first, I say what Love, counselled by Reason,
tells me when I am near the Lady. In the second, I set
forth the state of my heart by the example of the face. In
the third, I say how all ground of trust fails me. In the
fourth, I say that he sins who shows not pity of me, which
would give me some comfort. In the last, I say why
people should take pity ; namely, for the piteous look which
comes into mine eyes ; which piteous look is destroyed, that
is, appeareth not unto others, through the jeering of this
lady, who draws to the like action those who peradventure
would see this piteousness. The second part begins here,
" My face shows " ; the third, "Till, in the drunken terror";
the fourth, " It were a grievous sin " ; the fifth, " For the
great anguish."*

Thereafter, this sonnet bred in me desire to write
down in verse four other things touching my condition,
the which things it seemed to me that I had not yet
made manifest. The first among these was the grief
that possessed me very often, remembering the strange-
ness which Love wrought in me; the second was, how
Love many times assailed me so suddenly and with such
strength that I had no other life remaining except a
thought which spake of my lady; the third was, how,
when Love did battle with me in this wise, I would rise
up all colourless, if so I might see my lady, conceiving
that the sight of her would defend me against the assault
of Love, and altogether forgetting that which her presence
brought unto me ; and the fourth was, how, when I saw
her, the sight not only defended me not, but took away
the little life that remained to me. And I said these
four things in a sonnet, which is this :—

AT whiles (yea oftentimes) I muse over
   The quality of anguish that is mine
   Through Love : then pity makes my voice to pine,

Saying, " Is any else thus, anywhere ? "
Love smiteth me, whose strength is ill to bear ;
   So that of all my life is left no sign
   Except one thought; and that, because 'tis thine,
Leaves not the body but abideth there.
And then if I, whom other aid forsook,
   Would aid myself, and innocent of art
    Would fain have sight of thee as a last hope,
No sooner do I lift mine eyes to look
   Than the blood seems as shaken from my heart,
    And all my pulses beat at once and stop.

This sonnet is divided into four parts, four things being therein narrated ; and as these are set forth above, I only proceed to distinguish the parts by their beginnings.   Wherefore I say that the second part begins, " Love smiteth me" ; the third, " And then if I" ; the fourth, " No sooner do I lift."

After I had written these three last sonnets, wherein I spake unto my lady, telling her almost the whole of my condition, it seemed to me that I should be silent, having said enough concerning myself. But albeit I spake not to her again, yet it behoved me afterward to write of another matter, more noble than the foregoing. And for that the occasion of what I then wrote may be found pleasant in the hearing, I will relate it as briefly as I may.

Through the sore change in mine aspect, the secret of my heart was now understood of many. Which thing being thus, there came a day when certain ladies to whom it was well known (they having been with me at divers times in my trouble) were met together for the pleasure of gentle company. And as I was going that way by chance, (but I think rather by the will of fortune,) I heard one of them call unto me, and she that called was a lady of very sweet speech. And when I had come close up with them, and perceived that they had

not among them mine excellent lady, I was reassured;
and saluted them, asking of their pleasure. The ladies
were many; divers of whom were laughing one to
another, while divers gazed at me as though I should
speak anon. But when I still spake not, one of them,
who before had been talking with another, addressed me
by my name, saying, "To what end lovest thou this lady,
seeing that thou canst not support her presence? Now
tell us this thing, that we may know it: for certainly the
end of such a love must be worthy of knowledge." And
when she had spoken these words, not she only, but all
they that were with her, began to observe me, waiting
for my reply. Whereupon I said thus unto them:—
"Ladies, the end and aim of my Love was but the
salutation of that lady of whom I conceive that ye are
speaking; wherein alone I found that beatitude which
is the goal of desire. And now that it hath pleased her
to deny me this, Love, my Master, of his great goodness,
hath placed all my beatitude there where my hope will
not fail me." Then those ladies began to talk closely
together; and as I have seen snow fall among the rain,
so was their talk mingled with sighs. But after a little,
that lady who had been the first to address me, addressed
me again in these words: "We pray thee that thou wilt
tell us wherein abideth this thy beatitude." And answer-
ing, I said but thus much: "In those words that do
praise my lady." To the which she rejoined: "If thy
speech were true, those words that thou didst write
concerning thy condition would have been written with
another intent."

Then I, being almost put to shame because of her
answer, went out from among them; and as I walked,
I said within myself: "Seeing that there is so much
beatitude in those words which do praise my lady,
wherefore hath my speech of her been different?" And
then I resolved that thenceforward I would choose for
the theme of my writings only the praise of this most
gracious being. But when I had thought exceedingly,

it seemed to me that I had taken to myself a theme
which was much too lofty, so that I dared not begin ;
and I remained during several days in the desire of
speaking, and the fear of beginning. After which it
happened, as I passed one day along a path which lay
beside a stream of very clear water, that there came
upon me a great desire to say somewhat in rhyme : but
when I began thinking how I should say it, methought
that to speak of her were unseemly, unless I spoke to
other ladies in the second person ; which is to say, not
to *any* other ladies, but only to such as are so called
because they are gentle, let alone for mere womanhood.
Whereupon I declare that my tongue spake as though
by its own impulse, and said, " Ladies that have intel-
ligence in love." These words I laid up in my mind
with great gladness, conceiving to take them as my
commencement. Wherefore, having returned to the city
I spake of, and considered thereof during certain days,
I began a poem with this beginning, constructed in the
mode which will be seen below in its division. The
poem begins here :—

LADIES that have intelligence in love,
  Of mine own lady I would speak with you ;
  Not that I hope to count her praises through,
    But telling what I may, to ease my mind.
And I declare that when I speak thereof,
Love sheds such perfect sweetness over me
That if my courage failed not, certainly
    To him my listeners must be all resign'd.
    Wherefore I will not speak in such large kind
That mine own speech should foil me, which were
      base ;
But only will discourse of her high grace
    In these poor words, the best that I can find,
With you alone, dear dames and damozels :
'Twere ill to speak thereof with any else.

An Angel, of his blessed knowledge, saith
  To God : " Lord, in the world that Thou hast made,
  A miracle in action is display'd,
    By reason of a soul whose splendours fare
Even hither : and since Heaven requireth
  Nought saving her, for her it prayeth Thee,
  Thy Saints crying aloud continually."
    Yet Pity still defends our earthly share
    In that sweet soul; God answering thus the prayer.
" My well-belovèd, suffer that in peace
Your hope remain, while so My pleasure is,
    There where one dwells who dreads the loss of her :
And who in Hell unto the doomed shall say,
' I have looked on that for which God's chosen pray.' "

My lady is desired in the high Heaven :
  Wherefore, it now behoveth me to tell,
  Saying : Let any maid that would be well
    Esteemed keep with her : for as she goes by,
Into foul hearts a deathly chill is driven
By Love, that makes ill thought to perish there :
While any who endures to gaze on her
    Must either be ennobled, or else die.
    When one deserving to be raised so high
Is found, 'tis then her power attains its proof,
Making his heart strong for his soul's behoof
    With the full strength of meek humility.
Also this virtue owns she, by God's will :
Who speaks with her can never come to ill.

Love saith concerning her : " How chanceth it
  That flesh, which is of dust, should be thus pure ? "
  Then, gazing always, he makes oath : " Forsure,
    This is a creature of God till now unknown." .
She hath that paleness of the pearl that's fit
In a fair woman, so much and not more ;
She is as high as Nature's skill can soar ;
    Beauty is tried by her comparison.

Whatever her sweet eyes are turned upon,
Spirits of love do issue thence in flame,
Which through their eyes who then may look on them
    Pierce to the heart's deep chamber every one.
And in her smile Love's image you may see ;
Whence none can gaze upon her steadfastly.

Dear Song, I know thou wilt hold gentle speech
    With many ladies, when I send thee forth :
    Wherefore (being mindful that thou hadst thy birth
        From Love, and art a modest, simple child,)
Whomso thou meetest, say thou this to each :
" Give me good speed ! To her I wend along
In whose much strength my weakness is made strong."
    And if, i' the end, thou wouldst not be beguiled
    Of all thy labour, seek not the defiled
And common sort ; but rather choose to be
Where man and woman dwell in courtesy.
    So to the road thou shalt be reconciled,
And find the lady, and with the lady, Love.
Commend thou me to each, as doth behove.

This poem, that it may be better understood, I will divide more subtly than the others preceding; and therefore I will make three parts of it. The first part is a proem to the words following. The second is the matter treated of. The third is, as it were, a handmaid to the preceding words. The second begins here, " An angel" ; the third here, " Dear Song, I know." The first part is divided into four. In the first, I say to whom I mean to speak of my Lady, and wherefore I will so speak. In the second, I say what she appears to myself to be when I reflect upon her excellence, and what I would utter if I lost not courage. In the third, I say what it is I purpose to speak so as not to be impeded by faintheartedness. In the fourth, repeating to whom I purpose speaking, I tell the reason why I speak to them The second begins here, " And I declare" ; the third here,

" *Wherefore I will not speak* " ; *the fourth here,* " *With you alone.*" *Then, when I say* " *An angel,*" *I begin treating of this lady : and this part is divided into two. In the first, I tell what is understood of her in heaven. In the second, I tell what is understood of her on earth : here,* " *My lady is desired.*" *This second part is divided into two ; for, in the first, I speak of her as regards the nobleness of her soul, relating some of her virtues proceeding from her soul; in the second, I speak of her as regards the nobleness of her body, narrating some of her beauties : here,* " *Love saith concerning her.*" *This second part is divided into two, for, in the first, I speak of certain beauties which belong to the whole person ; in the second, I speak of certain beauties which belong to a distinct part of the person : here,* " *Whatever her sweet eyes.*" *This second part is divided into two ; for, in the one, I speak of the eyes, which are the beginning of love ; in the second, I speak of the mouth, which is the end of love. And that every vicious thought may be discarded herefrom, let the reader remember that it is above written that the greeting of this lady, which was an act of her mouth, was the goal of my desires, while I could receive it. Then, when I say,* " *Dear Song, I know,*" *I add a stanza as it were handmaid to the others, wherein I say what I desire from this my poem. And because this last part is easy to understand, I trouble not myself with more divisions. I say, indeed, that the further to open the meaning of this poem, more minute divisions ought to be used ; but nevertheless he who is not of wit enough to understand it by these which have been already made is welcome to leave it alone ; for certes, I fear I have communicated its sense to too many by these present divisions, if it so happened that many should hear it.*

When this song was a little gone abroad, a certain one of my friends, hearing the same, was pleased to question me, that I should tell him what thing love is; it may be, conceiving from the words thus heard a hope of me beyond my desert. Wherefore I, thinking that after such discourse it were well to say somewhat of the nature of Love, and also in accordance with my friend's desire, proposed to myself to write certain words in the which I should treat of this argument. And the sonnet that I then made is this :—

> Love and the gentle heart are one same thing,
>> Even as the wise man * in his ditty saith :
>> Each, of itself, would be such life in death
> As rational soul bereft of reasoning.
> 'Tis Nature makes them when she loves : a king
>> Love is, whose palace where he sojourneth
>> Is called the Heart ; there draws he quiet breath
> At first, with brief or longer slumbering.
> Then beauty seen in virtuous womankind
>> Will make the eyes desire, and through the heart
>> Send the desiring of the eyes again ;
> Where often it abides so long enshrin'd
>> That Love at length out of his sleep will start.
>> And women feel the same for worthy men.

This sonnet is divided into two parts. In the first, I speak of him according to his power. In the second, I speak of him according as his power translates itself into act. The second part begins here, " Then beauty seen." The first is divided into two. In the first, I say in what subject this power exists. In the second, I say how this subject and this power are produced together, and how the one regards the other, as form does matter. The second begins here, "'Tis Nature." Afterwards when I say, " Then beauty seen in virtuous womankind," I say how this power translates itself into act ; and, first, how it so translates itself in a man, then how it so translates itself in a woman: here, "And women feel."

Having treated of love in the foregoing, it appeared to

---

* Guido Guinicelli, in the canzone which begins, "Within the gentle heart Love shelters him." (See *Part II.* page 264.)

me that I should also say something in praise of my lady,
wherein it might be set forth how love manifested itself
when produced by her ; and how not only she could
awaken it where it slept, but where it was not she
could marvellously create it. To the which end I wrote
another sonnet ; and it is this :—

> My lady carries love within her eyes ;
>   All that she looks on is made pleasanter ;
>   Upon her path men turn to gaze at her ;
> He whom she greeteth feels his heart to rise,
> And droops his troubled visage, full of sighs,
>   And of his evil heart is then aware :
> Hate loves, and pride becomes a worshiper.
> O women, help to praise her in somewise.
> Humbleness, and the hope that hopeth well,
>   By speech of hers into the mind are brought,
>   And who beholds is blessèd oftenwhiles.
>   The look she hath when she a little smiles
>   Cannot be said, nor holden in the thought ;
> · 'Tis such a new and gracious miracle.

*This sonnet has three sections. In the first, I say how
this lady brings this power into action by those most noble
features, her eyes ; and, in the third, I say this same as to
that most noble feature, her mouth. And between these two
sections is a little section, which asks, as it were, help for the
previous section and the subsequent ; and it begins here, " O
women, help." The third begins here, " Humbleness." The
first is divided into three ; for, in the first, I say how she
with power makes noble that which she looks upon ; and this
is as much as to say that she brings Love, in power, thither
where he is not. In the second, I say how she brings Love,
in act, into the hearts of all those whom she sees. In the
third, I tell what she afterwards, with virtue, operates upon
their hearts. The second begins, " Upon her path " ; the third,
" He whom she greeteth." Then, when I say " O women,*

*help," I intimate to whom it is my intention to speak, calling
on women to help me to honour her. Then, when I say,
"Humbleness," I say that same which is said in the first
part, regarding two acts of her mouth, one whereof is
her most sweet speech, and the other her marvellous smile.
Only, I say not of this last how it operates upon the hearts
of others, because memory cannot retain this smile, nor its
operation.*

Not many days after this (it being the will of the most
High God, who also from Himself put not away death),
the father of wonderful Beatrice, going out of this life,
passed certainly into glory.   Thereby it happened, as of
very sooth it might not be otherwise, that this lady was
made full of the bitterness of grief : seeing that such a
parting is very grievous unto those friends who are left,
and that no other friendship is like to that between
a good parent and a good child ; and furthermore con-
sidering that this lady was good in the supreme degree,
and her father (as by many it hath been truly averred) of
exceeding goodness.   And because it is the usage of that
city that men meet with men in such a grief, and women
with women, certain ladies of her companionship gathered
themselves unto Beatrice, where she kept alone in her
weeping : and as they passed in and out, I could hear
them speak concerning her, how she wept.   At length
two of them went by me, who said : "Certainly she
grieveth in such sort that one might die for pity, behold-
ing her."   Then, feeling the tears upon my face, I put up
my hands to hide them : and had it not been that I hoped
to hear more concerning her (seeing that where I sat,
her friends passed continually in and out), I should
assuredly have gone thence to be alone, when I felt the
tears come.   But as I still sat in that place, certain ladies
again passed near me, who were saying among them-
selves : "Which of us shall be joyful any more, who have
listened to this lady in her piteous sorrow ?"   And there
were others who said as they went by me : "He that
sitteth here could not weep more if he had beheld her

as we have beheld her ;" and again : " He is so altered
that he seemeth not as himself." And still as the ladies
passed to and fro, I could hear them speak after this
fashion of her and of me.

Wherefore afterwards, having considered and per-
ceiving that there was herein matter for poesy, I resolved
that I would write certain rhymes in the which should be
contained all that those ladies had said. And because I
would willingly have spoken to them if it had not been
for discreetness, I made in my rhymes as though I had
spoken and they had answered me. And thereof I wrote
two sonnets ; in the first of which I addressed them as I
would fain have done; and in the second related their
answer, using the speech that I had heard from them, as
though it had been spoken unto myself. And the sonnets
are these :—

I.

You that thus wear a modest countenance
  With lids weigh'd down by the heart's heaviness,
  Whence come you, that among you every face
Appears the same, for its pale troubled glance ?
Have you beheld my lady's face, perchance,
  Bow'd with the grief that Love makes full of grace ?
  Say now, " This thing is thus " ; as my heart says,
Marking your grave and sorrowful advance.
And if indeed you come from where she sighs
  And mourns, may it please you (for his heart's relief)
    To tell how it fares with her unto him
Who knows that you have wept, seeing your eyes, *
  And is so grieved with looking on your grief
    That his heart trembles and his sight grows dim ?

*This sonnet is divided into two parts. In the first, I
call and ask these ladies whether they come from her, telling
them that I think they do, because they return the nobler.*

*In the second, I pray them to tell me of her ; and the second
begins here, " And if indeed."*

II.

CANST thou indeed be he that still would sing
    Of our dear lady unto none but us ?   .
    For though thy voice confirms that it is thus,
Thy visage might another witness bring.
And wherefore is thy grief so sore a thing
    That grieving thou mak'st others dolorous ?
    Hast thou too seen her weep, that thou from us
Canst not conceal thine inward sorrowing ?
Nay, leave our woe to us : let us alone :
    'Twere sin if one should strive to soothe our woe,
    For in her weeping we have heard her speak ·
Also her look's so full of her heart's moan
    That they who should behold her, looking so,
    Must fall aswoon, feeling all life grow weak.

*This sonnet has four parts, as the ladies in whose
person I reply had four forms of answer. And, because
these are sufficiently shown above, I stay not to explain the
purport of the parts, and therefore I only discriminate them.
The second begins here, " And wherefore is thy grief"; the
third here, " Nay, leave our woe"; the fourth, " Also her
look."*

A few days after this, my body became afflicted with
a painful infirmity, whereby I suffered bitter anguish for
many days, which at last brought me unto such weakness
that I could no longer move. And I remember that on
the ninth day, being overcome with intolerable pain, a
thought came into my mind concerning my lady : but
when it had a little nourished this thought, my mind
returned to its brooding over mine enfeebled body. And
then perceiving how frail a thing life is, even though
health keep with it, the matter seemed to me so pitiful

that I could not choose but weep; and weeping I said within myself: "Certainly it must some time come to pass that the very gentle Beatrice will die." Then, feeling bewildered, I closed mine eyes; and my brain began to be in travail as the brain of one frantic, and to have such imaginations as here follow.

And at the first, it seemed to me that I saw certain faces of women with their hair loosened, which called out to me, "Thou shalt surely die"; after the which, other terrible and unknown appearances said unto me, "Thou art dead." At length, as my phantasy held on in its wanderings, I came to be I knew not where, and to behold a throng of dishevelled ladies wonderfully sad, who kept going hither and thither weeping. Then the sun went out, so that the stars showed themselves, and they were of such a colour that I knew they must be weeping: and it seemed to me that the birds fell dead out of the sky, and that there were great earthquakes. With that, while I wondered in my trance, and was filled with a grievous fear, I conceived that a certain friend came unto me and said: "Hast thou not heard? She that was thine excellent lady hath been taken out of life." Then I began to weep very piteously; and not only in mine imagination, but with mine eyes, which were wet with tears. And I seemed to look towards Heaven, and to behold a multitude of angels who were returning upwards, having before them an exceedingly white cloud: and these angels were singing together gloriously, and the words of their song were these: "*Osanna in excelsis*"; and there was no more that I heard. Then my heart that was so full of love said unto me: "It is true that our lady lieth dead;" and it seemed to me that I went to look upon the body wherein that blessed and most noble spirit had had its abiding-place. And so strong was this idle imagining, that it made me to behold my lady in death, whose head certain ladies seemed to be covering with a white veil; and who was so humble of her aspect that it was as though she had

said, " I have attained to look on the beginning of peace."
And therewithal I came unto such humility by the sight
of her, that I cried out upon Death, saying : " Now come
unto me, and be not bitter against me any longer : surely,
there where thou hast been, thou hast learned gentleness.
Wherefore come now unto me who do greatly desire
thee : seest thou not that I wear thy colour already ? "
And when I had seen all those offices performed that
are fitting to be done unto the dead, it seemed to me
that I went back unto mine own chamber, and looked
up towards Heaven.   And so strong was my phantasy
that I wept again in very truth, and said with my true
voice : " O excellent soul ! how blessed is he that now
looketh upon thee ! "

And as I said these words, with a painful anguish of
sobbing and another prayer unto Death, a young and
gentle lady, who had been standing beside me where
I lay, conceiving that I wept and cried out because of
the pain of mine infirmity, was taken with trembling
and began to shed tears.   Whereby other ladies, who
were about the room, becoming aware of my discomfort
by reason of the moan that she made (who indeed was
of my very near kindred), led her away from where I
was, and then set themselves to awaken me, thinking
that I dreamed, and saying : " Sleep no longer, and be
not disquieted."

Then, by their words, this strong imagination was
brought suddenly to an end, at the moment that I was
about to say, " O Beatrice ! peace be with thee."   And
already I had said, " O Beatrice ! " when being aroused,
I opened mine eyes, and knew that it had been a
deception.   But albeit I had indeed uttered her name,
yet my voice was so broken with sobs, that it was not
understood by these ladies ; so that in spite of the
sore shame that I felt, I turned towards them by
Love's counselling.   And when they beheld me, they
began to say, " He seemeth as one dead," and to
whisper among themselves, " Let us strive if we may not

comfort him." Whereupon they spake to me many
soothing words, and questioned me moreover touching
the cause of my fear. Then I, being somewhat reassured,
and having perceived that it was a mere phantasy, said
unto them, "This thing it was that made me afeard;"
and told them of all that I had seen, from the beginning
even unto the end, but without once speaking the name
of my lady. Also, after I had recovered from my sick-
ness, I bethought me to write these things in rhyme;
deeming it a lovely thing to be known. Whereof I wrote
this poem :

A VERY pitiful lady, very young,
    Exceeding rich in human sympathies,
        Stood by, what time I clamour'd upon Death
And at the wild words wandering on my tongue
    And at the piteous look within mine eyes
        She was affrighted, that sobs choked her breath.
        So by her weeping where I lay beneath,
Some other gentle ladies came to know
My state, and made her go :
Afterward, bending themselves over me,
One said, "Awaken thee !"
        And one, "What thing thy sleep disquieteth ?"
With that, my soul woke up from its eclipse,
The while my lady's name rose to my lips :

But utter'd in a voice so sob-broken,
    So feeble with the agony of tears,
        That I alone might hear it in my heart;
And though that look was on my visage then
    Which he who is ashamed so plainly wears,
        Love made that I through shame held not apart,
        But gazed upon them. And my hue was such
That they look'd at each other and thought of death;
Saying under their breath
Most tenderly, "O let us comfort him :"

5

Then unto me : " What dream
    Was thine, that it hath shaken thee so much ?"
And when I was a little comforted,
" This, ladies, was the dream I dreamt," I said.

" I was a-thinking how life fails with us
    Suddenly after such a little while ;
        When Love sobb'd in my heart, which is his home.
Whereby my spirit wax'd so dolorous
    That in myself I said, with sick recoil :
        ' Yea, to my lady too this Death must come.'
        And therewithal such a bewilderment
Possess'd me, that I shut mine eyes for peace ;
And in my brain did cease
Order of thought, and every healthful thing.
Afterwards, wandering
    Amid a swarm of doubts that came and went,
Some certain women's faces hurried by,
And shrieked to me, ' Thou too shalt die, shalt die !'

" Then saw I many broken hinted sights
    In the uncertain state I stepp'd into.
        Meseem'd to be I know not in what place,
Where ladies through the streets, like mournful lights,
    Ran with loose hair, and eyes that frighten'd you,
        By their own terror, and a pale amaze :
        The while, little by little, as I thought,
The sun ceased, and the stars began to gather,
And each wept at the other ;
And birds dropp'd in mid-flight out of the sky ;
And earth shook suddenly ;
    And I was 'ware of one, hoarse and tired out,
Who ask'd of me : ' Hast thou not heard it said ? . . .
Thy lady, she that was so fair, is dead.'

" Then lifting up mine eyes, as the tears came,
    I saw the Angels, like a rain of manna,

In a long flight flying back Heavenward ;
Having a little cloud in front of them,
    After the which they went and said, ' Hosanna ' ;
    And if they had said more, you should have heard.
    Then Love said, ' Now shall all things be made
      clear :
Come and behold our lady where she lies.'
These 'wildering phantasies
Then carried me to see my lady dead.
Even as I there was led,
    Her ladies with a veil were covering her ;
And with her was such very humbleness
That she appeared to say, ' I am at peace.'

" And I became so humble in my grief,
    Seeing in her such deep humility,
      That I said : ' Death, I hold thee passing good
Henceforth, and a most gentle sweet relief,
    Since my dear love has chosen to dwell with thee :
      Pity, not hate, is thine, well understood.
      Lo ! I do so desire to see thy face
That I am like as one who nears the tomb ;
My soul entreats thee, Come.'
Then I departed, having made my moan ;
And when I was alone
    I said, and cast my eyes to the High Place :
' Blessed is he, fair soul, who meets thy glance !'
  . . . Just then you woke me, of your complai-
    saùnce."

*This poem has two parts. In the first, speaking to a
person undefined, I tell how I was aroused from a vain
phantasy by certain ladies, and how I promised them to tell
what it was. In the second, I say how I told them. The
second part begins here, " I was a-thinking." The first part
divides into two. In the first, I tell that which certain
ladies, and which one singly, did and said because of my
phantasy, before I had returned into my right senses. In*

the second, I tell what these ladies said to me after I had left off this wandering: and it begins here, " But uttered in a voice." Then, when I say, " I say a-thinking," I say how I told them this my imagination; and concerning this I have two parts. In the first, I tell, in order, this imagination. In the second, saying at what time they called me, I covertly thank them : and this part begins here, " Just then you woke me."

After this empty imagining, it happened on a day, as I sat thoughtful, that I was taken with such a strong trembling at the heart, that it could not have been otherwise in the presence of my lady. Whereupon I perceived that there was an appearance of Love beside me, and I seemed to see him coming from my lady; and he said, not aloud but within my heart : "Now take heed that thou bless the day when I entered into thee; for it is fitting that thou shouldst do so." And with that my heart was so full of gladness, that I could hardly believe it to be of very truth mine own heart and not another.

A short while after these words which my heart spoke to me with the tongue of Love, I saw coming towards me a certain lady who was very famous for her beauty, and of whom that friend whom I have already called the first among my friends had long been enamoured. This lady's right name was Joan ; but because of her comeliness (or at least it was so imagined) she was called of many *Primavera* (Spring), and went by that name among them. Then looking again, I perceived that the most noble Beatrice followed after her. And when both these ladies had passed by me, it seemed to me that Love spake again in my heart, saying : "She that came first was called Spring, only because of that which was to happen on this day. And it was I myself who caused that name to be given her ; seeing that as the Spring cometh first in the year, so should she come first on this day,* when Beatrice was to show herself after the vision

* There is a play in the original upon the words *Primavera*

of her servant. And even if thou go about to consider
her right name, it is also as one should say, 'She shall
come first': inasmuch as her name, Joan, is taken from
that John who went before the True Light, saying:
'*Ego vox clamantis in deserto: Parate viam Domini.*'"
And also it seemed to me that he added other words, to
wit: "He who should inquire delicately touching this
matter, could not but call Beatrice by mine own name,
which is to say, Love; beholding her so like unto
me."

Then I, having thought of this, imagined to write it
with rhymes and send it unto my chief friend; but
setting aside certain words † which seemed proper to be
set aside, because I believed that his heart still regarded
the beauty of her that was called Spring. And I wrote
this sonnet :—

> I FELT a spirit of love begin to stir
>   Within my heart, long time unfelt till then;
>   And saw Love coming towards me fair and fain,
> (That I scarce knew him for his joyful cheer),
> Saying, "Be now indeed my worshiper!"
>   And in his speech he laugh'd and laugh'd again.
>   Then, while it was his pleasure to remain,
> I chanced to look the way he had drawn near,
> And saw the Ladies Joan and Beatrice
>   Approach me, this the other following,
>   One and a second marvel instantly.

(Spring) and *prima verrà* (she shall come first), to which I have
given as near an equivalent as I could.

  * "I am the voice of one crying in the wilderness: 'Prepare ye
the way of the Lord.'"

  † That is (as I understand it), suppressing, from delicacy to-
wards his friend, the words in which Love describes Joan as merely
the forerunner of Beatrice. And perhaps in the latter part of this
sentence a reproach is gently conveyed to the fickle Guido Caval-
canti, who may already have transferred his homage (though Dante
had not then learned it) from Joan to Mandetta. (See his .Poems.)

And even as now my memory speaketh this,
　　Love spake it then : " The first is christen'd Spring;
　　The second Love, she is so like to me."

This sonnet has many parts : whereof the first tells how
I felt awakened within my heart the accustomed tremor, and
how it seemed that Love appeared to me joyful from afar.
The second says how it appeared to me that Love spake
within my heart, and what was his aspect. The third
tells how, after he had in such wise been with me a space, I
saw and heard certain things. The second part begins here,
" Saying, ' Be now ' " ; the third here, " Then, while it was
his pleasure." The third part divides into two. In the
first, I say what I saw. In the second, I say what I
heard ; and it begins here, " Love spake it then."
　　It might be here objected unto me, (and even by one
worthy of controversy,) that I have spoken of Love as
though it were a thing outward and visible : not only
a spiritual essence, but as a bodily substance also. The
which thing, in absolute truth, is a fallacy ; Love not
being of itself a substance, but an accident of substance.
Yet that I speak of Love as though it were a thing
tangible and even human, appears by three things which
I say thereof. And firstly, I say that I perceived Love
coming towards me ; whereby, seeing that *to come* be-
speaks locomotion, and seeing also how philosophy
teacheth us that none but a corporeal substance hath
locomotion, it seemeth that I speak of Love as of a cor-
poreal substance. And secondly, I say that Love smiled :
and thirdly, that Love spake ; faculties (and especially
the risible faculty) which appear proper unto man :
whereby it further seemeth that I speak of Love as of a
man. Now that this matter may be explained, (as is
fitting), it must first be remembered that anciently they
who wrote poems of Love wrote not in the vulgar tongue,
but rather certain poets in the Latin tongue. I mean,
among us, although perchance the same may have been
among others, and although likewise, as among the

Greeks, they were not writers of spoken language, but men of letters treated of these things.* And indeed it is not a great number of years since poetry began to be made in the vulgar tongue ; the writing of rhymes in spoken language corresponding to the writing in metre of Latin verse, by a certain analogy. And I say that it is but a little while, because if we examine the language of *oco* and the language of *sì*, † we shall not find in those tongues any written thing of an earlier date than the last hundred and fifty years. Also the reason why certain of a very mean sort obtained at the first some fame as poets is, that before them no man has written verses in the language of *sì :* and of these, the first was moved to the writing of such verses by the wish to make himself understood of a certain lady, unto whom Latin poetry was difficult. This thing is against such as rhyme concerning other matters than love; that mode of speech having been first used for the expression of love alone. ‡ Wherefore, seeing that poets have a license allowed them that is not allowed unto the writers of prose, and

---

* On reading Dante's treatise *De Vulgari Eloquio*, it will be found that the distinction which he intends here is not between one language, or dialect, and another ; but between " vulgar speech " (that is, the language handed down from mother to son without any conscious use of grammar or syntax), and language as regulated by grammarians and the laws of literary composition, and which Dante calls simply "Grammar." A great deal might be said on the bearings of the present passage, but it is no part of my plan to enter on such questions.

† *I.e.*, the languages of Provence and Tuscany.

‡ It strikes me that this curious passage furnishes a reason, hitherto (I believe) overlooked, why Dante put such of his lyrical poems as relate to philosophy into the form of love-poems. He liked writing in Italian rhyme rather than Latin metre ; he thought Italian rhyme ought to be confined to love-poems : therefore whatever he wrote (at this age) had to take the form of a love-poem. Thus any poem by Dante not concerning love is later than his twenty-seventh year (1291-2), when he wrote the prose of the *Vita Nuova ;* the poetry having been written earlier, at the time of the events referred to.

seeing also that they who write in rhyme are simply
poets in the vulgar tongue, it becomes fitting and reason-
able that a larger license should be given to these than
to other modern writers; and that any metaphor or
rhetorical similitude which is permitted unto poets, should
also be counted not unseemly in the rhymers of the
vulgar tongue. Thus, if we perceive that the former
have caused inanimate things to speak as though they
had sense and reason, and to discourse one with another;
yea, and not only actual things, but such also as have
no real existence (seeing that they have made things
which are not, to speak; and oftentimes written of those
which are merely accidents as though they were sub-
stances and things human); it should therefore be
permitted to the latter to do the like; which is to say,
not inconsiderately, but with such sufficient motive as
may afterwards be set forth in prose.

  That the Latin poets have done thus, appears through
Virgil, where he saith that Juno (to wit, a goddess hostile
to the Trojans) spake unto Æolus, master of the Winds;
as it is written in the first book of the Æneid, *Æole,
namque tibi, etc.;* and that this master of the Winds
made reply: *Tuus, o regina, quid optes—Explorare labor,
mihi jussa capessere fas est.* And through the same poet,
the inanimate thing speaketh unto the animate, in the
third book of the Æneid, where it is written: *Dardanidæ
duri, etc.* With Lucan, the animate thing speaketh to the
inanimate; as thus: *Multum, Roma, tamen debes civilibus
armis.* In Horace, man is made to speak to his own
intelligence as unto another person; (and not only hath
Horace done this, but herein he followeth the excellent
Homer,) as thus in his Poetics: *Dic mihi, Musa, virum,
etc.* Through Ovid, Love speaketh as a human creature,
in the beginning of his discourse *De Remediis Amoris:*
as thus: *Bella mihi, video, bella parantur, ait.* By which
ensamples this thing shall be made manifest unto such
as may be offended at any part of this my book. And
lest some of the common sort should be moved to jeering

hereat, I will here add, that neither did these ancient poets speak thus without consideration, nor should they who are makers of rhyme in our day write after the same fashion, having no reason in what they write; for it were a shameful thing if one should rhyme under the semblance of metaphor or rhetorical similitude, and afterwards, being questioned thereof, should be unable to rid his words of such semblance, unto their right understanding. Of whom, (to wit, of such as rhyme thus foolishly,) myself and the first among my friends do know many.

But returning to the matter of my discourse. This excellent lady of whom I spake in what hath gone before, came at last into such favour with all men, that when she passed anywhere folk ran to behold her; which thing was a deep joy to me: and when she drew near unto any, so much truth and simpleness entered into his heart, that he dared neither to lift his eyes nor to return her salutation: and unto this, many who have felt it can bear witness. She went along crowned and clothed with humility, showing no whit of pride in all that she heard and saw: and when she had gone by, it was said of many, "This is not a woman, but one of the beautiful angels of Heaven:" and there were some that said: "This is surely a miracle; blessed be the Lord, who hath power to work thus marvellously." I say, of very sooth, that she showed herself so gentle and so full of all perfection, that she bred in those who looked upon her a soothing quiet beyond any speech; neither could any look upon her without sighing immediately. These things, and things yet more wonderful, were brought to pass through her miraculous virtue. Wherefore I, considering thereof and wishing to resume the endless tale of her praises, resolved to write somewhat wherein I might dwell on her surpassing influence; to the end that not only they who had beheld her, but others also, might know as much concerning her as words could give to the understanding. And it was then that I wrote this sonnet :—

My lady looks so gentle and so pure
  When yielding salutation by the way,
  That the tongue trembles and has nought to say,
And the eyes, which fain would see, may not endure.
And still, amid the praise she hears secure,
  She walks with humbleness for her array;
  Seeming a creature sent from Heaven to stay
On earth, and show a miracle made sure.
She is so pleasant in the eyes of men
That through the sight the inmost heart doth gain
  A sweetness which needs proof to know it by:
And from between her lips there seems to move
A soothing essence that is full of love,
  Saying for ever to the spirit, "Sigh!"

This sonnet is so easy to understand, from what is afore narrated, that it needs no division; and therefore, leaving it, I say also that this excellent lady came into such favour with all men, that not only she herself was honoured and commended, but through her companionship, honour and commendation came unto others. Wherefore I, perceiving this, and wishing that it should also be made manifest to those that beheld it not, wrote the sonnet here following; wherein is signified the power which her virtue had upon other ladies:—

For certain he hath seen all perfectness
  Who among other ladies hath seen mine:
  They that go with her humbly should combine
To thank their God for such peculiar grace.
So perfect is the beauty of her face
  That it begets in no wise any sign
  Of envy, but draws round her a clear line
Of love, and blessed faith, and gentleness.
Merely the sight of her makes all things bow:
  Not she herself alone is holier
    Than all; but hers, through her, are raised above.

From all her acts such lovely graces flow
  That truly one may never think of her
  Without a passion of exceeding love.

This sonnet has three parts. In the first, I say in what company this lady appeared most wondrous. In the second, I say how gracious was her society. In the third, I tell of the things which she, with power, worked upon others. The second begins here, " They that go with her" ; the third here, "So perfect." This last part divides into three. In the first, I tell what she operated upon women, that is, by their own faculties. In the second, I tell what she operated in them through others. In the third, I say how she not only operated in women, but in all people ; and not only while herself present, but, by memory of her, operated wondrously. The second begins here, " Merely the sight" ; the third here, " From all her acts."

Thereafter on a day, I began to consider that which I had said of my lady : to wit, in these two sonnets aforegone : and becoming aware that I had not spoken of her immediate effect on me at that especial time, it seemed to me that I had spoken defectively. Whereupon I resolved to write somewhat of the manner wherein I was then subject to her influence, and of what her influence then was. And conceiving that I should not be able to say these things in the small compass of a sonnet, I began therefore a poem with this beginning :—

LOVE hath so long possessed me for his own
  And made his lordship so familiar
That he, who at first irked me, is now grown
  Unto my heart as its best secrets are.
And thus, when he in such sore wise doth mar
My life that all its strength seems gone from it,
Mine inmost being then feels throughly quit
  Of anguish, and all evil keeps afar.

Love also gathers to such power in me
   That my sighs speak, each one a grievous thing,
   Always soliciting
My lady's salutation piteously.
Whenever she beholds me, it is so,
Who is more sweet than any words can show.

*   *   *   *   *   *
*   *   *   *   *   *

*Quomodo sedet sola civitas plena populo ! facta est quasi
vidua domina gentium !* *

I was still occupied with this poem, (having composed
thereof only the above written stanza,) when the Lord
God of justice called my most gracious lady unto Him-
self, that she might be glorious under the banner of that
blessed Queen Mary, whose name had always a deep
reverence in the words of holy Beatrice. And because
haply it might be found good that I should say some-
what concerning her departure, I will herein declare
what are the reasons which make that I shall not do so.

And the reasons are three. The first is, that such
matter belongeth not of right to the present argument; if
one consider the opening of this little book. The second
is, that even though the present argument required it,
my pen doth not suffice to write in a fit manner of this
thing. And the third is, that were it both possible and
of absolute necessity, it would still be unseemly for me
to speak thereof, seeing that thereby it must behove me
to speak also mine own praises : a thing that in who-
soever doeth it is worthy of blame. For the which
reasons, I will leave this matter to be treated of by some
other than myself.

Nevertheless, as the number nine, which number hath

---

* " How doth the city sit solitary, that was full of people ! how
is she become as a widow, she that was great among the nations !"
—*Lamentations of Jeremiah*, i. 1.

often had mention in what hath gone before, (and not, as it might appear, without reason,) seems also to have borne a part in the manner of her death : it is therefore right that I should say somewhat thereof. And for this cause, having first said what was the part it bore herein, I will afterwards point out a reason which made that this number was so closely allied unto my lady.

I say, then, that according to the division of time in Italy her most noble spirit departed from among us in the first hour of the ninth day of the month ; and according to the division of time in Syria, in the ninth month of the year : seeing that Tismim, which with us is October, is there the first month. Also she was taken from among us in that year of our reckoning (to wit, of the years of our Lord) in which the perfect number was nine times multiplied within that century wherein she was born into the world : which is to say, the thirteenth century of Christians.*

And touching the reason why this number was so closely allied unto her, it may peradventure be this. According to Ptolemy, (and also to the Christian verity,) the revolving heavens are nine ; and according to the common opinion among astrologers, these nine heavens together have influence over the earth. Wherefore it would appear that this number was thus allied unto her for the purpose of signifying that, at her birth, all these nine heavens were at perfect unity with each other as to their influence. This is one reason that may be brought : but more narrowly considering, and according to the infallible truth, this number was her own self : that is to say, by similitude. As thus. The number three is the

---

* Beatrice Portinari will thus be found to have died during the first hour of the 9th of June, 1290. And from what Dante says at the commencement of this work, (viz. that she was younger than himself by eight or nine months,) it may also be gathered that her age, at the time of her death, was twenty-four years and three months. The "perfect number" mentioned in the present passage is the number ten.

root of the number nine; seeing that without the inter-
position of any other number, being multiplied merely
by itself, it produceth nine, as we manifestly perceive
that three times three are nine. Thus, three being of
itself the efficient of nine, and the Great Efficient of
Miracles being of Himself Three Persons (to wit: the
Father, the Son, and the Holy Spirit), which, being
Three, are also One :—this lady was accompanied by the
number nine to the end that men might clearly perceive
her to be a nine, that is, a miracle, whose only root is
the Holy Trinity. It may be that a more subtile person
would find for this thing a reason of greater subtilty :
but such is the reason that I find, and that liketh me best.

After this most gracious creature had gone out from
among us, the whole city came to be as it were widowed
and despoiled of all dignity. Then I, left mourning in
this desolate city, wrote unto the principal persons
thereof, in an epistle, concerning its condition; taking
for my commencement those words of Jeremias : *Quo-
modo sedet sola civitas ! etc.* And I make mention of this,
that none may marvel wherefore I set down these words
before, in beginning to treat of her death. Also if any
should blame me, in that I do not transcribe that epistle
whereof I have spoken, I will make it mine excuse that
I began this little book with the intent that it should
be written altogether in the vulgar tongue; wherefore,
seeing that the epistle I speak of is in Latin, it belongeth
not to mine undertaking: more especially as I know that
my chief friend, for whom I write this book, wished also
that the whole of it should be in the vulgar tongue.

When mine eyes had wept for some while, until they
were so weary with weeping that I could no longer
through them give ease to my sorrow, I bethought me
that a few mournful words might stand me instead of
tears. And therefore I proposed to make a poem, that
weeping I might speak therein of her for whom so much
sorrow had destroyed my spirit ; and I then began " The
eyes that weep."

*That this poem may seem to remain the more widowed
at its close, I will divide it before writing it; and this
method I will observe henceforward. I say that this poor
little poem has three parts. The first is a prelude. In the
second, I speak of her. In the third, I speak pitifully to the
poem. The second begins here, "Beatrice is gone up"; the
third here, "Weep, pitiful Song of mine." The first
divides into three. In the first, I say what moves me to
speak. In the second, I say to whom I mean to speak. In
the third, I say of whom I mean to speak. The second
begins here, "And because often, thinking"; the third
here, "And I will say." Then, when I say, "Beatrice is
gone up," I speak of her; and concerning this I have two
parts. First, I tell the cause why she was taken away
from us: afterwards, I say how one weeps her parting;
and this part commences here, "Wonderfully." This part
divides into three. In the first, I say who it is that weeps
her not. In the second, I say who it is that doth weep her.
In the third, I speak of my condition. The second begins
here, "But sighing comes, and grief"; the third, "With
sighs." Then, when I say, "Weep, pitiful Song of mine,"
I speak to this my song, telling it what ladies to go to, ana
stay with.*

THE eyes that weep for pity of the heart
    Have wept so long that their grief languisheth,
      And they have no more tears to weep withal:
And now, if I would ease me of a part
    Of what, little by little, leads to death,
      It must be done by speech, or not at all.
      And because often, thinking, I recall
How it was pleasant, ere she went afar,
    To talk of her with you, kind damozels,
      I talk with no one else,
But only with such hearts as women's are.
    And I will say,—still sobbing as speech fails,—
That she hath gone to Heaven suddenly,
And hath left Love below, to mourn with me.

Beatrice is gone up into high Heaven,
 The kingdom where the angels are at peace;
  And lives with them : and to her friends is dead.
Not by the frost of winter was she driven
 Away, like others; nor by summer-heats;
  But through a perfect gentleness, instead.
  For from the lamp of her meek lowlihead
Such an exceeding glory went up hence
 That it woke wonder in the Eternal Sire,
 Until a sweet desire
Entered Him for that lovely excellence,
 So that He bade her to Himself aspire;
Counting this weary and most evil place
Unworthy of a thing so full of grace.

Wonderfully out of the beautiful form
 Soared her clear spirit, waxing glad the while;
  And is in its first home, there where it is.
Who speaks thereof, and feels not the tears warm
 Upon his face, must have become so vile
  As to be dead to all sweet sympathies.
  Out upon him! an abject wretch like this
May not imagine anything of her,—
 He needs no bitter tears for his relief.
 But sighing comes, and grief,
And the desire to find no comforter,
 (Save only Death, who makes all sorrow brief,)
To him who for a while turns in his thought
How she hath been among us, and is not.

With sighs my bosom always laboureth
 In thinking, as I do continually,
  Of her for whom my heart now breaks apace;
And very often when I think of death,
 Such a great inward longing comes to me
  That it will change the colour of my face;
  And, if the idea settles in its place,

All my limbs shake as with an ague-fit :
   Till, starting up in wild bewilderment,
   I do become so shent
That I go forth, lest folk misdoubt of it.
   Afterward, calling with a sore lament
On Beatrice, I ask, "Canst thou be dead?"
And calling on her, I am comforted.

Grief with its tears, and anguish with its sighs,
   Come to me now whene'er I am alone ;
    So that I think the sight of me gives pain.
And what my life hath been, that living dies,
   Since for my lady the New Birth's begun,
    I have not any language to explain.
    And so, dear ladies, though my heart were fain,
I scarce could tell indeed how I am thus.
   All joy is with my bitter life at war ;
   Yea, I am fallen so far
That all men seem to say, "Go out from us,"
   Eyeing my cold white lips, how dead they are.
But she, though I be bowed unto the dust,
Watches me ; and will guerdon me, I trust.

Weep, pitiful Song of mine, upon thy way,
   To the dames going and the damozels
   For whom and for none else
Thy sisters have made music many a day.
Thou, that art very sad and not as they
   Go dwell thou with them as a mourner dwells.

After I had written this poem, I received the visit of
a friend whom I counted as second unto me in the
degrees of friendship, and who, moreover, had been
united by the nearest kindred to that most gracious
creature. And when we had a little spoken together,
he began to solicit me that I would write somewhat

6

in memory of a lady who had died; and he disguised his speech, so as to seem to be speaking of another who was but lately dead: wherefore I, perceiving that his speech was of none other than that blessed one herself, told him that it should be done as he required. Then afterwards, having thought thereof, I imagined to give vent in a sonnet to some part of my hidden lamentations; but in such sort that it might seem to be spoken by this friend of mine, to whom I was to give it. And the sonnet saith thus; "Stay now with me," etc.

This sonnet has two parts. In the first, I call the Faithful of Love to hear me. In the second, I relate my miserable condition. The second begins here, "Mark how they force."

STAY now with me, and listen to my sighs,
　　Ye piteous hearts, as pity bids ye do.
　　Mark how they force their way out and press through;
If they be once pent up, the whole life dies.
Seeing that now indeed my weary eyes
　　Oftener refuse than I can tell to you
　　(Even though my endless grief is ever new,)
To weep and let the smothered anguish rise.
Also in sighing ye shall hear me call
　　On her whose blessed presence doth enrich
　　　The only home that well befitteth her:
And ye shall hear a bitter scorn of all
　　Sent from the inmost of my spirit in speech
　　　That mourns its joy and its joy's minister.

But when I had written this sonnet, bethinking me who he was to whom I was to give it, that it might appear to be his speech, it seemed to me that this was but a poor and barren gift for one of her so near kindred. Wherefore, before giving him this sonnet, I wrote two stanzas of a poem: the first being written in very sooth as though it were spoken by him, but the other being

mine own speech, albeit, unto one who should not look
closely, they would both seem to be said by the same
person. Nevertheless, looking closely, one must perceive
that it is not so, inasmuch as one does not call this
most gracious creature *his lady*, and the other does, as
is manifestly apparent. And I gave the poem and the
sonnet unto my friend, saying that I had made them
only for him.

*The poem begins, " Whatever while," and has two parts.
In the first, that is, in the first stanza, this my dear friend,
her kinsman, laments. In the second, I lament ; that is,
in the other stanza, which begins, " For ever." And thus
it appears that in this poem two persons lament, of whom
one laments as a brother, the other as a servant.*

WHATEVER while the thought comes over me
　　That I may not again
　　　Behold that lady whom I mourn for now,
About my heart my mind brings constantly
　　So much of extreme pain
　　　That I say, Soul of mine, why stayest thou ?
　　　Truly the anguish, soul, that we must bow
Beneath, until we win out of this life,
　　Gives me full oft a fear that trembleth :
　　So that I call on Death
Even as on Sleep one calleth after strife,
Saying, Come unto me. Life showeth grim
And bare ; and if one dies, I envy him.

For ever, among all my sighs which burn,
　　There is a piteous speech
　　　That clamours upon death continually :
Yea, unto him doth my whole spirit turn
　　Since first his hand did reach
　　　My lady's life with most foul cruelty.
　　　But from the height of woman's fairness, she,
Going up from us with the joy we had,

Grew perfectly and spiritually fair ;
That so she spreads even there
A light of Love which makes the Angels glad,
And even unto their subtle minds can bring
A certain awe of profound marvelling.

On that day which fulfilled the year since my lady
had been made of the citizens of eternal life, remem-
bering me of her as I sat alone, I betook myself to
draw the resemblance of an angel upon certain tablets.
And while I did thus, chancing to turn my head, I
perceived that some were standing beside me to whom
I should have given courteous welcome, and that they
were observing what I did : also I learned afterwards
that they had been there a while before I perceived
them. Perceiving whom, I arose for salutation, and
said : " Another was with me." *

Afterwards, when they had left me, I set myself
again to mine occupation, to wit, to the drawing figures
of angels : in doing which, I conceived to write of this
matter in rhyme, as for her anniversary, and to address
my rhymes unto those who had just left me. It was
then that I wrote the sonnet which saith, "That lady" :
and as this sonnet hath two commencements, it be-
hoveth me to divide it with both of them here.

*I say that, according to the first, this sonnet has three
parts. In the first, I say that this lady was then in my
memory. In the second, I tell what Love therefore did
with me. In the third, I speak of the effects of Love. The
second begins here, " Love knowing " ; the third here,
" Forth went they." This part divides into two. In the
one, I say that all my sighs issued speaking. In the other,
I say how some spoke certain words different from the
others. The second begins here, " And still." In this*

---

* Thus according to some texts. The majority, however, add
the words, "And therefore was I in thought :" but the shorter
speech is perhaps the more forcible and pathetic.

*same manner is it divided with the other beginning, save
that, in the first part, I tell when this lady had thus come
into my mind, and this I say not in the other.*

THAT lady of all gentle memories
   Had lighted on my soul ;—whose new abode
   Lies now, as it was well ordained of God,
Among the poor in heart, where Mary is.
Love, knowing that dear image to be his,
   Woke up within the sick heart sorrow-bow'd,
   Unto the sighs which are its weary load
Saying, " Go forth."   And they went forth, I wis ;
Forth went they from my breast that throbbed and ached ;
   With such a pang as oftentimes will bathe
    Mine eyes with tears when I am left alone.
   And still those sighs which drew the heaviest breath
Came whispering thus : " O noble intellect !
   It is a year to-day that thou art gone."

SECOND COMMENCEMENT.

THAT lady of all gentle memories
   Had lighted on my soul ;—for whose sake flowed
   The tears of Love ; in whom the power abode
Which led you to observe while I did this.
Love, knowing that dear image to be his, etc.

Then, having sat for some space sorely in thought
because of the time that was now past, I was so filled
with dolorous imaginings that it became outwardly mani-
fest in mine altered countenance. Whereupon, feeling
this and being in dread lest any should have seen me,
I lifted mine eyes to look ; and then perceived a young
and very beautiful lady, who was gazing upon me from
a window with a gaze full of pity, so that the very sum
of pity appeared gathered together in her. And seeing
that unhappy persons, when they beget compassion in

others, are then most moved unto weeping, as though
they also felt pity for themselves, it came to pass that
mine eyes began to be inclined unto tears. Wherefore,
becoming fearful lest I should make manifest mine
abject condition, I rose up, and went where I could not
be seen of that lady; saying afterwards within myself:
"Certainly with her also must abide most noble Love."
And with that, I resolved upon writing a sonnet, wherein,
speaking unto her, I should say all that I have just said.
And as this sonnet is very evident, I will not divide it :—

MINE eyes beheld the blessed pity spring
   Into thy countenance immediately
   A while agone, when thou beheldst in mc
The sickness only hidden grief can bring;
And then I knew thou wast considering
   How abject and forlorn my life must be;
   And I became afraid that thou shouldst see
My weeping, and account it a base thing.
Therefore I went out from thee; feeling how
   The tears were straightway loosened at my heart
     Beneath thine eyes' compassionate control.
   And afterwards I said within my soul :
  "Lo! with this lady dwells the counterpart
Of the same Love who holds me weeping now."

It happened after this that whensoever I was seen of
this lady, she became pale and of a piteous countenance,
as though it had been with love; whereby she remem-
bered me many times of my own most noble lady, who
was wont to be of a like paleness. And I know that
often, when I could not weep nor in any way give ease
unto mine anguish, I went to look upon this lady, who
seemed to bring the tears into my eyes by the mere sight
of her. Of the which thing I bethought me to speak
unto her in rhyme, and then made this sonnet: which
begins, "Love's pallor," and which is plain without being
divided, by its exposition aforesaid :—

LOVE's pallor and the semblance of deep ruth
  Were never yet shown forth so perfectly
  In any lady's face, chancing to see
Grief's miserable countenance uncouth,
As in thine, lady, they have sprung to soothe,
  When in mine anguish thou hast looked on me ;
  Until sometimes it seems as if, through thee,
My heart might almost wander from its truth.
Yet so it is, I cannot hold mine eyes
  From gazing very often upon thine
    In the sore hope to shed those tears they keep ;
And at such time, thou mak'st the pent tears rise
  Even to the brim, till the eyes waste and pine ;
    Yet cannot they, while thou art present, weep.

At length, by the constant sight of this lady, mine eyes began to be gladdened overmuch with her company ; through which thing many times I had much unrest, and rebuked myself as a base person : also, many times I cursed the unsteadfastness of mine eyes, and said to them inwardly : " Was not your grievous condition of weeping wont one while to make others weep ? And will ye now forget this thing because a lady looketh upon you ? who so looketh merely in compassion of the grief ye then showed for your own blessed lady. But whatso ye can, that do ye, accursed eyes ! many a time will I make you remember it ! for never, till death dry you up, should ye make an end of your weeping." And when I had spoken thus unto mine eyes, I was taken again with extreme and grievous sighing. And to the end that this inward strife which I had undergone might not be hidden from all saving the miserable wretch who endured it, I proposed to write a sonnet, and to comprehend in it this horrible condition. And I wrote this which begins, " The very bitter weeping."

The sonnet has two parts. In the first, I speak to my eyes, as my heart spoke within myself. In the second, I remove a difficulty, showing who it is that speaks thus : and this part begins here, " So far." It well might receive other divisions also ; but this would be useless, since it is manifest by the preceding exposition.

"THE very bitter weeping that ye made
  So long a time together, eyes of mine,
  Was wont to make the tears of pity shine
In other eyes full oft, as I have said.
But now this thing were scarce rememberèd
  If I, on my part, foully would combine
  With you, and not recall each ancient sign
Of grief, and her for whom your tears were shed.
It is your fickleness that doth betray
  My mind to fears, and makes me tremble thus
    What while a lady greets me with her eyes.
Except by death, we must not any way
  Forget our lady who is gone from us."
    So far doth my heart utter, and then sighs.

The sight of this lady brought me into so unwonted a condition that I often thought of her as of one too dear unto me ; and I began to consider her thus : " This lady is young, beautiful, gentle, and wise : perchance it was Love himself who set her in my path, that so my life might find peace." And there were times when I thought yet more fondly, until my heart consented unto its reasoning. But when it had so consented, my thought would often turn round upon me, as moved by reason, and cause me to say within myself : " What hope is this which would console me after so base a fashion, and which hath taken the place of all other imagining ? " Also there was another voice within me, that said : " And wilt thou, having suffered so much tribulation through Love, not escape while yet thou mayst from so much bitterness ? Thou must surely know that this thought carries with it the desire of Love, and drew its life from the gentle eyes of that lady who vouchsafed

thee so much pity." Wherefore I, having striven sorely
and very often with myself, bethought me to say some-
what thereof in rhyme. And seeing that in the battle
of doubts, the victory most often remained with such as
inclined towards the lady of whom I speak, it seemed to
me that I should address this sonnet unto her : in the
first line whereof, I call that thought which spake of her
a gentle thought, only because it spoke of one who was
gentle ; being of itself most vile.*

*In this sonnet I make myself into two, according as my
thoughts were divided one from the other. The one part I
call Heart, that is, appetite; the other, Soul, that is, reason ;
and I tell what one saith to the other. And that it is fitting
to call the appetite Heart, and the reason Soul, is manifest
enough to them to whom I wish this to be open. True it is
that, in the preceding sonnet, I take the part of the Heart
against the Eyes ; and that appears contrary to what I say
in the present ; and therefore I say that, there also, by the
Heart I mean appetite, because yet greater was my desire to
remember my most gentle lady than to see this other, although
indeed I had some appetite towards her, but it appeared
slight : wherefrom it appears that the one statement is not
contrary to the other. This sonnet has three parts. In the
first, I begin to say to this lady how my desires turn all
towards her. In the second, I say how the soul, that is the
reason, speaks to the Heart, that is, to the appetite. In the
third, I say how the latter answers. The second begins
here, "And what is this?" the third here, "And the
heart answers."*

---

* Boccaccio tells us that Dante was married to Gemma Donati
about a year after the death of Beatrice. Can Gemma then be "the
lady of the window," his love for whom Dante so contemns ? Such
a passing conjecture (when considered together with the inter-
pretation of this passage in Dante's later work, the *Convito*) would
of course imply an admission of what I believe to lie at the heart
of all true Dantesque commentary; that is, the existence always
of the actual events even where the allegorical superstructure has
been raised by Dante himself.

A GENTLE thought there is will often start,
   Within my secret self, to speech of thee :
   Also of Love it speaks so tenderly
That much in me consents and takes its part:
" And what is this," the soul saith to the heart,
   " That cometh thus to comfort thee and me,
   And thence where it would dwell, thus potently
Can drive all other thoughts by its strange art ? "
And the heart answers : " Be no more at strife
   'Twixt doubt and doubt : this is Love's messenger
     And speaketh but his words, from him received ;
And all the strength it owns and all the life
   It draweth from the gentle eyes of her
     Who, looking on our grief, hath often grieved."

But against this adversary of reason, there rose up in me on a certain day, about the ninth hour, a strong visible phantasy, wherein I seemed to behold the most gracious Beatrice, habited in that crimson raiment which she had worn when I had first beheld her; also she appeared to me of the same tender age as then. Whereupon I fell into a deep thought of her : and my memory ran back, according to the order of time, unto all those matters in the which she had borne a part ; and my heart began painfully to repent of the desire by which it had so basely let itself be possessed during so many days, contrary to the constancy of reason.

And then, this evil desire being quite gone from me, all my thoughts turned again unto their excellent Beatrice. And I say most truly that from that hour I thought constantly of her with the whole humbled and ashamed heart ; the which became often manifest in sighs, that had among them the name of that most gracious creature, and how she departed from us. Also it would come to pass very often, through the bitter anguish of some one thought, that I forgot both it, and myself, and where I was. By this increase of sighs, my weeping, which before had been somewhat lessened, increased in like manner ;

so that mine eyes seemed to long only for tears and to
cherish them, and came at last to be circled about with
red as though they had suffered martyrdom : neither
were they able to look again upon the beauty of any face
that might again bring them to shame and evil : from
which things it will appear that they were fitly guer-
doned for their unsteadfastness.   Wherefore I (wishing
that mine abandonment of all such evil desires and vain
temptations should be certified and made manifest,
beyond all doubts which might have been suggested by
the rhymes aforewritten) proposed to write a sonnet
wherein I should express this purport.   And I then
wrote, " Woe's me ! "

*I said, " Woe's me ! " because I was ashamed of the
trifling of mine eyes.   This sonnet I do not divide, since its
purport is manifest enough.*

Woe's me ! by dint of all these sighs that come
    Forth of my heart, its endless grief to prove,
    Mine eyes are conquered, so that even to move
Their lids for greeting is grown troublesome,
They wept so long that now they are grief's home,
    And count their tears all laughter far above ;
    They wept till they are circled now by Love
With a red circle in sign of martyrdom.
These musings, and the sighs they bring from me,
    Are grown at last so constant and so sore
        That love swoons in my spirit with faint breath ;
Hearing in those sad sounds continually
    The most sweet name that my dead lady bore,
        With many grievous words touching her death.

About this time, it happened that a great number of
persons undertook a pilgrimage, to the end that they
might behold that blessed portraiture bequeathed unto us
by our Lord Jesus Christ as the image of His beautiful
countenance * (upon which countenance my dear lady

---

* The Veronica (*Vera icon*, or true image) ; that is, the napkin

now looketh continually).   And certain among these pilgrims, who seemed very thoughtful, passed by a path which is well-nigh in the midst of the city where my most gracious lady was born, and abode, and at last died.

Then I, beholding them, said within myself : " These pilgrims seen to be come from very far ; and I think they cannot have heard speak of this lady, or know anything concerning her.   Their thoughts are not of her, but of other things ; it may be, of their friends who are far distant, and whom we, in our turn, know not."   And I went on to say : " I know that if they were of a country near unto us, they would in some wise seem disturbed, passing through this city which is so full of grief."   And I said also : " If I could speak with them a space, I am certain that I should make them weep before they went forth of this city ; for those things that they would hear from me must needs beget weeping in any."

And when the last of them had gone by me, I bethought me to write a sonnet, showing forth mine inward speech ; and that it might seem the more pitiful, I made as though I had spoken it indeed unto them.   And I wrote this sonnet, which beginneth : " Ye pilgrim-folk." I made use of the word *pilgrim* for its general signification ; for " pilgrim " may be understood in two senses, one general, and one special.   General, so far as any man may be called a pilgrim who leaveth the place of his birth ; whereas, more narrowly speaking, he only is

---

with which a woman was said to have wiped our Saviour's face on His way to the cross, and which miraculously retained its likeness. Dante makes mention of it also in the *Commedia* (Parad. xxi. 103), where he says :—

> " Qual è colui che forse di Croazia
>   Viene a veder la Veronica nostra
> Che per l'antica fama non si sazia
>   Ma dice nel pensier fin che si mostra :
> Signor mio Gesù Cristo, Iddio verace,
>   Or fu sì fatta la sembianza vostra ? " etc.

a pilgrim who goeth towards or frowards the House of
St. James. For there are three separate denominations
proper unto those who undertake journeys to the glory of
God. They are called Palmers who go beyond the seas
eastward, whence often they bring palm-branches. And
Pilgrims, as I have said, are they who journey unto the
holy House of Gallicia ; seeing that no other apostle was
buried so far from his birth-place as was the blessed
Saint James. And there is a third sort who are called
Romers ; in that they go whither these whom I have
called pilgrims went : which is to say, unto Rome.

*This sonnet is not divided, because its own words suffi-
ciently declare it.*

YE pilgrim-folk, advancing pensively
    As if in thought of distant things, I pray,
    Is your own land indeed so far away—
As by your aspect it would seem to be—
That this our heavy sorrow leaves you free
    Though passing through the mournful town mid-way ;
    Like unto men that understand to-day
Nothing at all of her great misery ?
Yet if ye will but stay, whom I accost,
    And listen to my words a little space,
    At going ye shall mourn with a loud voice.
It is her Beatrice that she hath lost ;
    Of whom the least word spoken holds such grace
    That men weep hearing it, and have no choice.

A while after these things, two gentle ladies sent unto
me, praying that I would bestow upon them certain of
these my rhymes. And I (taking into account their
worthiness and consideration,) resolved that I would
write also a new thing, and send it them together with
those others, to the end that their wishes might be more
honourably fulfilled. Therefore I made a sonnet, which
narrates my condition, and which I caused to be con-
veyed to them, accompanied by the one preceding, and

with that other which begins, " Stay now with me and listen to my sighs." And the new sonnet is, " Beyond the sphere."

This sonnet comprises five parts. In the first, I tell whither my thought goeth, naming the place by the name of one of its effects. In the second, I say wherefore it goeth up, and who makes it go thus. In the third, I tell what it saw, namely, a lady honoured. And I then call it a " Pilgrim Spirit," because it goes up spiritually, and like a pilgrim who is out of his known country. In the fourth, I say how the spirit sees her such (that is, in such quality) that I cannot understand her ; that is to say my thought rises into the quality of her in a degree that my intellect cannot comprehend, seeing that our intellect is, towards those blessed souls, like our eye weak against the sun ; and this the Philosopher says in the Second of the Metaphysics. In the fifth, I say that, although I cannot see there whither my thought carries me—that is, to her admirable essence— I at least understand this, namely, that it is a thought of my lady, because I often hear her name therein. And, at the end of this fifth part, I say, " Ladies mine," to show that they are ladies to whom I speak. The second part begins, "A new perception " ; the third, "When it hath reached"; the fourth, " It sees her such"; the fifth, " And yet I know." It might be divided yet more nicely, and made yet clearer ; but this division may pass, and therefore I stay not to divide it further.

BEYOND the sphere which spreads to widest space
   Now soars the sigh that my heart sends above ;
   A new perception born of grieving Love
Guideth it upward the untrodden ways.
When it hath reached unto the end, and stays,
   It sees a lady round whom splendours move
   In homage ; till, by the great light thereof
Abashed, the pilgrim spirit stands at gaze.
It sees her such, that when it tells me this

Which it hath seen, I understand it not,
  It hath a speech so subtile and so fine.
And yet I know its voice within my thought
Often remembereth me of Beatrice :
  So that I understand it, ladies mine.

After writing this sonnet, it was given unto me to behold a very wonderful vision : * wherein I saw things which determined me that I would say nothing further of this most blessed one, until such time as I could discourse more worthily concerning her. And to this end I labour all I can ; as she well knoweth. Wherefore if it be His pleasure through whom is the life of all things, that my life continue with me a few years, it is my hope that I shall yet write concerning her what hath not before been written of any woman. After the which, may it seem good unto Him who is the Master of Grace, that my spirit should go hence to behold the glory of its lady : to wit, of that blessed Beatrice who now gazeth continually on His countenance *qui est per omnia sæcula benedictus.* † *Laus Deo.*

---

* This we may believe to have been the Vision of Hell, Purgatory, and Paradise, which furnished the triple argument of the *Divina Commedia.* The Latin words ending the *Vita Nuova* are almost identical with those at the close of the letter in which Dante, on concluding the *Paradise*, and accomplishing the hope here expressed, dedicates his great work to Can Grande della Scala.
† " Who is blessed throughout all ages."

THE END OF THE NEW LIFE.

I.

TO BRUNETTO LATINI.

SONNET.

Sent with the Vita Nuova.

MASTER BRUNETTO, this my little maid
   Is come to spend her Easter-tide with you;
   Not that she reckons feasting as her due,—
Whose need is hardly to be fed, but read.
Not in a hurry can her sense be weigh'd,
   Nor mid the jests of any noisy crew:
   Ah! and she wants a little coaxing too
Before she'll get into another's head.
But if you do not find her meaning clear,
   You've many Brother Alberts* hard at hand,
   Whose wisdom will respond to any call.
Consult with them and do not laugh at her;
   And if she still is hard to understand,
   Apply to Master Janus last of all.

---

* Probably in allusion to Albert of Cologne. Giano (Janus),
which follows, was in use as an Italian name, as for instance Giano
della Bella; but it seems probable that Dante is merely playfully
advising his preceptor to avail himself of the twofold insight of
Janus the double-faced.

II.

SONNET.*

Of Beatrice de' Portinari, on All Saints' Day.

LAST All Saints' holy-day, even now gone by,
  I met a gathering of damozels :
  She that came first, as one doth who excels,
Had Love with her, bearing her company :
A flame burned forward through her steadfast eye,
  As when in living fire a spirit dwells :
  So, gazing with the boldness which prevails
O'er doubt, I knew an angel visibly.
As she passed on, she bowed her mild approof
  And salutation to all men of worth,
Lifting the soul to solemn thoughts aloof.
  In Heaven itself that lady had her birth,
I think, and is with us for our behoof: .
  Blessed are they who meet her on the earth.

---

* This and the six following pieces (with the possible exception
of the canzone at page 101) seem so certainly to have been written
at the same time as the poetry of the *Vita Nuova*, that it becomes
difficult to guess why they were omitted from that work. Other
poems in Dante's *Canzoniere* refer in a more general manner to
his love for Beatrice, but each among those I allude to bears
the impress of some special occasion.

III.

SONNET.

*To certain Ladies; when Beatrice was lamenting
her Father's Death.*[*]

WHENCE come you, all of you so sorrowful?
  An it may please you, speak for courtesy.
  I fear for my dear lady's sake, lest she
Have made you to return thus filled with dule.
O gentle ladies, be not hard to school
  In gentleness, but to some pause agree,
  And something of my lady say to me,
For with a little my desire is full.
Howbeit it be a heavy thing to hear:
  For Love now utterly has thrust me forth,
With hand for ever lifted, striking fear.
  See if I be not worn unto the earth;
Yea, and my spirit must fail from me here,
  If, when you speak, your words are of no worth.

---

[*] See the *Vita Nuova*, at page 60.

IV.

SONNET.

To the same Ladies ; with their Answer.

YE ladies, walking past me piteous-eyed,
   Who is the lady that lies prostrate here ?
   Can this be even she my heart holds dear ?
Nay, if it be so, speak, and nothing hide.
Her very aspect seems itself beside,
   And all her features of such altered cheer
   That to my thinking they do not appear
Hers who makes others seem beatified.

" If thou forget to know our lady thus,
   Whom grief o'ercomes, we wonder in no wise,
For also the same thing befalleth us.
   Yet if thou watch the movement of her eyes,
Of her thou shalt be straightway conscious.
   O weep no more ; thou art all wan with sighs."

V.

BALLATA.

He will gaze upon Beatrice.

BECAUSE mine eyes can never have their fill
Of looking at my lady's lovely face,
   I will so fix my gaze
That I may become blessed, beholding her

Even as an angel, up at his great height
Standing amid the light,
   Becometh blessed by only seeing God :—
So, though I be a simple earthly wight,
Yet none the less I might,
   Beholding her who is my heart's dear load,
   Be blessed, and in the spirit soar abroad.
Such power abideth in that gracious one ;
Albeit felt of none
   Save of him who, desiring, honours her.

VI.

CANZONE.*

A Complaint of his Lady's scorn.

LOVE, since it is thy will that I return
'Neath her usurped control
  Who is thou know'st how beautiful and proud;
Enlighten thou her heart, so bidding burn
    Thy flame within her soul
  That she rejoice not when my cry is loud.
  Be thou but once endowed
With sense of the new peace, and of this fire,
  And of the scorn wherewith I am despised,
And wherefore death is my most fierce desire;
    And then thou'lt be apprised
Of all. So if thou slay me afterward,
Anguish unburthened shall make death less hard.

O Lord, thou knowest very certainly
    That thou didst make me apt
  To serve thee. But I was not wounded yet,
When under heaven I beheld openly
    The face which thus hath rapt
My soul. Then all my spirits ran elate
    Upon her will to wait.
And she, the peerless one who o'er all worth
  Is still her proper beauty's worshiper,

---

* This poem seems probably referable to the time during which
Beatrice denied her salutation to Dante. (See the *Vita Nuona*, at
page 41 *et seq.*)

Made semblance then to guide them safely forth:
   And they put faith in her:
Till, gathering them within her garment all,
She turned their blessed peace to tears and gall.

Then I (for I could hear how they complained,)
    As sympathy impelled,
  Full oft to seek her presence did arise.
And mine own soul (which better had refrained)
    So much my strength upheld
  That I could steadily behold her eyes.
  This in thy knowledge lies,
Who then didst call me with so mild a face
  That I hoped solace from my greater load:
And when she turned the key on my dark place,
    Such ruth thy grace bestowed
Upon my grief, and in such piteous kind,
That I had strength to bear, and was resign'd.

For love of the sweet favour's comforting
    Did I become her thrall;
  And still her every movement gladdened me
With triumph that I served so sweet a thing:
    Pleasures and blessings all
  I set aside, my perfect hope to see:
  Till her proud contumely—
That so mine aim might rest unsatisfied—
  Covered the beauty of her countenance.
So straightway fell into my living side,
    To slay me, the swift lance:
While she rejoiced and watched my bitter end,
Only to prove what succour thou wouldst send.

I therefore, weary with my love's constraint,
    To death's deliverance ran,
  That out of terrible grief I might be brought:
For tears had broken me and left me faint
    Beyond the lot of man,

Until each sigh must be my last, I thought.
   Yet still this longing wrought
So much of torment for my soul to bear,
   That with the pang I swooned and fell to earth.
Then, as in trance, 'twas whispered at mine ear,
   How in this constant girth
Of anguish, I indeed at length must die :
So that I dreaded Love continually.

    Master, thou knowest now
The life which in thy service I have borne :
   Not that I tell it thee to disallow
Control, who still to thy behest am sworn.
   Yet if through this my vow
I remain dead, nor help they will confer,
Do thou at least, for God's sake, pardon her.

VII.

CANZONE.

He beseeches Death for the Life of Beatrice.

DEATH, since I find not one with whom to grieve,
   Nor whom this grief of mine may move to tears,
     Whereso I be or whitherso I turn :
Since it is thou who in my soul wilt leave
   No single joy, but chill'st it with just fears
     And makest it in fruitless hopes to burn :
     Since thou, Death, and thou only, canst decern
Wealth to my life, or want, at thy free choice :—
It is to thee that I lift up my voice,
   Bowing my face that's like a face just dead.
I come to thee, as to one pitying,
In grief for that sweet rest which nought can bring
   Again, if thou but once be entered
Into her life whom my heart cherishes
Even as the only portal of its peace.

Death, how most sweet the peace is that thy grace
   Can grant to me, and that I pray thee for,
     Thou easily mayst know by a sure sign,
If in mine eyes thou look a little space
   And read in them the hidden dread they store,—
     If upon all thou look which proves me thine.
     Since the fear only maketh me to pine
After this sort,—what will mine anguish be
When her eyes close, of dreadful verity,
   In whose light is the light of mine own eyes?

But now I know that thou wouldst have my life
As hers, and joy'st thee in my fruitless strife.
   Yet I do think this which I feel implies
That soon, when I would die to flee from pain,
I shall find none by whom I may be slain.

Death, if indeed thou smite this gentle one
   Whose outward worth but tells the intellect
     How wondrous is the miracle within,—
Thou biddest Virtue rise up and begone,
   Thou dost away with Mercy's best effect,
     Thou spoil'st the mansion of God's sojourning.
     Yea, unto nought her beauty thou dost bring
Which is above all other beauties, even
In so much as befitteth one whom Heaven
   Sent upon earth in token of its own.
Thou dost break through the perfect trust which hath
Been alway her companion in Love's path:
   The light once darkened which was hers alone,
Love needs must say to them he ruleth o'er,
"I have lost the noble banner that I bore."

Death, have some pity then for all the ill
   Which cannot choose but happen if she die,
     And which will be the sorest ever known.
Slacken the string, if so it be thy will,
   That the sharp arrow leave it not,—thereby
     Sparing her life, which if it flies is flown.
     O Death, for God's sake, be some pity shown!
Restrain within thyself, even at its height,
The cruel wrath which moveth thee to smite
   Her in whom God hath set so much of grace.
Show now some ruth if 'tis a thing thou hast!
I seem to see Heaven's gate, that is shut fast,
   Open, and angels filling all the space
About me,—come to fetch her soul whose laud
Is sung by saints and angels before God.

Song, thou must surely see how fine a thread
　　This is that my last hope is holden by,
　　　　And what I should be brought to without her.
Therefore for thy plain speech and lowlihead
　　Make thou no pause : but go immediately,
　　　　(Knowing thyself for my heart's minister,)
　　　　And with that very meek and piteous air
Thou hast, stand up before the face of Death,
To wrench away the bar that prisoneth
　　And win unto the place of the good fruit.
And if indeed thou shake by thy soft voice
Death's mortal purpose,—haste thee and rejoice
　　Our lady with the issue of thy suit.
So yet awhile our earthly nights and days
Shall keep the blessed spirit that I praise.

VIII.

SONNET.

On the 9th of June 1290.

UPON a day, came Sorrow in to me,
  Saying, " I've come to stay with thee a while ;"
  And I perceived that she had ushered Bile
And Pain into my house for company.
Wherefore I said, " Go forth—away with thee !"
  But like a Greek she answered, full of guile,
  And went on arguing in an easy style.
Then, looking, I saw Love come silently,
Habited in black raiment, smooth and new,
  Having a black hat set upon his hair ;
And certainly the tears he shed were true.
  So that I asked, " What ails thee, trifler ?"
Answering he said : " A grief to be gone through ;
  For our own lady's dying, brother dear."

IX.

TO CINO DA PISTOIA.

SONNET.

He rebukes Cino for Fickleness.

I THOUGHT to be for ever separate,
   Fair Master Cino, from these rhymes of yours;
   Since further from the coast, another course,
My vessel now must journey with her freight.*
Yet still, because I hear men name your state
   As his whom every lure doth straight beguile,
   I pray you lend a very little while
Unto my voice your ear grown obdurate.
The man after this measure amorous,
   Who still at his own will is bound and loosed,
     How slightly Love him wounds is lightly known.
If on this wise your heart in homage bows,
   I pray you for God's sake it be disused,
     So that the deed and the sweet words be one.

---

  * This might seem to suggest that the present sonnet was written about the same time as the close of the *Vita Nuova*, and that an allusion may also here be intended to the first conception of Dante's great work.

CINO DA PISTOIA TO DANTE ALIGHIERI.

SONNET.

He answers Dante, confessing his unsteadfast heart.

DANTE, since I from my own native place
   In heavy exile have turned wanderer,
   Far distant from the purest joy which e'er
Had issued from the Fount of joy and grace,
I have gone weeping through the world's dull space,
   And me proud Death, as one too mean, doth spare ;
   Yet meeting Love, Death's neighbour, I declare
That still his arrows hold my heart in chase.
Nor from his pitiless aim can I get free,
   Nor from the hope which comforts my weak will,
     Though no true aid exists which I could share.
One pleasure ever binds and looses me ;
   That so, by one same Beauty lured, I still
     Delight in many women here and there.

X.

TO CINO DA PISTOIA.

SONNET.

Written in Exile.

BECAUSE I find not whom to speak withal
  Anent that lord whose I am as thou art,
  Behoves that in thine ear I tell some part
Of this whereof I gladly would say all.
And deem thou nothing else occasional
  Of my long silence while I kept apart,
  Except this place, so guilty at the heart
That the right has not who will give it stall.
Love comes not here to any woman's face,
  Nor any man here for his sake will sigh,
    For unto such, "Thou fool!" were straightway said.
Ah! Master Cino, how the time turns base,
  And mocks at us, and on our rhymes says " Fie ! "
    Since truth has been thus thinly harvested.

CINO DA PISTOIA TO DANTE ALIGHIERI.

SONNET.

He answers the foregoing Sonnet, and prays Dante, in the name of Beatrice, to continue his great Poem.

I KNOW not, Dante, in what refuge dwells
   The truth, which with all men is out of mind;
   For long ago it left this place behind,
Till in its stead at last God's thunder swells.
Yet if our shifting life most clearly tells
   That here the truth has no reward assign'd,—
   'Twas God, remember, taught it to mankind,
And even among the fiends preached nothing else.
Then, though the kingdoms of the earth be torn,
   Where'er thou set thy feet, from Truth's control,
   Yet unto me thy friend this prayer accord :—
Beloved, O my brother, sorrow-worn,
   Even in that lady's name who is thy goal,
   Sing on till thou redeem thy plighted word ! *

---

* That is, the pledge given at the end of the *Vita Nuova*. This may perhaps have been written in the early days of Dante's exile, before his resumption of the interrupted *Commedia*.

XI.

Sonnet.

Of Beauty and Duty.

Two ladies to the summit of my mind
　　Have clomb, to hold an argument of love.
　　The one has wisdom with her from above,
For every noblest virtue well designed :
The other, beauty's tempting power refined
　　And the high charm of perfect grace approve :
　　And I, as my sweet Master's will doth move,
At feet of both their favours am reclined.
Beauty and Duty in my soul keep strife,
　　At question if the heart such course can take
　　And 'twixt two ladies hold its love complete.
　　　The fount of gentle speech yields answer meet,
　　That Beauty may be loved for gladness' sake,
And Duty in the lofty ends of life.

XII.

SESTINA.*

Of the Lady Pietra degli Scrovigni.

To the dim light and the large circle of shade
I have clomb, and to the whitening of the hills,
There where we see no colour in the grass.   ·
Nathless my longing loses not its green,
It has so taken root in the hard stone
Which talks and hears as though it were a lady.

Utterly frozen is this youthful lady,
Even as the snow that lies within the shade ;
For she is no more moved than is the stone
By the sweet season which makes warm the hills
And alters them afresh from white to green,
Covering their sides again with flowers and grass.

When on her hair she sets a crown of grass
The thought has no more room for other lady ,

---

* I have translated this piece both on account of its great and
peculiar beauty, and also because it affords an example of a form
of composition which I have met with in no Italian writer before
Dante's time, though it is not uncommon among the Provençal
poets (see Dante, *De Vulg. Eloq.*). I have headed it with the name
of a Paduan lady, to whom it is surmised by some to have been
addressed during Dante's exile ; but this must be looked upon as
a rather doubtful conjecture, and I have adopted the name chiefly
to mark it at once as not referring to Beatrice.

8

Because she weaves the yellow with the green
So well that Love sits down there in the shade,—
Love who has shut me in among low hills
Faster than between walls of granite-stone.

She is more bright than is a precious stone;
The wound she gives may not be healed with grass:
I therefore have fled far o'er plains and hills
For refuge from so dangerous a lady;
But from her sunshine nothing can give shade,—
Not any hill, nor wall, nor summer-green.

A while ago, I saw her dressed in green,—
So fair, she might have wakened in a stone
This love which I do feel even for her shade;
And therefore, as one woos a graceful lady,
I wooed her in a field that was all grass
Girdled about with very lofty hills.

Yet shall the streams turn back and climb the hills
Before Love's flame in this damp wood and green
Burn, as it burns within a youthful lady,
For my sake, who would sleep away in stone
My life, or feed like beasts upon the grass,
Only to see her garments cast a shade.

How dark soe'er the hills throw out their shade,
Under her summer-green the beautiful lady
Covers it, like a stone covered in grass.

XIII.

SONNET.*

A Curse for a fruitless Love

My curse be on the day when first I saw
  The brightness in those treacherous eyes of thine,—
The hour when from my heart thou cam'st to draw
  My soul away, that both might fail and pine :
  My curse be on the skill that smooth'd each line
Of my vain songs,—the music and just law
  Of art, by which it was my dear design
That the whole world should yield thee love and awe.
Yea, let me curse mine own obduracy,
  Which firmly holds what doth itself confound—
    To wit, thy fair perverted face of scorn :
    For whose sake Love is oftentimes forsworn
So that men mock at him : but most at me
  Who would hold fortune's wheel and turn it round.

---

* I have separated this sonnet from the pieces bearing on the
Vita Nuova, as it is naturally repugnant to connect it with
Beatrice. I cannot, however, but think it possible that it may
have been the bitter fruit of some bitterest moment in those hours
when Dante endured her scorn.

GUIDO CAVALCANTI.

I.

TO DANTE ALIGHIERI.

SONNET.

*He interprets Dante's Dream, related in the first Sonnet of
the Vita Nuova.**

UNTO my thinking, thou beheld'st all worth,
  All joy, as much of good as man may know,
  If thou wert in his power who here below
Is honour's righteous lord throughout this earth.
Where evil dies, even there he has his birth,
  Whose justice out of pity's self doth grow.
  Softly to sleeping persons he will go,
And, with no pain to them, their hearts draw forth.
Thy heart he took, as knowing well, alas!
  That Death had claimed thy lady for a prey:
    In fear whereof, he fed her with thy heart.
    But when he seemed in sorrow to depart,
  Sweet was thy dream; for by that sign, I say,
Surely the opposite shall come to pass.†

---

  * See the *Vita Nuova*, at page 33.
  † This may refer to the belief that, towards morning, dreams go
by contraries.

II.

SONNET.

To his Lady Joan, of Florence.

FLOWERS hast thou in thyself, and foliage,
   And what is good, and what is glad to see ;
The sun is not so bright as thy visàge ;
   All is stark naught when one hath looked on thee ;
There is not such a beautiful personage
   Anywhere on the green earth verily ;
If one fear love, thy bearing sweet and sage
   Comforteth him, and no more fear hath he.
Thy lady friends and maidens ministering
   Are all, for love of thee, much to my taste :
And much I pray them that in everything
   They honour thee even as thou meritest,
And have thee in their gentle harbouring :
   Because among them all thou art the best.

III.

..

SONNET.

He compares all Things with his Lady, and finds them
wanting.

BEAUTY in woman; the high will's decree;
    Fair knighthood armed for manly exercise;
    The pleasant song of birds; love's soft replies;
The strength of rapid ships upon the sea;
The serene air when light begins to be;
    The white snow, without wind that falls and lies;
    Fields of all flower; the place where waters rise;
Silver and gold; azure in jewellery :—
Weighed against these, the sweet and quiet worth
    Which my dear lady cherishes at heart
        Might seem a little matter to be shown;
    Being truly, over these, as much apart
As the whole heaven is greater than this earth.
        All good to kindred natures cleaveth soon.

IV.

SONNET.

A Rapture concerning his Lady.

Who is she coming, whom all gaze upon,
  Who makes the air all tremulous with light,
And at whose side is Love himself? that none
  Dare speak, but each man's sighs are infinite.
  Ah me! how she looks round from left to right,
Let Love discourse : I may not speak thereon.
Lady she seems of such high benison
  As makes all others graceless in men's sight.
The honour which is hers cannot be said ;
  To whom are subject all things virtuous,
    While all things beauteous own her deity.
Ne'er was the mind of man so nobly led,
  Nor yet was such redemption granted us
    That we should ever know her perfectly.

V.

BALLATA.

Of his Lady among other Ladies.

WITH other women I beheld my love ;—
  Not that the rest were women to mine eyes,
Who only as her shadows seemed to move.

I do not praise her more than with the truth,
  Nor blame I these if it be rightly read.

But while I speak, a thought I may not soothe
  Says to my senses : "Soon shall ye be dead,
  If for my sake your tears ye will not shed."

And then the eyes yield passage, at that thought,
To the heart's weeping, which forgets her not.

VI.

TO GUIDO ORLANDI.

SONNET.

Of a consecrated Image resembling his Lady.

GUIDO, an image of my lady dwells
  At San Michele in Orto, consecrate
  And duly worshiped.   Fair in holy state
She listens to the tale each sinner tells :
And among them that come to her, who ails
  The most, on him the most doth blessing wa
  She bids the fiend men's bodies abdicate ;
Over the curse of blindness she prevails,
And heals sick languors in the public squares.
  A multitude adores her reverently :
    Before her face two burning tapers are ;
    Her voice is uttered upon paths afar.
  Yet through the Lesser Brethren's* jealousy
She is named idol ; not being one of theirs.

---

* The Franciscans, in profession of deeper poverty and humility
than belonged to other Orders, called themselves *Fratres minores.*

GUIDO ORLANDI TO GUIDO CAVALCANTI.

MADRIGAL.

In answer to the foregoing Sonnet.

IF thou hadst offered, friend, to blessed Mary
    A pious voluntary,
  As thus : " Fair rose, in holy garden set " :
Thou then hadst found a true similitude :
    Because all truth and good
  Are hers, who was the mansion and the gate
Wherein abode our High Salvation,
    Conceived in her, a Son,
  Even by the angel's greeting whom she met.
Be thou assured that if one cry to her,
    Confessing, " I did err,"
  For death she gives him life ; for she is great.

Ah ! how mayst thou be counselled to implead
    With God thine own misdeed,
  And not another's ?   Ponder what thou art ;
    And humbly lay to heart
That Publican who wept his proper need.
The Lesser Brethren 'cherish the divine
    Scripture and church-doctrine ;
Being appointed keepers of the faith
    Whose preaching succoureth :
For what they preach is our best medicine.

VII.

SONNET.

Of the Eyes of a certain Mandetta, of Thoulouse, which resemble those of his Lady Joan, of Florence.

A CERTAIN youthful lady in Thoulouse,
 Gentle and fair, of cheerful modesty,
 Is in her eyes, with such exact degree,
Of likeness unto mine own lady, whose
I am, that through the heart she doth abuse
 The soul to sweet desire. It goes from me
 To her; yet, fearing, saith not who is she
That of a truth its essence thus subdues.
This lady looks on it with the sweet eyes
 Whose glance did erst the wounds of Love anoint
  Through its true lady's eyes which are as they.
Then to the heart returns it, full of sighs,
 Wounded to death by a sharp arrow's point
  Wherewith this lady speeds it on its way.

VIII.

Ballata.

He reveals, in a Dialogue, his increasing Love for Mandetta.

Being in thought of love, I chanced to see
    Two youthful damozels.
  One sang : " Our life inhales
  All love continually."

Their aspect was so utterly serene,
    So courteous, of such quiet nobleness,
That I said to them : " Yours, I may well ween,
    'Tis of all virtue to unlock the place.
    Ah ! damozels, do not account him base
      Whom thus his wound subdues :
      Since I was at Thoulouse,
        My heart is dead in me."

They turned their eyes upon me in so much
    As to perceive how wounded was my heart ;
While, of the spirits born of tears, one such
    Had been begotten through the constant smart.
    Then seeing me, abashed, to turn apart,
      One of them said, and laugh'd :
      " Love, look you, by his craft
        Holds this man thoroughly."

But with grave sweetness, after a brief while,
    She who at first had laughed on me replied,
Saying : "This lady, who by Love's great guile
    Her countenance in thy heart has glorified,
    Look'd thee so deep within the eyes, Love sigh'd
        And was awakened there.
        If it seem ill to bear,
           In him thy hope must be."

The second piteous maiden, of all ruth,
    Fashioned for sport in Love's own image, said :
" This stroke, whereof thy heart bears trace in sooth,
    From eyes of too much puissance was shed,
    Whence in thy heart such brightness enterèd,
        'Thou mayst not look thereon.
        Say, of those eyes that shone
           Canst thou remember thee ? "

Then said I, yielding answer therewithal
    Unto this virgin's difficult behest :
" A lady of Thoulouse, whom Love doth call
    Mandetta, sweetly kirtled and enlac'd,
    I do remember to my sore unrest.
        Yea, by her eyes indeed
        My life has been decreed
           To death inevitably."

Go, Ballad, to the city, even Thoulouse,
    And softly entering the Dauràde,* look round
    And softly call, that so there may be found
Some lady who for compleasaunce may choose
To show thee her who can my life confuse.
        And if she yield thee way,
        Lift thou thy voice and say :
           "For grace I come to thee."

---

* The ancient church of the Dauràde still exists at Thoulouse.
It was so called from the golden effect of the mosaics adorning it.

DANTE ALIGHIERI TO GUIDO CAVALCANTI.

He imagines a pleasant Voyage for Guido, Lapo Gianni,
and himself, with their three Ladies.

GUIDO, I wish that Lapo, thou, and I,
    Could be by spells conveyed, as it were now,
    Upon a barque, with all the winds that blow
Across all seas at our good will to hie.
So no mischance nor temper of the sky
    Should mar our course with spite or cruel slip;
    But we, observing old companionship,
To be companions still should long thereby.
And Lady Joan, and Lady Beatrice,
    And her the thirtieth on my roll,* with us
        Should our good wizard set, o'er seas to move
        And not to talk of anything but love :
And they three ever to be well at ease,
    As we should be, I think, if this were thus.

---

   * That is, his list of the sixty most beautiful ladies of Florence,
referred to in the *Vita Nuova;* among whom Lapo Gianni's lady,
Lagia, would seem to have stood thirtieth.

IX.

TO DANTE ALIGHIERI.

Sonnet.

*Guido answers the foregoing Sonnet, speaking with shame
of his changed Love.*

If I were still that man, worthy to love,
   Of whom I have but the remembrance now,
   Or if the lady bore another brow,
To hear this thing might bring me joy thereof.
But thou, who in Love's proper court dost move,
   Even there where hope is born of grace,—see how
   My very soul within me is brought low :
For a swift archer, whom his feats approve,
Now bends the bow, which Love to him did yield,
   In such mere sport against me, it would seem
     As though he held his lordship for a jest.
     Then hear the marvel which is sorriest :—
   My sorely wounded soul forgiveth him,
Yet knows that in his act her strength is kill'd.

X.

TO DANTE ALIGHIERI.

SONNET.

He reports, in a feigned Vision, the successful Issue of Lapo Gianni's Love.

DANTE, a sigh that rose from the heart's core
    Assailed me, while I slumbered, suddenly:
So that I woke o' the instant, fearing sore
    Lest it came thither in Love's company:
Till, turning, I beheld the servitor
    Of Lady Lagia: "Help me," so said he,
"O help me, Pity." Though he said no more,
    So much of Pity's essence entered me,
That I was ware of Love, those shafts he wields
    A-whetting, and preferred the mourner's quest
        To him, who straightway answered on this wise:
"Go tell my servant that the lady yields,
    And that I hold her now at his behest:
        If he believe not, let him note her eyes."

XI.

TO DANTE ALIGHIERI.

SONNET.

He mistrusts the Love of Lapo Gianni.

I PRAY thee, Dante, shouldst thou meet with Love
  In any place where Lapo then may be,
  That there thou fail not to mark heedfully
If Love with lover's name that man approve;
If to our Master's will his lady move
  Aright, and if himself show fealty :
  For ofttimes, by ill custom, ye may see
This sort profess the semblance of true love.
Thou know'st that in the court where Love holds sway
  A law subsists, that no man who is vile
    Can service yield to a lost woman there.
    If suffering aught avail the sufferer,
  Thou straightway shalt discern our lofty style
Which needs the badge of honour must display.

XIL

SONNET.

*On the Detection of a false Friend.**

LOVE and the Lady Lagia, Guido and I,
    Unto a certain lord are bounden all,
    Who has released us—know ye from whose thrall?
Yet I'll not speak, but let the matter die :
Since now these three no more are held thereby,
    Who in such homage at his feet did fall
    That I myself was not more whimsical,
In him conceiving godship from on high.
Let Love be thanked the first, who first discern'd
    The truth ; and that wise lady afterward,
      Who in fit time took back her heart again ;
And Guido next, from worship wholly turn'd ;
    And I, as he.   But if ye have not heard,
      I shall not tell how much I loved him then.

---

* I should think, from the mention of Lady Lagia, that this
might refer again to Lapo Gianni, who seems (one knows not
why) to have fallen into disgrace with his friends.   The Guido
mentioned is probably Guido Orlandi.

XIII.

SONNET.

He speaks of a third Love of his.

O THOU that often hast within thine eyes
 A Love who holds three shafts,—know thou from me
 That this my sonnet would commend to thee
(Come from afar) a soul in heavy sighs,
Which even by Love's sharp arrow wounded lies.
 Twice did the Syrian archer shoot, and he
 Now bends his bow the third time, cunningly
That, thou being here, he wound me in no wise.
Because the soul would quicken at the core
 Thereby, which now is near to utter death,
  From those two shafts, a triple wound that yield.
The first gives pleasure, yet disquieteth ;
And with the second is the longing for
  The mighty gladness by the third fulfill'd.

XIV.

BALLATA.

Of a continual Death in Love.

THOUGH thou, indeed, hast quite forgotten ruth,
Its steadfast truth my heart abandons not;
But still its thought yields service in good part
    To that hard heart in thee.

Alas! who hears believes not I am so.
Yet who can know? of very surety, none.
From Love is won a spirit, in some wise,
    Which dies perpetually:

And, when at length in that strange ecstasy
    The heavy sigh will start,
    There rains upon my heart
    A love so pure and fine,
That I say: "Lady, I am wholly thine." *

---

* I may take this opportunity of mentioning that, in every case
where an abrupt change of metre occurs in one of my translations,
it is so also in the original poem.

XV.

SONNET

To a Friend who does not pity his Love.

IF I entreat this lady that all grace
  Seem not unto her heart an enemy,
  Foolish and evil thou declarest me,
And desperate in idle stubbornness.
Whence is such cruel judgment thine, whose face,
  To him that looks thereon, professeth thee
  Faithful, and wise, and of all courtesy,
And made after the way of gentleness?
Alas! my soul within my heart doth find
  Sighs, and its grief by weeping doth enhance,
    That, drowned in bitter tears, those sighs depart:
And then there seems a presence in the mind,
  As of a lady's thoughtful countenance
    Come to behold the death of the poor heart.

XVI.

BALLATA.

He perceives that his highest Love is gone from him.

THROUGH this my strong and new misaventure,
          All now is lost to me
Which most was sweet in Love's supremacy.

So much of life is dead in its control,
     That she, my pleasant lady of all grace,
Is gone out of the devastated soul :
     I see her not, nor do I know her place ;
     Nor even enough of virtue with me stays
          To understand, ah me !
The flower of her exceeding purity.

Because there comes—to kill that gentle thought
     With saying that I shall not see her more—
This constant pain wherewith I am distraught,
     Which is a burning torment very sore,
     Wherein I know not whom I should implore.
          Thrice thanked the Master be
Who turns the grinding wheel of misery !

Full of great anguish in a place of fear
     The spirit of my heart lies sorrowing,
Through Fortune's bitter craft.   She lured it here,
     And gave it o'er to Death, and barbed the sting ;
     She wrought that hope which was a treacherous thing ;
          In Time, which dies from me,
She made me lose mine hour of ecstasy.

For you, perturbed and fearful words of mine,
   Whither yourselves may please, even thither go;
But always burthened with shame's troublous sign,
   And on my lady's name still calling low.
   For me, I must abide in such deep woe
      That all who look shall see
Death's shadow on my face assuredly.

XVII.

SONNET.

Of his Pain from a new Love.

WHY from the danger did mine eyes not start,—
  Why not become even blind,—ere through my sight
  Within my soul thou ever couldst alight
To say : " Dost thou not hear me in thy heart ? "
New torment then, the old torment's counterpart,
  Filled me at once with such a sore affright,
  That, Lady, lady, (I said,) destroy not quite
Mine eyes and me ! O help us where thou art !
Thou hast so left mine eyes, that love is fain—
  Even Love himself—with pity uncontroll'd
    To bend above them, weeping for their loss :
Saying : " If any man feel heavy pain,
  This man's more painful heart let him behold :
    Death has it in her hand, cut like a cross."

GUIDO ORLANDI TO GUIDO CAVALCANTI.

PROLONGED SONNET.

He finds fault with the Conceits of the foregoing Sonnet.

FRIEND, well I know thou knowest well to bear
    Thy sword's-point, that it pierce the close-locked mail :
    And like a bird to flit from perch to pale :
And out of difficult ways to find the air :
Largely to take and generously to share :
    Thrice to secure advantage : to regale
    Greatly the great, and over lands prevail.
In all thou art, one only fault is there :
For still among the wise of wit thou say'st
    That Love himself doth weep for thine estate ;
        And yet, no eyes no tears : lo now, thy whim !
Soft, rather say : This is not held in haste ;
    But bitter are the hours and passionate,
        To him that loves, and love is not for him.

For me, (by usage strengthened to forbear
From carnal love,) I fall not in such snare.

GIANNI ALFANI TO GUIDO CAVALCANTI.

SONNET.*

On the part of a Lady of Pisa.

GUIDO, that Gianni who, a day agone,
    Sought thee, now greets thee (ay and thou mayst
       laugh !)
On that same Pisan beauty's sweet behalf
Who can deal love-wounds even as thou hast done.
She asked me whether thy good will were prone
    For service unto Love who troubles her,
    If she to thee in suchwisè should repair
That, save by him and Gualtier, 'twere not known :—
For thus her kindred of ill augury
    Should lack the means wherefrom there might be
      plann'd
    Worse harm than lying speech that smites afar.
I told her that thou hast continually
    A goodly sheaf of arrows to thy hand,
    Which well should stead her in such gentle war.

---

* From a passage in Ubaldini's Glossary (1640) to the " Documenti d'Amore " of Francesco Barberino (1300), I judge that Guido answered the above sonnet, and that Alfani made a rejoinder, from which a scrap there printed appears to be taken. The whole piece existed, in Ubaldini's time, among the Strozzi MSS.

BERNARDO DA BOLOGNA TO
GUIDO CAVALCANTI.

SONNET.

*He writes to Guido, telling him of the Love which a certain
Pinella showed on seeing him.*

UNTO that lowly lovely maid, I wis,
  So poignant in the heart was thy salute,
  That she changed countenance, remaining mute.
Wherefore I asked : " Pinella, how is this ?
Hast heard of Guido ? know'st thou who he is ? "
  She answered, " Yea ; " then paused, irresolute;
  But I saw well how the love-wounds acute
Were widened, and the star which Love calls his
Filled her with gentle brightness perfectly.
  " But, friend, an't please thee, I would have it told,"
She said, " how I am known to him through thee.
  Yet since, scarce seen, I knew his name of old,--
Even as the riddle is read, so must it be.
  Oh ! send him love of mine a thousand-fold ! "

XVIII.

TO BERNARDO DA BOLOGNA.

SONNET.

Guido answers, commending Pinella, and saying that the Love he can offer her is already shared by many noble Ladies.

THE fountain-head that is so bright to see
  Gains as it runs in virtue and in sheen,
Friend Bernard; and for her who spoke with thee,
  Even such the flow of her young life has been:
So that when Love discourses secretly
  Of things the fairest he has ever seen,
He says there is no fairer thing than she,
  A lowly maid as lovely as a queen.
And for that I am troubled, thinking of
  That sigh wherein I burn upon the waves
    Which drift her heart,—poor barque, so ill bested!—
Unto Pinella a great river of love
  I send, that's full of sirens, and whose slaves
    Are beautiful and richly habited.

DINO COMPAGNI TO GUIDO CAVALCANTI.

SONNET.

He reproves Guido for his Arrogance in Love.

No man may mount upon a golden stair,
    Guido my master, to Love's palace-sill:
No key of gold will fit the lock that's there,
    Nor heart there enter without pure goodwill.
Not if he miss one courteous duty, dare
    A lover hope he should his love fulfil;
But to his lady must make meek repair,
    Reaping with husbandry her favours still.
And thou but know'st of Love (I think) his name:
    Youth holds thy reason in extremities:
    Only on thine own face thou turn'st thine eyes;
Fairer than Absalom's account'st the same;
And think'st, as rosy moths are drawn by flame,
    To draw the women from their balconies.*

---

* It is curious to find these poets perpetually rating one another for the want of constancy in love. Guido is rebuked, as above, by Dino Compagni; Cino da Pistoia by Dante (p. 108); and Dante by Guido (p. 144), who formerly, as we have seen (p. 129) had confided to him his doubts of Lapo Gianni.

XIX.

TO GUIDO ORLANDI.

Sonnet

In praise of Guido Orlandi's Lady.

A LADY in whom love is manifest—
  That love which perfect honour doth adorn—
Hath ta'en the living heart out of thy breast,
  Which in her keeping to new life is born :
For there by such sweet power it is possest
  As even is felt of Indian unicorn : *
And all its virtue now, with fierce unrest,
  Unto thy soul makes difficult return.
For this thy lady is virtue's minister
  In suchwise that no fault there is to show,
    Save that God made her mortal on this ground.
    And even herein His wisdom shall be found :
  For only thus our intellect could know
That heavenly beauty which resembles her.

---

  * In old representations, the unicorn is often seen with his head in a virgin's lap.

GUIDO ORLANDI TO GUIDO CAVALCANTI.

SONNET.

He answers the foregoing Sonnet, declaring himself his Lady's Champion.

To sound of trumpet rather than of horn,
   I in Love's name would hold a battle-play
   Of gentlemen in arms on Easter Day ;
And, sailing without oar or wind, be borne
Unto my joyful beauty; all that morn
   To ride round her, in her cause seeking fray
   Of arms with all but thee, friend, who dost say
The truth of her, and whom all truths adorn.
And still I pray Our Lady's grace above,
   Most reverently, that she whom my thoughts bear
     In sweet remembrance own her Lord supreme.
Holding her honour dear, as doth behove,—
   In God who therewithal sustaineth her
     Let her abide, and not depart from Him.

XX.

TO DANTE ALIGHIERI.

SONNET.

*He rebukes Dante for his way of Life, after the Death of Beatrice.**

I COME to thee by daytime constantly,
   But in thy thoughts too much of baseness find :
   Greatly it grieves me for thy gentle mind,
And for thy many virtues gone from thee.
It was thy wont to shun much company,
   Unto all sorry concourse ill inclin'd :
   And still thy speech of me, heartfelt and kind,
Had made me treasure up thy poetry.
But now I dare not, for thine abject life,
   Make manifest that I approve thy rhymes ;
     Nor come I in such sort that thou mayst know.
Ah! prythee read this sonnet many times :
So shall that evil one who bred this strife
     Be thrust from thy dishonoured soul and go.

---

* This interesting sonnet must refer to the same period of
Dante's life regarding which he has made Beatrice address him
in words of noble reproach when he meets her in Eden. (*Purg.*
C. xxx.)

XXI.

BALLATA.

Concerning a Shepherd-maid.

WITHIN a copse I met a shepherd-maid,
More fair, I said, than any star to see.

She came with waving tresses pale and bright,
  With rosy cheer, and loving eyes of flame,
Guiding the lambs beneath her wand aright.
  Her naked feet still had the dews on them,
  As, singing like a lover, so she came;
Joyful, and fashioned for all ecstasy.

I greeted her at once, and question made
  What escort had she through the woods in spring?
But with soft accents she replied and said
  That she was all alone there, wandering;
  Moreover: "Do you know, when the birds sing,
My heart's desire is for a mate," said she.

While she was telling me this wish of hers,
  The birds were all in song throughout the wood.
"Even now then," said my thought, "the time recurs,
  With mine own longing to assuage her mood."
  And so, in her sweet favour's name, I sued
That she would kiss there and embrace with me.

10

She took my hand to her with amorous will,
   And answered that she gave me all her heart,
And drew me where the leaf is fresh and still,
   Where spring the wood-flowers in the shade apart.
   And on that day, by Joy's enchanted art,
There Love in very presence seemed to be.*

---

* The glossary to Barberino, already mentioned, refers to the existence, among the Strozzi MSS., of a poem by Lapo di Farinata degli Uberti, written in answer to the above ballata of Cavalcanti. As this respondent was no other than Guido's brother-in-law, one feels curious to know what he said to the peccadilloes of his sister's husband. But I fear the poem cannot yet have been published, as I have sought for it in vain at all my printed sources of information.

XXII.

SONNET.

Of an ill-favoured Lady.

JUST look, Manetto, at that wry-mouthed minx ;
   Merely take notice what a wretch it is ;
   How well contrived in her deformities,
How beastly favoured when she scowls and blinks.
Why, with a hood on (if one only thinks)
   Or muffle of prim veils and scapularies,—
   And set together, on a day like this,
Some pretty lady with the odious sphinx ;—
Why, then thy sins could hardly have such weight,
   Nor thou be so subdued from Love's attack,
   Nor so possessed in Melancholy's sway,
But that perforce thy peril must be great
   Of laughing till the very heart-strings crack :
     Either thou'dst die, or thou must run away

XXIII.

TO POPE BONIFACE VIII.

*After the Pope's Interdict, when the great Houses were
leaving Florence.*

NERO, thus much for tidings in thine ear.
   They of the Buondelmonti quake with dread,
   Nor by all Florence may be comforted,
Noting in thee the lion's ravenous cheer ;
Who more than any dragon giv'st them fear,
   In ancient evil stubbornly array'd ;
   Neither by bridge nor bulwark to be stay'd,
But only by King Pharaoh's sepulchre.
O in what monstrous sin dost thou engage,—
   All these which are of loftiest blood to drive
     Away, that none dare pause but all take wing !
Yet sooth it is, thou might'st redeem the pledge
   Even yet, and save thy naked soul alive,
     Wert thou but patient in the bargaining.

XXIV.

BALLATA.

In Exile at Sarzana.

BECAUSE I think not ever to return,
   Ballad, to Tuscany,—
   Go therefore thou for me
      Straight to my lady's face,
      Who, of her noble grace,
   Shall show thee courtesy.

Thou seekest her in charge of many sighs,
   Full of much grief and of exceeding fear.
But have good heed thou come not to the eyes
   Of such as are sworn foes to gentle cheer :
   For, certes, if this thing should chance,—from her
      Thou then couldst only look
      For scorn, and such rebuke
      As needs must bring me pain ;—
      Yea, after death again
      Tears and fresh agony.

Surely thou knowest, Ballad, how that Death
   Assails me, till my life is almost sped :
Thou knowest how my heart still travaileth
   Through the sore pangs which in my soul are bred :—
   My body being now so nearly dead,
      It cannot suffer more.

Then, going, I implore
That this my soul thou take
(Nay, do so for my sake,)
When my heart sets it free.

Ah! Ballad, unto thy dear offices
  I do commend my soul, thus trembling;
That thou mayst lead it, for pure piteousness,
  Even to that lady's presence whom I sing.
  Ah! Ballad, say thou to her, sorrowing,
      Whereso thou meet her then :—
      "This thy poor handmaiden
      Is come, nor will be gone,
      Being parted now from one
      Who served Love painfully."

Thou also, thou bewildered voice and weak,
  That goest forth in tears from my grieved heart,
Shalt, with my soul and with this ballad, speak
  Of my dead mind, when thou dost hence depart,
  Unto that lady (piteous as thou art!)
      Who is so calm and bright,
      It shall be deep delight
      To feel her presence there.
      And thou, Soul, worship her
      Still in her purity.

XXV.

CANZONE.*

A Song of Fortune.

Lo! I am she who makes the wheel to turn;
  Lo! I am she who gives and takes away;
    Blamed idly, day by day,
  In all mine acts by you, ye humankind.
For whoso smites his visage and doth mourn,
  What time he renders back my gifts to me,
    Learns then that I decree
  No state which mine own arrows may not find.
  Who clomb must fall :—this bear ye well in mind,
Nor say, because he fell, I did him wrong.
    Yet mine is a vain song :
For truly ye may find out wisdom when
King Arthur's resting-place is found of men.

Ye make great marvel and astonishment ·
  What time ye see the sluggard lifted up
    And the just man to drop,
  And ye complain on God and on my sway.
O humankind, ye sin in your complaint :

---

* .This and the three following Canzoni are only to be found in
the later collections of Guido Cavalcanti's poems. I have included
them on account of their interest, if really his, and especially for
the beauty of the last .among them ; but must confess to some
doubts of their authenticity.

For He, that Lord who made the world to live,
    Lets me not take or give
By mine own act, but as He wills I may.
   Yet is the mind of man so castaway,
That it discerns not the supreme behest.
       Alas ! ye wretchedest,
And chide ye at God also ?   Shall not He
Judge between good and evil righteously ?

Ah ! had ye knowledge how God evermore,
    With agonies of soul and grievous heats,
      As on an anvil beats
On them that in this earth hold high estate,—
Ye would choose little rather than much store,
    And solitude than spacious palaces ;
      Such is the sore disease
Of anguish that on all their days doth wait.
Behold if they be not unfortunate,
When oft the father dares not trust the son !
      O wealth, with thee is won
A worm to gnaw for ever on his soul
Whose abject life is laid in thy control !

If also ye take note what piteous death
    They ofttimes make, whose hoards were manifold,
      Who cities had and gold
    And multitudes of men beneath their hand ;
Then he among you that most angereth
    Shall bless me, saying, "Lo ! I worship thee
      That I was not as he
  Whose death is thus accurst throughout the land."
But now your living souls are held in band
Of avarice, shutting you from the true light
      Which shows how sad and slight
Are this world's treasured riches and array
That still change hands a hundred times a-day.

For me,—could envy enter in my sphere,
    Which of all human taint is clean and quit,—
        I well might harbour it
    When I behold the peasant at his toil.
Guiding his team, untroubled, free from fear,
    He leaves his perfect furrow as he goes,
        And gives his field repose
    From thorns and tares and weeds that vex the soil :
    Thereto he labours, and without turmoil
Entrusts his work to God, content if so
        Such guerdon from it grow
That in that year his family shall live :
Nor care nor thought to other things will give.

But now ye may no more have speech of me,
    For this mine office craves continual use :
        Ye therefore deeply muse
    Upon those things which ye have heard the while :
Yea, and even yet remember heedfully
    How this my wheel a motion hath so fleet,
        That in an eyelid's beat
    Him whom it raised it maketh low and vile.
    None was, nor is, nor shall be of such guile,
Who could, or can, or shall, I say, at length
        Prevail against my strength.
But still those men that are my questioners
In bitter torment own their hearts perverse.

Song, that wast made to carry high intent
    Dissembled in the garb of humbleness,—
        With fair and open face
To Master Thomas let thy course be bent.
Say that a great thing scarcely may be pent
    In little room : yet always pray that he
        Commend us, thee and me,
To them that are more apt in lofty speech :
For truly one must learn ere he can teach.

XXVI.

CANZONE.

A Song against Poverty.

O POVERTY, by thee the soul is wrapp'd
  With hate, with envy, dolefulness, and doubt.
      Even so be thou cast out,
  And even so he that speaks thee otherwise.
I name thee now, because my mood is apt
To curse thee, bride of every lost estate,
      Through whom are desolate
  On earth all honourable things and wise.
  Within thy power each blest condition dies :
By thee, men's minds with sore mistrust are made
      Fantastic and afraid :—
Thou, hated worse than Death, by just accord,
And with the loathing of all hearts abhorr'd.

Yea, rightly art thou hated worse than Death,
  For he at length is longed for in the breast.
      But not with thee, wild beast,
  Was ever aught found beautiful or good.
For life is all that man can lose by death,
Not fame and the fair summits of applause ;
      His glory shall not pause,
  But live in men's perpetual gratitude.
  While he who on thy naked sill has stood,
Though of great heart and worthy everso,
      He shall be counted low.
Then let the man thou troublest never hope
To spread his wings in any lofty scope.

Hereby my mind is laden with a fear,
   And I will take some thought to shelter me.
      For this I plainly see :—
   Through thee, to fraud the honest man is led ;
To tyranny the just lord turneth here,
And the magnanimous soul to avarice.
      Of every bitter vice
   Thou, to my thinking, art the fount and head ;
   From thee no light in any wise is shed,
Who bringest to the paths of dusky hell.
      I therefore see full well,
That death, the dungeon, sickness, and old age,
Weighed against thee, are blessèd heritage.

And what though many a goodly hypocrite,
   Lifting to thee his veritable prayer,
      Call God to witness there
   How this thy burden moved not Him to wrath.
Why, who may call (of them that muse aright)
Him poor, who of the whole can say, 'Tis Mine ?
      Methinks I well divine
   That want, to such, should seem an easy path.
   God, who made all things, all things had and hath ;
Nor any tongue may say that He was poor,
      What while He did endure
For man's best succour among men to dwell :
Since to have all, with Him, was possible.

Song, thou shalt wend upon thy journey now:
   And, if thou meet with folk who rail at thee,
      Saying that poverty
Is not even sharper than thy words allow,—
Unto such brawlers briefly answer thou,
To tell them they are hypocrites ; and then
      Say mildly, once again,
That I, who am nearly in a beggar's case,
Might not presume to sing my proper praise

XXVII.

Canzone.

He laments the Presumption and Incontinence of his Youth.

The devastating flame of that fierce plague,
    The foe of virtue, fed with others' peace
      More than itself foresees,
    Being still shut in to gnaw its own desire ;
Its strength not weakened, nor its hues more vague,
    For all the benison that virtue sheds,
      But which for ever spreads
    To be a living curse that shall not tire :
      Or yet again, that other idle fire
Which flickers with all change as winds may please :
      One whichsoe'er of these
At length has hidden the true path from me
      Which twice man may not see,
And quenched the intelligence of joy, till now
All solace but abides in perfect woe.

Alas ! the more my painful spirit grieves,
    The more confused with miserable strife
      Is that delicious life
    Which sighing it recalls perpetually :
But its worst anguish, whence it still receives
    More pain than death, is sent, to yield the sting
      Of perfect suffering,
    By him who is my lord and governs me ;
    Who holds all gracious truth in fealty,
Being nursed in those four sisters' fond caress
      Through whom comes happiness.

He now has left me ; and I draw my breath
  Wound in the arms of Death,
Desirous of her : she is cried upon
In all the prayers my heart puts up alone.

How fierce aforetime and how absolute
  That wheel of flame which turned within my head,
    May never quite be said,
  Because there are not words to speak the whole.
It slew my hope whereof I lack the fruit,
  And stung the blood within my living flesh
    To be an intricate mesh
  Of pain beyond endurance or control ;
  Withdrawing me from God, who gave my soul
To know the sign where honour has its seat
    From honour's counterfeit.
So in its longing my heart finds not hope,
    Nor knows what door to ope ;
Since, parting me from God, this foe took thought
To shut those paths wherein He may be sought.

My second enemy, thrice armed in guile,
  As wise and cunning to mine overthrow
    As her smooth face doth show,
  With yet more shameless strength holds mastery.
My spirit, naked of its light and vile,
  Is lit by her with her own deadly gleam,
    Which makes all anguish seem
  As nothing to her scourges that I see.
  O thou the body of grace, abide with me
As thou wast once in the once joyful time ;
    And though thou hate my crime,
Fill not my life with torture to the end ;
    But in thy mercy, bend
My steps, and for thine honour, back again ;
Till, finding joy through thee, I bless my pain.

Since that first frantic devil without faith
   Fell, in thy name, upon the stairs that mount
     Unto the limpid fount
Of thine intelligence,—withhold not now
Thy grace, nor spare my second foe from death.
   For lo! on this my soul has set her trust ;
     And failing this, thou must
Prove false to truth and honour, seest thou !
   Then, saving light and throne of strength, allow
My prayer, and vanquish both my foes at last ;
     That so I be not cast
Into that woe wherein I fear to end.
     Yet if it is ordain'd
That I must die ere this be perfected,—
Ah ! yield me comfort after I am dead.

Ye unadornèd words obscure of sense,
   With weeping and with sighing go from me,
     And bear mine agony
(Not to be told by words, being too intense,)
     To His intelligence
Who moved by virtue shall fulfil my breath
In human life or compensating death.

XXVIII.

CANZONE.

A Dispute with Death.

"O SLUGGISH, hard, ingrate, what doest thou ?
  Poor sinner, folded round with heavy sin,
    Whose life to find out joy alone is bent.
I call thee, and thou fall'st to deafness now ;
  And, deeming that my path whereby to win
    Thy seat is lost, there sitt'st thee down content,
    And hold'st me to thy will subservient.
But I into thy heart have crept disguised :
    Among thy senses and thy sins I went,
By roads thou didst not guess, unrecognised.
Tears will not now suffice to bid me go,
Nor countenance abased, nor words of woe."

Now, when I heard the sudden dreadful voice
  Wake thus within to cruel utterance,
    Whereby the very heart of hearts did fail,
My spirit might not any more rejoice,
  But fell from its courageous pride at once,
    And turned to fly, where flight may not avail.
    Then slowly 'gan some strength to re-inhale
The trembling life which heard that whisper speak,
    And had conceived the sense with sore travail;
Till in the mouth it murmured, very weak,
Saying : "Youth, wealth, and beauty, these have I
O Death ! remit thy claim,—I would not die.'

Small sign of pity in that aspect dwells
 Which then had scattered all my life abroad
  Till there was comfort with no single sense :
And yet almost in piteous syllables,
 When I had ceased to speak, this answer flow'd :
  " Behold what path is spread before thee hence ;
  Thy life has all but a day's permanence.
And is it for the sake of youth there seems
 In loss of human years such sore offence ?
Nay, look unto the end of youthful dreams.
What present glory does thy hope possess,
That shall not yield ashes and bitterness ?"

But, when I looked on Death made visible,
 From my heart's sojourn brought before mine eyes,
  And holding in her hand my grievous sin,
I seemed to see my countenance, that fell,
 Shake like a shadow : my heart uttered cries,
  And my soul wept the curse that lay therein.
  Then Death : "Thus much thine urgent prayer
   shall win :—
I grant thee the brief interval of youth
 At natural pity's strong soliciting."
And I (because I knew that moment's ruth
But left my life to groan for a frail space)
Fell in the dust upon my weeping face.

So, when she saw me thus abashed and dumb,
 In loftier words she weighed her argument,
  That new and strange it was to hear her speak ;
Saying : "The path thy fears withhold thee from
Is thy best path.   To folly be not shent,
 Nor shrink from me because thy flesh is weak.
 Thou seest how man is sore confused, and eke
How ruinous Chance makes havoc of his life,
 And grief is in the joys that he doth seek ;

Nor ever pauses the perpetual strife
'Twixt fear and rage; until beneath the sun
His perfect anguish be fulfilled and done."

" O Death ! thou art so dark and difficult,
    That never human creature might attain
        By his own will to pierce thy secret sense,
Because, foreshadowing thy dread result,
He may not put his trust in heart or brain,
        Nor power avails him, nor intelligence.
        Behold how cruelly thou takest hence
These forms so beautiful and dignified,
        And chain'st them in thy shadow chill and dense,
And forcest them in narrow graves to hide;
With pitiless hate subduing still to thee
The strength of man and woman's delicacy."

"Not for thy fear the less I come at last,
    For this thy tremor, for thy painful sweat.
        Take therefore thought to leave (for lo ! I call)
Kinsfolk and comrades, all thou didst hold fast,—
    Thy father and thy mother,—to forget
        All these thy brethren, sisters, children, all.
        Cast sight and hearing from thee; let hope fall;
Leave every sense and thy whole intellect,
        These things wherein thy life made festival :
For I have wrought thee to such strange effect
That thou hast no more power to dwell with these
    As living man.   Let pass thy soul in peace."

Yea, Lord.   O thou, the Builder of the spheres,
    Who, making me, didst shape me, of thy grace,
        In thine own image and high counterpart;
Do thou subdue my spirit, long perverse,
    To weep within thy will a certain space,
        Ere yet thy thunder come to rive my heart.
        Set in my hand some sign of what thou art,

II

Lord God, and suffer me to seek out Christ,—
    Weeping, to seek Him in thy ways apart;
Until my sorrow have at length suffic'd
In some accepted instant to atone
For sins of thought, for stubborn evil done.

Dishevelled and in tears, go, song of mine,
    To break the hardness of the heart of man :
        Say how his life began
From dust, and in that dust doth sink supine :
    Yet, say, the unerring spirit of grief shall guide
        His soul, being purified,
To seek its Maker at the heavenly shrine.

CINO DA PISTOIA.

I.

TO DANTE ALIGHIERI.

SONNET.

*He interprets Dante's Dream, related in the first Sonnet of the Vita Nuova.**

EACH lover's longing leads him naturally
    Unto his lady's heart his heart to show ;
    And this it is that Love would have thee know
By the strange vision which he sent to thee.
With thy heart therefore, flaming outwardly,
    In humble guise he fed thy lady so,
    Who long had lain in slumber, from all woe
Folded within a mantle silently.
Also, in coming, Love might not repress
    His joy, to yield thee thy desire achieved,
        Whence heart should unto heart true service bring.
But understanding the great love-sickness
    Which in thy lady's bosom was conceived,
        He pitied her, and wept in vanishing.

---

* See *ante*, page 33.

II.

TO DANTE ALIGHIERI.

CANZONE.

On the Death of Beatrice Portinari.

ALBEIT my prayers have not so long delay'd,
    But craved for thee, ere this, that Pity and Love
    Which only bring our heavy life some rest;
Yet is not now the time so much o'erstay'd
    But that these words of mine which tow'rds thee move
        Must find thee still with spirit dispossess'd,
        And say to thee: " In Heaven she now is bless'd,
Even as the blessèd name men called her by;"
        While thou dost ever cry,
" Alas! the blessing of mine eyes is flown!"
        Behold, these words set down
Are needed still, for still thou sorrowest.
Then hearken; I would yield advisedly
Some comfort: Stay these sighs; give ear to me.

We know for certain that in this blind world
    Each man's subsistence is of grief and pain,
        Still trailed by fortune through all bitterness.
Blessèd the soul which, when its flesh is furl'd
    Within a shroud, rejoicing doth attain
        To Heaven itself, made free of earthly stress.
        Then wherefore sighs thy heart in abjectness,
Which for her triumph should exult aloud?
        For He the Lord our God

Hath called her, hearkening what her Angel said,
    To have Heaven perfected.
  Each saint for a new thing beholds her face,
And she the face of our Redemption sees,
Conversing with immortal substances.

Why now do pangs of torment clutch thy heart
  Which with thy love should make thee overjoy'd,
    As him whose intellect hath passed the skies ?
Behold, the spirits of thy life depart
  Daily to Heaven with her, they so are buoy'd .
    With their desire, and Love so bids them rise.
    O God ! and thou, a man whom God made wise,
To nurse a charge of care, and love the same !
      I bid thee in His Name
From sin of sighing grief to hold thy breath,
      Nor let thy heart to death,
  Nor harbour death's resemblance in thine eyes.
God hath her with Himself eternally,
Yet she inhabits every hour with thee.

Be comforted, Love cries, be comforted !
  Devotion pleads, Peace, for the love of God !
    O yield thyself to prayers so full of grace ;
And make thee naked now of this dull weed
  Which 'neath thy foot were better to be trod ;
    For man through grief despairs and ends his days.
    How ever shouldst thou see the lovely face
If any desperate death should once be thine ?
      From justice so condign
Withdraw thyself even now ; that in the end
      Thy heart may not offend
  Against thy soul, which in the holy place,
In Heaven, still hopes to see her and to be
Within her arms.   Let this hope comfort thee.

Look thou into the pleasure wherein dwells
  Thy lovely lady who is in Heaven crown'd,

Who is herself thy hope in Heaven, the while
To make thy memory hallowed she avails ;
   Being a soul within the deep Heaven bound,
    A face on thy heart painted, to beguile
    Thy heart of grief which else should turn it vile.
Even as she seemed a wonder here below,
        On high she seemeth so,—
Yea, better known, is there more wondrous yet.
        And even as she was met
    First by the angels with sweet song and smile,
Thy spirit bears her back upon the wing,
Which often in those ways is journeying.

Of thee she entertains the blessèd throngs,
   And says to them : " While yet my body thrave
   On earth, I gat much honour which he gave,
Commending me in his commended songs."
   Also she asks alway of God our Lord
   To give thee peace according to His word.

III.

TO DANTE ALIGHIERI.

SONNET.

*He conceives of some Compensation in Death.**

DANTE, whenever this thing happeneth,—
  That Love's desire is quite bereft of Hope,
  (Seeking in vain at ladies' eyes some scope
Of joy, through what the heart for ever saith,)—
I ask thee, can amends be made by Death?
  Is such sad pass the last extremity?—
  Or may the Soul that never feared to die
Then in another body draw new breath?
Lo! thus it is through her who governs all
  Below,—that I, who entered at her door,
    Now at her dreadful window must fare forth.
Yea, and I think through her it doth befall
  That even ere yet the road is travelled o'er
    My bones are weary and life is nothing worth.

---

* Among Dante's Epistles there is a Latin letter to Cino, which
I should judge was written in reply to this Sonnet.

IV.

MADRIGAL.

To his Lady Selvaggia Vergiolesi ; likening his Love to a Search for Gold.

I ᴀᴍ all-bent to glean the golden ore
   Little by little from the river-bed ;
      Hoping the day to see
When Crœsus shall be conquered in my store.
   Therefore, still sifting where the sands are spread,
      I labour patiently :
Till, thus intent on this thing and no more,—
   If to a vein of silver I were led,
      It scarce could gladden me.
And, seeing that no joy's so warm i' the core
   As this whereby the heart is comforted
      And the desire set free,—
Therefore thy bitter love is still my scope,
   Lady, from whom it is my life's sore theme
More painfully to sift the grains of hope
      Than gold out of that stream.

V.

SONNET.

To Love, in great Bitterness.

O LOVE, O thou that, for my fealty,
  Only in torment dost thy power employ,
  Give me, for God's sake, something of thy joy,
That I may learn what good there is in thee.
Yea, for, if thou art glad with grieving me,
  Surely my very life thou shalt destroy
  When thou renew'st my pain, because the joy
Must then be wept for with the misery.
He that had never sense of good, nor sight,
  Esteems his ill estate but natural,
    Which so is lightlier borne : his case is mine.
    But, if thou wouldst uplift me for a sign,
  Bidding me drain the curse and know it all,
I must a little taste its opposite.

VI.

SONNET.

Death is not without but within him.

THIS fairest lady, who, as well I wot,
   Found entrance by her beauty to my soul,
   Pierced through mine eyes my heart, which erst was
        whole,
Sorely, yet makes as though she knew it not ;
Nay turns upon me now, to anger wrought ;
   Dealing me harshness for my pain's best dole,
   And is so changed by her own wrath's control,
That I go thence, in my distracted thought
Content to die ; and, mourning, cry abroad
   On Death, as upon one afar from me ;
      But Death makes answer from within my heart.
   Then, hearing her so hard at hand to be,
I do commend my spirit unto God ;
      Saying to her too, " Ease and peace thou art."

VII.

SONNET.

A Trance of Love.

VANQUISHED and weary was my soul in me,
  And my heart gasped after its much lament,
  When sleep at length the painful languor sent.
And, as I slept (and wept incessantly),—
Through the keen fixedness of memory
  Which I had cherished ere my tears were spent,
  I passed to a new trance of wonderment;
Wherein a visible spirit I could see,
Which caught me up, and bore me to a place
  Where my most gentle lady was alone;
    And still before us a fire seemed to move,
  Out of the which methought there came a moan
Uttering, "Grace, a little season, grace!
    I am of one that hath the wings of Love."

VIII. '

SONNET.

Of the Grave of Selvaggia, on the Monte della Sambuca.

I WAS upon the high and blessed mound,
  And kissed, long worshiping, the stones and grass,
  There on the hard stones prostrate, where, alas!
That pure one laid her forehead in the ground.
Then were the springs of gladness sealed and bound,
  The day that unto Death's most bitter pass
  My sick heart's lady turned her feet, who was
Already in her gracious life renown'd.
So in that place I spake to Love, and cried:
  " O sweet my god, I am one whom Death may claim
    Hence to be his; for lo! my heart lies here."
  Anon, because my Master lent no ear,
Departing, still I called Selvaggia's name.
So with my moan I left the mountain-side.

IX.

CANZONE.

His Lament for Selvaggia.

Ay me, alas ! the beautiful bright hair
  That shed reflected gold
    O'er the green growths on either side the way :
Ay me ! the lovely look, open and fair,
  Which my heart's core doth hold
    With all else of that best-remembered day ;
    Ay me ! the face made gay
With joy that Love confers ;
Ay me ! that smile of hers
  Where whiteness as of snow was visible
Among the roses at all seasons red !
    Ay me ! and was this well,
O Death, to let me live when she is dead ?

Ay me ! the calm, erect, dignified walk ;
  Ay me ! the sweet salute,—
    The thoughtful mind,—the wit discreetly worn ;
Ay me ! the clearness of her noble talk,
  Which made the good take root
    In me, and for the evil woke my scorn ;
    Ay me ! the longing born
Of so much loveliness,—
The hope, whose eager stress
  Made other hopes fall back to let it pass,
Even till my load of love grew light thereby !
    These thou hast broken, as glass,
O Death, who makest me, alive, to die !

Ay me! Lady, the lady of all worth ;—
  Saint, for whose single shrine
    All other shrines I left, even as Love will'd ;—
Ay me! what precious stone in the whole earth,
  For that pure fame of thine
    Worthy the marble statue's base to yield ?
    Ay me ! fair vase fulfill'd
With more than this world's good,—
By cruel chance and rude
  Cast out upon the steep path of the mountains
Where Death has shut thee in between hard stones !
  Ay me ! two languid fountains
Of weeping are these eyes, which joy disowns.

Ay me, sharp Death ! till what I ask is done
  And my whole life is ended utterly,—
Answer—must I weep on
  Even thus, and never cease to moan Ay me ?

X.

TO GUIDO CAVALCANTI.

SONNET.

He owes nothing to Guido as a Poet.

WHAT rhymes are thine which I have ta'en from thee,
　Thou Guido, that thou ever say'st I thieve ?*
'Tis true, fine fancies gladly I receive,
But when was aught found beautiful in thee?
Nay, I have searched my pages diligently,
　And tell the truth, and lie not, by your leave.
From whose rich store my web of songs I weave
Love knoweth well, well knowing them and me. ·
No artist I,—all men may gather it ;
　Nor do I work in ignorance of pride,
　　(Though the world reach alone the coarser sense ;)
But am a certain man of humble wit
　Who journeys with his sorrow at his side,
　　For a heart's sake, alas ! that is gone hence.

---

* I have not examined Cino's poetry with special reference to
this accusation ; but there is a Canzone of his in which he speaks
of having conceived an affection for another lady from her resem-
blance to Selvaggia. Perhaps Guido considered this as a sort of
plagiarism *de facto* on his own change of love through Mandetta's
likeness to Giovanna.

XI.

SONNET.

He impugns the verdicts of Dante's Commedia.

THIS book of Dante's, very sooth to say,
  Is just a poet's lovely heresy,
  Which by a lure as sweet as sweet can be
Draws other men's concerns beneath its sway ;
While, among stars' and comets' dazzling play,
  It beats the right down, lets the wrong go free,
  Shows some abased, and others in great glee,
Much as with lovers is Love's ancient way.
Therefore his vain decrees, wherein he lied,
  Fixing folks' nearness to the Fiend their foe,
Must be like empty nutshells flung aside.
  Yet through the rash false witness set to grow,
French and Italian vengeance on such pride
  May fall, like Antony's on Cicero.

XII.

SONNET.

He condemns Dante for not naming, in the Commedia, his
friend Onesto di Boncima, and his Lady Selvaggia.

AMONG the faults we in that book descry
   Which has crowned Dante lord of rhyme and thought,
   Are two so grave that some attaint is brought
Unto the greatness of his soul thereby.
One is, that holding with Sordello high
   Discourse, and with the rest who sang and taught,
   He of Onesto di Boncima * nought
Has said, who was to Arnauld Daniel † nigh.
The other is, that when he says he came
   To see, at summit of the sacred stair,
   His Beatrice among the heavenly signs,—
He, looking in the bosom of Abraham,
   Saw not that highest of all women there
     Who joined Mount Sion to the Apennines.‡

---

  * Between this poet and Cino various friendly sonnets were
interchanged, which may be found in the Italian collections. There
is also one sonnet by Onesto to Cino, with his answer, both of
which are far from being affectionate or respectful. They are
very obscure, however, and not specially interesting.
  † The Provençal poet, mentioned in C. xxvi. of the *Purgatory.*
  ‡ That is, sanctified the Apennines by her burial on the Monte
della Sambuca.

DANTE DA MAIANO.

I.

TO DANTE ALIGHIERI.

SONNET.

*He interprets Dante Alighieri's Dream, related in the
first Sonnet of the Vita Nuova.**

OF that wherein thou art a questioner
  Considering, I make answer briefly thus,
  Good friend, in wit but little prosperous:
And from my words the truth thou shalt infer,—
So hearken to thy dream's interpreter.
  If, sound of frame, thou soundly canst discuss
  In reason,—then, to expel this overplus
Of vapours which hath made thy speech to err,
See that thou lave and purge thy stomach soon.
    But if thou art afflicted with disease,
    Know that I count it mere delirium.
    Thus of my thought I write thee back the sum:
  Nor my conclusions can be changed from these
Till to the leach thy water I have shown.

---

* See *ante*, page 33.

II.

SONNET.

He craves interpreting of a Dream of his.

THOU that art wise, let wisdom minister
   Unto my dream, that it be understood.
To wit : A lady, of her body fair,
   And whom my heart approves in womanhood,
   Bestowed on me a wreath of flowers, fair-hued
And green in leaf, with gentle loving air ;
   After the which, meseemed I was stark nude
Save for a smock of hers that I did wear.
Whereat, good friend, my courage gat such growth
   That to mine arms I took her tenderly :
With no rebuke the beauty laughed unloth,
   And as she laughed I kissed continually.
I say no more, for that I pledged mine oath,
   And that my mother, who is dead, was by.

GUIDO ORLANDI TO DANTE DA MAIANO.

SONNET.

He interprets the Dream* related in the foregoing Sonnet.

On the last words of what you write to me
   I give you my opinion at the first,
   To see the dead must prove corruption nursed
Within you, by your heart's own vanity.
The soul should bend the flesh to its decree :
   Then rule it, friend, as fish by line amerced.
   As to the smock, your lady's gift, the worst
Of words were not too bad for speech so free.
It is a thing unseemly to declare
   The love of gracious dame or damozel,
      And therewith for excuse to say, I dream'd.
      Tell us no more of this, but think who seem'd
   To call you : mother came to whip you well.
Love close, and of Love's joy you'll have your share.

---

* There exist no fewer than six answers by different poets, interpreting Dante da Maiano's dream. I have chosen Guido Orlandi's, much the most matter-of-fact of the six, because it is diverting to find the writer again in his antagonistic mood. Among the five remaining answers, in all of which the vision is treated as a very mysterious matter, one is attributed to Dante Alighieri, but seems so doubtful that I have not translated it. Indeed, it would do the greater Dante, if he really wrote it, little credit as a lucid interpreter of dreams; though it might have some interest, as giving him (when compared with the sonnet at page 178) a decided advantage over his lesser namesake in point of courtesy.

III.

Sonnet.

To his Lady Nina, of Sicily.

So greatly thy great pleasaunce pleasured me,
    Gentle my lady, from the first of all,
    That counting every other blessing small
I gave myself up wholly to know thee :
And since I was made thine, thy courtesy
    And worth, more than of earth, celestial,
    I learned, and from its freedom did enthrall
My heart, the servant of thy grace to be.
Wherefore I pray thee, joyful countenance,
    Humbly, that it incense or irk thee not,
If I, being thine, do wait upon thy glance.
More to solicit, I am all afraid :
    Yet, lady, twofold is the gift, we wot,
Given to the needy unsolicited.

.IV.

SONNET.

He thanks his Lady for the Joy he has had from her.

WONDERFUL countenance and royal neck,
  I have not found your beauty's parallel !
  Nor at her birth might any yet prevail
The likeness of these features to partake.
Wisdom is theirs, and mildness : for whose sake
  All grace seems stol'n, such perfect grace to swell ;
  Fashioned of God beyond delight to dwell
Exalted. And herein my pride I take
Who of this garden have possession,
  So that all worth subsists for my behoof
    And bears itself according to my will.
    Lady, in thee such pleasaunce hath its fill
That whoso is content to rest thereon
  Knows not of grief, and holds all pain aloof.

CECCO ANGIOLIERI, DA SIENA.

I.

TO DANTE ALIGHIERI.

Sonnet.

*On the last Sonnet of the Vita Nuova.**

Dante Alighieri, Cecco, your good friend
  And servant, gives you greeting as his lord,
  And prays you for the sake of Love's accord,
(Love being the Master before whom you bend,)
That you will pardon him if he offend,
  Even as your gentle heart can well afford.
  All that he wants to say is just one word
Which partly chides your sonnet at the end.
For where the measure changes, first you say
  You do not understand the gentle speech
  A spirit made touching your Beatrice:
And next you tell your ladies how, straightway,
  You understand it. Wherefore (look you) each
  Of these your words the other's sense denies.

* See *ante*, page 94.

II.

SONNET.

He will not be too deeply in Love.

I AM enamoured, and yet not so much
    But that I'd do without it easily ;
    And my own mind thinks all the more of me
That Love has not quite penned me in his hutch.
Enough if for his sake I dance and touch
    The lute, and serve his servants cheerfully :
    An overdose is worse than none would be :
Love is no lord of mine, I'm proud to vouch.
So let no woman who is born conceive
    That I'll be her liege slave, as I see some,
    Be she as fair and dainty as she will.
Too much of love makes idiots, I believe :
    I like not any fashion that turns glum
    The heart, and makes the visage sick and ill.

III.

SONNET.

Of Love in Men and Devils.

THE man who feels not, more or less, somewhat ·
   Of love in all the years his life goes round
   Should be denied a grave in holy ground ·
Except with usurers who will bate no groat:
Nor he himself should count himself a jot
   Less wretched than the meanest beggar found.
   Also the man who in Love's robe is gown'd
May say that Fortune smiles upon his lot.
Seeing how love has such nobility
   That if it entered in the lord of Hell
     'Twould rule him more than his fire's ancient sting;
He should be glorified to eternity,
   And all his life be always glad and well
     As is a wanton woman in the spring.

IV.

SONNET.

Of Love, in honour of his mistress Becchina.

WHATEVER good is naturally done
  Is born of Love as fruit is born of flower:
  By Love all good is brought to its full power:
Yea, Love does more than this; for he finds none
So coarse but from his touch some grace is won,
  And the poor wretch is altered in an hour.
  So let it be decreed that Death devour
The beast who says that Love's a thing to shun.
A man's just worth the good that he can hold,
  And where no love is found, no good is there;
    On that there's nothing that I would not stake.
So now, my Sonnet, go as you are told
    To lovers and their sweethearts everywhere,
    And say I made you for Becchina's sake.

V.

SONNET.

Of Becchina, the Shoemaker's Daughter.

WHY, if Becchina's heart were diamond,
  And all the other parts of her were steel,
  As cold to love as snows when they congeal
In lands to which the sun may not get round;
And if her father were a giant crown'd
  And not a donkey born to stitching shoes,
    Or I were but an ass myself;—to use
Such harshness, scarce could to her praise redound
Yet if she'd only for a minute hear,
  And I could speak if only pretty well,
    I'd let her know that I'm her happiness;
That I'm her life should also be made clear,
  With other things that I've no need to tell;
    And then I feel quite sure she'd answer Yes.

VI.

SONNET.

To Messer Angiolieri, his Father.

IF I'd a sack of florins, and all new,
  (Packed tight together, freshly coined and fine,)
  And Arcidosso and Montegiovi mine,*
And quite a glut of eagle-pieces too,—
It were but as three farthings to my view
  Without Becchina.   Why then all these plots
  To whip me, daddy ?   Nay, but tell me—what's
My sin, or all the sins of Turks, to you ?
For I protest (or may I be struck dead !)
  My love's so firmly planted in its place,
    Whipping nor hanging now could change the grain.
And if you want my reason on this head,
  It is that whoso looks her in the face,
    Though he were old, gets back his youth again.

---

* Perhaps the names of his father's estates.

VII.

SONNET.

Of the 20th June 1291.

I'M full of everything I do not want,
   And have not that wherein I should find ease;
   For alway till Becchina brings me peace
The heavy heart I bear must toil and pant;   ·
That so all written paper would prove scant
   (Though in its space the Bible you might squeeze,)
   To say how like the flames of furnaces
I burn, remembering what she used to grant.
Because the stars are fewer in heaven's span
   Than all those kisses wherewith I kept tune
      All in an instant (I who now have none!)
Upon her mouth (I and no other man!)
   So sweetly on the twentieth day of June
      In the new year * twelve hundred ninety-one.

---

* The year, according to the calendar of those days, began on
the 25th March. The alteration to 1st January was made in 1582
by the Pope, and immediately adopted by all Catholic countries,
but by England not till 1752. There is some added vividness in
remembering that Cecco's unplatonic love-encounter dates eleven
days after the first death-anniversary of Beatrice (9th of June 1291),
when Dante tells us that he " drew the resemblance of an angel
upon certain tablets." (See *ante*, p. 84.)

VIII.

SONNET.

In absence from Becchina.

My heart's so heavy with a hundred things
    That I feel dead a hundred times a-day;
Yet death would be the least of sufferings,
    For life's all suffering save what's slept away;
Though even in sleep there is no dream but brings
    From dream-land such dull torture as it may.
And yet one moment would pluck out these stings,
    If for one moment she were mine to-day
Who gives my heart the anguish that it has.
    Each thought that seeks my heart for its abode
        Becomes a wan and sorrow-stricken guest:
Sorrow has brought me to so sad a pass
    That men look sad to meet me on the road;
        Nor any road is mine that leads to rest.

IX.

SONNET.

Of Becchina in a rage.

WHEN I behold Becchina in a rage,
  Just like a little lad I trembling stand
  Whose master tells him to hold out his hand
Had I a lion's heart, the sight would wage
Such war against it, that in that sad stage
  I'd wish my birth might never have been plann'd,
  And curse the day and hour that I was bann'd
With such a plague for my life's heritage.
Yet even if I should sell me to the Fiend,
  I must so manage matters in some way
    That for her rage I may not care a fig ;
Or else from death I cannot long be screen'd.
  So I'll not blink the fact, but plainly say
    It's time I got my valour to grow big.

X.

Sonnet.

*He rails against Dante, who had censured his homage to
Becchina.*

DANTE ALIGHIERI in Becchina's praise
   Won't have me sing, and bears him like my lord.
   He's but a pinchbeck florin, on my word ;
Sugar he seems, but salt's in all his ways ;
He looks like wheaten bread, who's bread of maize ;
   He's but a sty, though like a tower in height ;
   A falcon, till you find that he's a kite ;
Call him a cock !—a hen's more like his case.
Go now to Florence, Sonnet of my own,
   And there with dames and maids hold pretty parles,
   And say that all he is doth only seem.
And I meanwhile will make him better known
   Unto the Count of Provence, good King Charles ; *
   And in this way we'll singe his skin for him.

---

  * This may be either Charles II., King of Naples and Count of
Provence, or more probably his son Charles Martel, King of Hun-
gary. We know from Dante that a friendship subsisted between
himself and the latter prince, who visited Florence in 1295, and
died in the same year, in his father's lifetime (*Paradise*, C. viii.)

XI.

SONNET.

Of his four Tormentors.

I'M caught, like any thrush the nets surprise,
    By Daddy and Becchina, Mammy and Love.
As to the first-named, let thus much suffice,—
    Each day he damns me, and each hour thereof;
Becchina wants so much of all that's nice,
    Not Mahomet himself could yield enough:
And Love still sets me doting in a trice
    On trulls who'd seem the Ghetto's proper stuff.
My mother don't do much because she can't,
    But I may count it just as good as done,
Knowing the way and not the will's her want.
    To-day I tried a kiss with her—just one—
To see if I could make her sulks avaunt:
    She said, "The devil rip you up, my son!"

XII.

SONNET.

Concerning his Father.

THE dreadful and the desperate hate I bear
   My father (to my praise, not to my shame,)
   Will make him live more than Methusalem ;
Of this I've long ago been made aware.
Now tell me, Nature, if my hate's not fair.
   A glass of some thin wine not worth a name
   One day I begged (he has whole butts o' the same,)
And he had almost killed me, I declare.
"Good Lord, if I had asked for vernage-wine !"
   Said I ; for if he'd spit into my face
   I wished to see for reasons of my own.
Now say that I mayn't hate this plague of mine !
   Why, if you knew what I know of his ways,
     You'd tell me that I ought to knock him down.*

---

* I have thought it necessary to soften one or two expressions
in this sonnet.

XIII.

SONNET.

Of all he would do.

IF I were fire, I'd burn the world away;
　If I were wind, I'd turn my storms thereon;
　If I were water, I'd soon let it drown;
If I were God, I'd sink it from the day;
If I were Pope, I'd never feel quite gay
　Until there was no peace beneath the sun;
　　If I were Emperor, what would I have done?—
I'd lop men's heads all round in my own way.
If I were Death, I'd look my father up;
　If I were Life, I'd run away from him;
　　And treat my mother to like calls and runs.
If I were Cecco (and that's all my hope),
　I'd pick the nicest girls to suit my whim,
　　And other folk should get the ugly ones.

XIV.

SONNET.

He is past all Help.

FOR a thing done, repentance is no good,
   Nor to say after, Thus would I have done:
In life, what's left behind is vainly rued;
   So let a man get used his hurt to shun;
For on his legs he hardly may be stood
   Again, if once his fall be well begun.
But to show wisdom's what I never could;
   So where I itch I scratch now, and all's one.
I'm down, and cannot rise in any way;
   For not a creature of my nearest kin
      Would hold me out a hand that I could reach.
I pray you do not mock at what I say;
   For so my love's good grace may I not win
      If ever sonnet held so true a speech!

XV.

SONNET.

Of why he is unhanged.

WHOEVER without money is in love
 Had better build a gallows and go hang;
 He dies not once, but oftener feels the pang
Than he who was cast down from Heaven above.
And certes, for my sins, it's plain enough,
 If Love's alive on earth, that he's myself,
 Who would not be so cursed with want of pelf
If others paid my proper dues thereof.
Then why am I not hanged by my own hands?
 I answer: for this empty narrow chink
  Of hope;—that I've a father old and rich,
And that if once he dies I'll get his lands;
 And die he must, when the sea's dry, I think.
  Meanwhile God keeps him whole and me i' the
   ditch.

XVI.

Sonnet.

Of why he would be a Scullion.

I AM so out of love through poverty
  That if I see my mistress in the street
  I hardly can be certain whom I meet,
And of her name do scarce remember me.
Also my courage it has made to be
  So cold, that if I suffered some foul cheat,
  Even from the meanest wretch that one could beat,
Save for the sin I think he should go free.
Ay, and it plays me a still nastier trick ;
  For, meeting some who erewhile with me took
  Delight, I seem to them a roaring fire.
So here's a truth whereat I need not stick ;—
  That if one could turn scullion to a cook,
  It were a thing to which one might aspire.

XVII.

Prolonged Sonnet.

When his Clothes were gone.

NEVER so bare and naked was church-stone
  As is my clean-stripped doublet in my grasp ;
  Also I wear a shirt without a clasp,
Which is a dismal thing to look upon.
Ah ! had I still but the sweet coins I won
  That time I sold my nag and staked the pay,
  I'd not lie hid beneath the roof to-day
And eke out sonnets with this moping moan.
Daily a thousand times stark mad am I
  At my dad's meanness who won't clothe me now,
For " How about the horse? " is still his cry.
  Till one thing strikes me as clear anyhow,—
No rag I'll get.   The wretch has sworn, I see,
Not to invest another doit in me.
And all because of the fine doublet's price
He gave me, when I vowed to throw no dice,
And for his damned nag's sake ! Well, this is nice !

XVIII.

SONNET.

He argues his case with Death.

GRAMERCY, Death, as you've my love to win,
  Just be impartial in your next assault ;
  And that you may not find yourself in fault,
Whate'er you do, be quick now and begin.
As oft may I be pounded flat and thin
  As in Grosseto there are grains of salt,
  If now to kill us both you be not call'd,—
'Both me and him who sticks so in his skin.
Or better still, look here ; for if I'm slain
  Alone,—his wealth, it's true, I'll never have,
Yet death is life to one who lives in pain :
  But if you only kill Saldagno's knave,
I'm left in Siena (don't you see your gain ?)
  Like a rich man who's made a galley-slave.*

---

* He means, possibly, that he should be more than ever tormented by his creditors, on account of their knowing his ability to pay them ; but the meaning seems very uncertain.

XIX.

SONNET.

Of Becchina, and of her Husband.

I WOULD like better in the grace to be
    Of the dear mistress whom I bear in mind
    (As once I was) than I should like to find
A stream that washed up gold continually :
Because no language could report of me
    The joys that round my heart would then be twin'd,
    Who now, without her love, do seem resign'd
To death that bends my life to its decree.
And one thing makes the matter still more sad :
    For all the while I know the fault's my own,
        That on her husband I take no revenge,
Who's worse to her than is to me my dad.
    God send grief has not pulled my courage down,
        That hearing this I laugh ; for it seems strange.

XX.

SONNET.

To Becchina's rich Husband. *

As thou wert loth to see, before thy feet,
  The dear broad coin roll all the hill-slope down,
  Till, gathering it from rifted clods, some clown
Should rub it oft and scarcely render it ;—
Tell me, I charge thee, if by generous heat
  Or clutching frost the fruits of earth be grown,
  And by what wind the blight is o'er them strown,
And with what gloom the tempest is replete.
Yet daily, in good sooth, as morn by morn
  Thou hear'st the voice of thy poor husbandman
  And those loud herds, his other family,—
I know, as surely as Becchina's born
  With a kind heart, she does the best she can
  To filch at least one new-bought prize from thee.

---

* This puzzling sonnet is printed in Italian collections with the name of Guido Cavalcanti. It must evidently belong to Angiolieri, and it has certain fine points which make me unwilling to omit it ; though partly as to rendering, and wholly as to application, I have been driven on conjecture.

XXI.

SONNET

On the Death of his Father.

LET not the inhabitants of Hell despair,
  For one's got out who seemed to be locked in;
  And Cecco's the poor devil that I mean,
Who thought for ever and ever to be there.
But the leaf's turned at last, and I declare
  That now my state of glory doth begin :
  For Messer Angiolieri's slipped his skin,
Who plagued me, summer and winter, many a year.
Make haste to Cecco, Sonnet, with a will,
  To him who no more at the Abbey dwells ;
    Tell him that Brother Henry's half dried up.*
He'll never more be down-at-mouth, but fill
  His beak at his own beck,† till his life swells
    To more than Enoch's or Elijah's scope.

---

  * It would almost seem as if Cecco, in his poverty, had at last taken refuge in a religious house under the name of Brother Henry (*Frate Arrigo*), and as if he here meant that Brother Henry was now decayed, so to speak, through the resuscitation of Cecco. (See *Introduction to Part I.*, p 23.)

  † In the original words, "Ma di tal cibo imbecchi lo suo becco," a play upon the name of Becchina seems intended, which I have conveyed as well as I could.

XXII.

SONNET.

He would slay all who hate their Fathers.

WHO utters of his father aught but praise,
   'Twere well to cut his tongue out of his mouth;
   Because the Deadly Sins are seven, yet doth
No one provoke such ire as this must raise.
Were I a priest, or monk in anyways,
   Unto the Pope my first respects were paid,
   Saying, "Holy Father, let a just crusade
Scourge each man who his sire's good name gainsays."
And if by chance a handful of such rogues
   At any time should come into our clutch,
     I'd have them cooked and eaten then and there,
If not by men, at least by wolves and dogs.
   The Lord forgive me! for I fear me much
     Some words of mine were rather foul than fair.

XXIII.

TO DANTE ALIGHIERI.

SONNET.

*He writes to Dante, then in exile at Verona, defying him as
no better than himself.*

DANTE ALIGHIERI, if I jest and lie,
　You in such lists might run a tilt with me :
　I get my dinner, you your supper, free ;
And if I bite the fat, you suck the fry ;
I shear the cloth and you the teazle ply ;
　If I've a strut, who's prouder than you are ?
　If I'm foul-mouthed, you're not particular ;
And you're turned Lombard, even if Roman I.
So that, 'fore Heaven ! if either of us flings
　Much dirt at the other, he must be a fool :
For lack of luck and wit we do these things.
　Yet if you want more lessons at my school,
Just say so, and you'll find the next touch stings—·
　For, Dante, I'm the goad and you're the bull.

GUIDO ORLANDI.*

Against the " White " Ghibellines.

Now of the hue of ashes are the Whites ;
   And they go following now after the kind
   Of creatures we call crabs, which, as some find,
Will only seek their natural food o' nights.
All day they hide ; their flesh has such sore frights
   Lest Death be come for them on every wind,
   Lest now the Lion's† wrath be so inclined
That they may never set their sin to rights.
Guelf were they once, and now are Ghibelline :
   Nothing but rebels henceforth be they named,—
   State-foes, as are the Uberti, every one.
Behold, against the Whites all men must sign
   Some judgment whence no pardon can be claim'd
   Excepting they were offered to Saint John.‡

---

  * Several 'other pieces by this author, addressed to Guido Caval-
canti and Dante da Maiano, will be found among their poems.
  † *I.e.* Florence.
  ‡ That is, presented at the high altar on the feast-day of St. John
the Baptist ; a ceremony attending the release of criminals, a cer-
tain number of whom were annually pardoned on that day in
Florence. This was the disgraceful condition annexed to that
recall to Florence which Dante received when in exile at the court
of Verona ; which others accepted, but which was refused by
him in a memorable epistle still preserved.

LAPO GIANNI.

I.

MADRIGAL.

What Love shall provide for him.

LOVE, I demand to have my lady in fee.

Fine balm let Arno be;
The walls of Florence all of silver rear'd,
And crystal pavements in the public way.

With castles make me fear'd,
Till every Latin soul have owned my sway.

Be the world peaceful; safe throughout each path;
No neighbour to breed wrath;
The air, summer and winter, temperate.

A thousand dames and damsels richly clad
Upon my choice to wait,
Singing by day and night to make me glad.

Let me have fruitful gardens of great girth,
Filled with the strife of birds,
With water-springs, and beasts that house i' the earth.

Let me seem Solomon for lore of words,
Samson for strength, for beauty Absalom.

Knights as my serfs be given;
And as I will, let music go and come;
Till at the last thou bring me into Heaven.

II.

BALLATA.

A Message in charge for his Lady Lagia.

BALLAD, since Love himself hath fashioned thee
    Within my mind where he doth make abode,
    Hie thee to her who through mine eyes bestow'd
Her blessing on my heart, which stays with me.

Since thou wast born a handmaiden of Love,
    With every grace thou should'st be perfected,
        And everywhere seem gentle, wise, and sweet.
And for that thine aspect gives sign thereof,
    I do not tell thee, "Thus much must be said:"—
        Hoping, if thou inheritest my wit,
        And com'st on her when speech may ill befit,
That thou wilt say no words of any kind:
But when her ear is graciously inclin'd,
    Address her without dread submissively.

Afterward, when thy courteous speech is done,
    (Ended with fair obeisance and salute
        To that chief forehead of serenest good,)
Wait thou the answer which, in heavenly tone,
    Shall haply stir between her lips, nigh mute
        For gentleness and virtuous womanhood.
        And mark that, if my homage please her mood,
No rose shall be incarnate in her cheek,
But her soft eyes shall seem subdued and meek,
    And almost pale her face for delicacy.

For, when at last thine amorous discourse
  Shall have possessed her spirit with that fear
  Of thoughtful recollection which in love
Comes first,—then say thou that my heart implores
  Only without an end to honour her,
    Till by God's will my living soul remove:
    That I take counsel oftentimes with Love;
For he first made my hope thus strong and rife,
Through whom my heart, my mind, and all my life,
  Are given in bondage to her seigniory.

Then shalt thou find the blessed refuge girt
  I' the circle of her arms, where pity and grace
  Have sojourn, with all human excellence:
Then shalt thou feel her gentleness exert
  Its rule (unless, alack! she deem thee base):
    Then shalt thou know her sweet intelligence:
    Then shalt thou see—O marvel most intense!—
What thing the beauty of the angels is,
And what are the miraculous harmonies
  Whereon Love rears the heights of sovereignty.

Move, Ballad, so that none take note of thee,
  Until thou set thy footsteps in Love's road.
  Having arrived, speak with thy visage bow'd,
And bring no false doubt back, or jealousy.

DINO FRESCOBALDI.

I.

Sonnet.

Of what his Lady is.

This is the damsel by whom love is brought
　To enter at his eyes that looks on her;
　This is the righteous maid, the comforter,
Whom every virtue honours unbesought.
Love, journeying with her, unto smiles is wrought,
　Showing the glory which surrounds her there;
　Who, when a lowly heart prefers its prayer,
Can make that its transgression come to nought.
And, when she giveth greeting, by Love's rule,
　With sweet reserve she somewhat lifts her eyes,
　　Bestowing that desire which speaks to us.
　　Alone on what is noble looks she thus,
　Its opposite rejecting in like wise,
This pitiful young maiden beautiful.

II.

SONNET.

Of the Star of his Love.

THAT star the highest seen in heaven's expanse
  Not yet forsakes me with its lovely light:
  It gave me her who from her heaven's pure height
Gives all the grace mine intellect demands.
Thence a new arrow of strength is in my hands
  Which bears good will whereso it may alight;
  So barbed, that no man's body or soul its flight
Has wounded yet, nor shall wound any man's.
Glad am I therefore that her grace should fall
  Not otherwise than thus; whose rich increase
    Is such a power as evil cannot dim.
My sins within an instant perished all
  When I inhaled the light of so much peace.
    And this Love knows; for I have told it him.

GIOTTO DI BONDONE.

Canzone.

Of the Doctrine of Voluntary Poverty.

Many there are, praisers of Poverty;
The which as man's best state is register'd
    When by free choice preferr'd,
With strict observance having nothing here.
For this they find certain authority
Wrought of an over-nice interpreting.
    Now as concerns such thing,
A hard extreme it doth to me appear,
    Which to commend I fear,
For seldom are extremes without some vice.
    Let every edifice,
Of work or word, secure foundation find;
    Against the potent wind,
And all things perilous, so well prepar'd
That it need no correction afterward.

Of poverty which is against the will,
It never can be doubted that therein
    Lies broad the way to sin.
For oftentimes it makes the judge unjust;
In dames and damsels doth their honour kill;
And begets violence and villanies,
    And theft and wicked lies,
And casts a good man from his fellows' trust.
    And for a little dust
Of gold that lacks, wit seems a lacking too.

If once the coat give view
Of the real back, farewell all dignity.
　　Each therefore strives that he
Should by no means admit her to his sight,
Who, only thought on, makes his face turn white.

Of poverty which seems by choice elect,
I may pronounce from plain experience,—
　　Not of mine own pretence,—
That 'tis observed or unobserved at will.
Nor its observance asks our full respect:
For no discernment, nor integrity,
　　Nor lore of life, nor plea
Of virtue, can her cold regard instil.
　　I call it shame and ill
To name as virtue that which stifles good.
　　I call it grossly rude,
On a thing bestial to make consequent
　　Virtue's inspired advènt
To understanding hearts acceptable :
For the most wise most love with her to dwell.

Here mayst thou find some issue of demur :
For lo ! our Lord commendeth poverty.
　　Nay, what His meaning be
Search well : His words are wonderfully deep,
Oft doubly sensed, asking interpreter.
The state for each most saving, is His will
　　For each.　Thine eyes unseal,
And look within, the inmost truth to reap.
　　Behold what concord keep
His holy words with His most holy life.
　　In Him the power was rife
Which to all things apportions time and place.
　　On earth He chose such case ;
And why ?　'Twas His to point a higher life.

But here, on earth, our senses show us still
How they who preach this thing are least at peace,
    And evermore increase
Much thought how from this thing they should escape.
For if one such a lofty station fill,
He shall assert his strength like a wild wolf,
    Or daily mask himself
Afresh, until his will be brought to shape ;
    Ay, and so wear the cape
That direst wolf shall seem like sweetest lamb
    Beneath the constant sham.
Hence, by their art, this doctrine plagues the world :
    And hence, till they be hurl'd
From where they sit in high hypocrisy,
No corner of the world seems safe to me.

Go, Song, to some sworn owls that we have known
And on their folly bring them to reflect :
    But if they be stiff-neck'd,
Belabour them until their heads are down.

SIMONE DALL' ANTELLA.

PROLONGED SONNET.

In the last Days of the Emperor Henry VII.

ALONG the road all shapes must travel by,
  How swiftly, to my thinking, now doth fare
  The wanderer who built his watchtower there
Where wind is torn with wind continually !
Lo ! from the world and its dull pain to fly,
  Unto such pinnacle did he repair,
  And of her presence was not made aware,
Whose face, that looks like Peace, is Death's own lie.
Alas, Ambition, thou his enemy,
  Who lurest the poor wanderer on his way,
But never bring'st him where his rest may be,—
  O leave him now, for he is gone astray
Himself out of his very self through thee,
  Till now the broken stems his feet betray,
And, caught with boughs before and boughs behind,
Deep in thy tangled wood he sinks entwin'd.

GIOVANNI QUIRINO TO DANTE ALIGHIERI.

SONNET.

He commends the work of Dante's life, then drawing
to its close ; and deplores his own deficiencies.

GLORY to God and to God's Mother chaste,
   Dear friend, is all the labour of thy days :
   Thou art as he who evermore uplays
That heavenly wealth which the worm cannot waste :
So shalt thou render back with interest
   The precious talent given thee by God's grace :
   While I, for my part, follow in their ways
Who by the cares of this world are possess'd.
For, as the shadow of the earth doth make
   The moon's globe dark, when so she is debarr'd
     From the bright rays which lit her in the sky,—
So now, since thou my sun didst me forsake,
   (Being distant from me), I grow dull and hard,
     Even as a beast of Epicurus' sty.

DANTE ALIGHIERI TO GIOVANNI QUIRINO.

SONNET.

*He answers the foregoing Sonnet; saying what he feels at
the approach of Death.*

THE King by whose rich grace His servants be
  With plenty beyond measure set to dwell
  Ordains that I my bitter wrath dispel
And lift mine eyes to the great consistory;
Till, noting how in glorious quires agree
  The citizens of that fair citadel,
  To the Creator I His creature swell
Their song, and all their love possesses me.
So, when I contemplate the great reward
  To which our God has called the Christian seed,
  I long for nothing else but only this.
And then my soul is grieved in thy regard,
  Dear friend, who reck'st not of thy nearest need,
  Renouncing for slight joys the perfect bliss.

APPENDIX TO PART I.

I.

FORESE DONATI.

WHAT follows relates to the very filmiest of all the will-o'-the-wisps which have beset me in making this book. I should be glad to let it lose itself in its own quagmire, but am perhaps bound to follow it as far as may be.

Ubaldini, in his Glossary to Barberino, (published in 1640, and already several times referred to here,) has a rather startling entry under the word *Vendetta*.

After describing this "custom of the country," he says :—

"To leave a vengeance unaccomplished was considered very shameful; and on this account Forese de' Donati sneers at Dante, who did not avenge his father Alighieri : saying to him ironically,—

'Ben sò che fosti figliuol d' Alighieri;
Ed accorgomen pure alla vendetta
Che facesti di lui sì bella e netta ;'

and hence perhaps Dante is menaced in Hell by the Spirit of one of his race."

Now there is no hint to be found anywhere that Dante's father, who died about 1270, in the poet's childhood, came by his death in any violent way. The spirit met in Hell (C. xxix.) is Geri son of Bello Alighieri, and Dante's great-uncle ; and he is there represented as passing his kinsman in contemptuous silence on account of *his own* death by the hand of one of the Sacchetti, which remained till then unavenged, and so continued till after Dante's death, when Cione Alighieri fulfilled the *vendetta* by slaying a Sacchetti at the door of his house. If Dante is really the person addressed in the sonnet quoted by Ubaldini, I think it probable (as I shall show presently when I give the whole sonnet) that the ironical allusion is to the death of Geri Alighieri. But indeed the real writer, the real subject, and the real object of this clumsy piece of satire, seem about equally puzzling.

Forese Donati, to whom this Sonnet and another I shall quote are attributed, was the brother of Gemma Donati, Dante's wife, and of Corso and Piccarda Donati. Dante introduces him in the Purgatory (C. xxiii.) as expiating the sin of gluttony. From what is there said, he seems to have been well known in youth to Dante, who speaks also of having wept his death; but at the same time he hints that the life they led together was disorderly and a subject for regret. This can hardly account for such violence as is shown in these sonnets, said to have been written from one to the other; but it is not impossible, of course, that a rancour, perhaps temporary, may have existed at some time between them, especially as Forese probably adhered with the rest of his family to the party hostile to Dante. At any rate, Ubaldini, Crescimbeni, Quadrio, and other writers on Italian Poetry, seem to have derived this impression from the poems which they had seen in MS. attributed to Forese. They all combine in stigmatizing Forese's supposed productions as very bad poetry, and in fact this seems the only point concerning them which is beyond a doubt. The four sonnets of which I now proceed to give such translations as I have found possible were first published together in 1812 by Fiacchi, who states that he had seen two separate ancient MSS. in both of which they were attributed to Dante and Forese.

In rendering them, I have no choice but to adopt in a positive form my conjectures as to their meaning; but that I view these only as conjectures will appear afterwards.

I.

DANTE ALIGHIERI TO FORESE DONATI.

He taunts Forese, by the nickname of Bicci.

O BICCI, pretty son of who knows whom
   Unless thy mother Lady Tessa tell,—
   Thy gullet is already crammed too well,
Yet others' food thou needs must now consume.
Lo! he that wears a purse makes ample room
   When thou goest by in any public place,
   Saying, "This fellow with the branded face
Is thief apparent from his mother's womb."
And I know one who's fain to keep his bed
   Lest thou shouldst filch it, at whose birth he stood
     Like Joseph when the world its Christmas saw.
Of Bicci and his brothers it is said
   That with the heat of misbegotten blood
     Among their wives they are nice brothers-in-law.

II.

FORESE DONATI TO DANTE ALIGHIERI.

He taunts Dante ironically for not avenging Geri Alighieri.

RIGHT well I know thou'rt Alighieri's son;
   Nay, that revenge alone might warrant it,

Which thou didst take, so clever and complete,
For thy great-uncle who awhile agone
Paid scores in full.   Why, if thou hadst hewn one
    In bits for it, 'twere early still for peace !
    But then thy head's so heaped with things like these
That they would weigh two sumpter-horses down.
Thou hast taught us a fair fashion, sooth to say,—
    That whoso lays a stick well to thy back,
        Thy comrade and thy brother he shall be.
As for their names who've shown thee this good play,
    I'll tell thee, so thou'lt tell me all the lack
        Thou hast of help, that I may stand by thee.

III.

DANTE ALIGHIERI TO FORESE DONATI.

He taunts him concerning his Wife.

To hear the unlucky wife of Bicci cough,
    (Bicci,—Forese as he's called, you know,—)
You'd fancy she had wintered, sure enough,
    Where icebergs rear themselves in constant snow :
    And Lord ! if in mid-August it is so,
How in the frozen months must she come off ?
    To wear her socks abed avails not,—no,
Nor quilting from Cortona, warm and tough.
Her cough, her cold, and all her other ills,
    Do not afflict her through the rheum of age,
        But through some want within her nest, poor spouse !
This grief, with other griefs, her mother feels,
    Who says, "Without much trouble, I'll engage,
        She might have married in Count Guido's house !"

IV.

FORESE DONATI TO DANTE ALIGHIERI.

He taunts him concerning the unavenged Spirit of Geri Alighieri.

THE other night I had a dreadful cough
  Because I'd got no bed-clothes over me ;
And so, when the day broke, I hurried off
  To seek some gain whatever it might be.
And such luck as I had I tell you of.
  For lo ! no jewels hidden in a tree
I find, nor buried gold, nor suchlike stuff,
  But Alighieri among the graves I see,
Bound by some spell, I know not at whose 'hest,—
  At Solomon's, or what sage's who shall say ?
Therefore I crossed myself towards the east ;
  And he cried out : " For Dante's love I pray
Thou loose me ! " But I knew not in the least
  How this were done, so turned and went my way

Now all this may be pronounced little better than
scurrilous doggrel, and I would not have introduced any
of it, had I not wished to include everything which could
possibly belong to my subject.

Even supposing that the authorship is correctly attri-
buted in each case, the insults heaped on Dante have of
course no weight, as coming from one who shows every
sign of being both foul-mouthed and a fool. That then
even the observance of the *vendetta* had its opponents
among the laity, is evident from a passage in Barberino's
Documenti d' Amore. The two sonnets bearing Dante's
name, if not less offensive than the others, are rather

more pointed ; but seem still very unworthy even of his least exalted mood.

Accordingly Fraticelli (in his *Minor Works of Dante*) settles to his own satisfaction that these four sonnets are not by Dante and Forese ; but I do not think his arguments conclusive enough to set the matter quite at rest. He first states positively that Sonnet I. (as above) is by Burchiello, the Florentine barber-poet of the fifteenth century. However, it is only to be found in one edition of Burchiello, and that a late one, of 1757, where it is placed among the pieces which are very doubtfully his. It becomes all the more doubtful when we find it there followed by Sonnet II. (as above), which would seem by all evidence to be at any rate written by a different person from the first, whoever the writers of both may be. Of this sonnet Fraticelli seems to state that he has seen it attributed in one MS. to a certain Bicci Novello ; and adds (but without giving any authority) that it was addressed to some descendant of the great poet, also bearing the name of Dante. Sonnet III. is pronounced by Fraticelli to be of uncertain authorship, though if the first is by Burchiello, so must this be. He also decides that the designation, "Bicci, vocati Forese," shows that Forese was the nickname and Bicci the real name ; but this is surely quite futile, as the way in which the name is put is to the full as likely to be meant in ridicule as in earnest. Lastly, of Sonnet IV. Fraticelli says nothing.

It is now necessary to explain that Sonnet II., as I translate it, is made up from two versions, the one printed by Fiacchi and the one given among Burchiello's poems ; while in one respect I have adopted a reading of my own. I would make the first four lines say—

> Ben sò che fosti figliuol d'Alighieri :
> Ed accorgomen pure alla vendetta
> Che facesti di lui, sì bella e netta,
> Dell' *avolin* che diè cambio l'altrieri.

Of the two printed texts one says, in the fourth line—

> Dell' aguglin ched ei cambiò l'altrieri ;

and the other,

> Degli auguglin che diè cambio l'altrieri.

"Aguglino" would be "eaglet," and with this, the whole sense of the line seems quite unfathomable: whereas at the same time "aguglino" would not be an unlikely corrupt transcription, or even corrupt version, of "avolino," which again (according to the often confused distinctions of Italian relationships,) might well be a modification of "avolo" (grandfather), meaning great-uncle. The reading would thus be, "La vendetta che facesti *di lui* (*i.e.*) *dell' avolino* che diè cambio l'altrier ; " translated literally, "The vengeance which you took for him,—for your great-uncle who gave change the other day.". Geri Alighieri might indeed have been said to "give change" or "pay scores in full" by his death, as he himself had been the aggressor in the first instance, having slain one of the Sacchetti, and been afterwards slain himself by another.

I should add that I do not think the possibility, however questionable, of these sonnets being authentically by Dante and Forese, depends solely on the admission of this word "avolino."

The rapacity attributed to the "Bicci" of Sonnet I. seems a tendency somewhat akin to the insatiable gluttony which Forese is represented as expiating in Dante's Purgatory. Mention is also there made of Forese's wife, though certainly in a very different strain from that of Sonnet III. ; but it is not impossible that the poet might have intended to make amends to her as well as in some degree to her husband's memory. I am really more than half ashamed of so many "possibles" and "not impossibles" ; but perhaps, having been led into the subject, am a little inclined that the reader should be worried with it like myself.

At any rate, considering that these Sonnets are attributed by various old manuscripts to Dante and Forese Donati ;—that various writers (beginning with Ubaldini, who seems to have ransacked libraries more than almost any one) have spoken of these and other sonnets by Forese against Dante,—that the feud between the Alighieri and Sacchetti, and the death of Geri, were certainly matters of unabated bitterness in Dante's lifetime, as we find the *vendetta* accomplished even after his death,—and lastly, that the sonnets attributed to Forese seem to be plausibly referable to this subject, —I have thought it pardonable towards myself and my readers to devote to these ill-natured and not very refined productions this very long and tiresome note.

Crescimbeni *(Storia della Volgar Poesia)* gives another sonnet against Dante as being written by Forese Donati, and it certainly resembles these in style. I should add that their obscurity of mere language is excessive, and that my translations therefore are necessarily guesswork here and there ; though as to this I may spare particulars except in what affects the question at issue. In conclusion, I hope I need hardly protest against the inference that my translations and statements might be shown to abound in dubious makeshifts and whimsical conjectures ; though it would be admitted, on going over the ground I have traversed, that it presents a difficulty of some kind at almost every step.

II.

CECCO D'ASCOLI.

THERE is one more versifier, contemporary with Dante, to whom I might be expected to refer. This is the ill-fated Francesco Stabili, better known as Cecco d'Ascoli,

15

who was burnt by the Inquisition at Florence in 1327, as a heretic, though the exact nature of his offence is involved in some mystery. He was a narrow, discontented, and self-sufficient writer; and his incongruous poem in *sesta rima*, called *L'Acerba*, contains various references to the poetry of Dante (whom he knew personally) as well as to that of Guido Cavalcanti, made chiefly in a supercilious spirit. These allusions have no poetical or biographical value whatever, so I need say no more of them or their author. And indeed perhaps the "Bicci" sonnets are quite enough of themselves in the way of absolute trash.

III.

GIOVANNI BOCCACCIO.

SEVERAL of the little-known sonnets of Boccaccio have reference to Dante, but, being written in the generation which followed his, do not belong to the body of my first division. I therefore place three of them here, together with a few more specimens from the same poet.

There is nothing which gives Boccaccio a greater claim to our regard than the enthusiastic reverence with which he loved to dwell on the *Commedia* and on the memory of Dante, who died when he was seven years old. This is amply proved by his Life of the Poet and Commentary on the Poem, as well as by other passages in his writings both in prose and poetry. The first of the three following sonnets relates to his public reading and elucidation of Dante, which took place at Florence, by a decree of the State, in 1373. The second sonnet shows how the greatest minds of the generation which immediately succeeded Dante already paid unhesitating tribute to his political as well as poetical greatness. In the third sonnet, it is interesting to note the personal love and confidence with which Boccaccio could address the spirit of his mighty master, unknown to him in the flesh.

I.

To one who had censured his public Exposition of Dante.

IF Dante mourns, there wheresoe'er he be,
    That such high fancies of a soul so proud
    Should be laid open to the vulgar crowd,
(As, touching my Discourse, I'm told by thee,)
This were my grievous pain ; and certainly
    My proper blame should not be disavow'd ;
    Though hereof somewhat, I declare aloud
Were due to others, not alone to me.
False hopes, true poverty, and therewithal
    The blinded judgment of a host of friends,
        And their entreaties, made that I did thus.
But of all this there is no gain at all
    Unto the thankless souls with whose base ends
        Nothing agrees that's great or generous.

II.

Inscription for a portrait of Dante.

DANTE ALIGHIERI, a dark oracle
    Of wisdom and of art, I am ; whose mind
    Has to my country such great gifts assign'd
That men account my powers a miracle.

My lofty fancy passed as low as Hell,
　　As high as Heaven, secure and unconfin'd;
　　And in my noble book doth every kind
Of earthly lore and heavenly doctrine dwell.
Renownèd Florence was my mother,—nay,
　　Stepmother unto me her piteous son,
　　　　Through sin of cursed slander's tongue and tooth.
Ravenna sheltered me so cast away;
　　My body is with her,—my soul with One
　　　　For whom no envy can make dim the truth.

III.

To Dante in Paradise, after Fiammetta's death.

DANTE, if thou within the sphere of Love,
　　As I believe, remain'st contemplating
　　Beautiful Beatrice, whom thou didst sing
Erewhile, and so wast drawn to her above;—
Unless from false life true life thee remove
　　So far that Love's forgotten, let me bring
　　One prayer before thee: for an easy thing
This were, to thee whom I do ask it of.
I know that where all joy doth most abound
　　In the Third Heaven, my own Fiammetta sees
　　　　The grief which I have borne since she is dead
O pray her (if mine image be not drown'd
　　In Lethe) that her prayers may never cease
　　　　Until I reach her and am comforted.

I add three further examples of Boccaccio's poetry,
chosen for their beauty alone. Two of these relate to
Maria d'Aquino, if she indeed be the lady whom, in his
writings, he calls Fiammetta. The third as a playful
charm very characteristic of the author of the *Decameron;*

while its beauty of colour (to our modern minds, privileged to review the whole pageant of Italian Art,) might recall the painted pastorals of Giorgione.

IV.

Of Fiammetta singing.

Love steered my course, while yet the sun rode high,
  On Scylla's waters to a myrtle-grove :
  The heaven was still and the sea did not move;
Yet now and then a little breeze went by
Stirring the tops of trees against the sky :
  And then I heard a song as glad as love,
  So sweet that never yet the like thereof
Was heard in any mortal company.
"A nymph, a goddess, or an angel sings
  Unto herself, within this chosen place,
    Of ancient loves ; " so said I at that sound.
And there my lady, 'mid the shadowings
  Of myrtle-trees, 'mid flowers and grassy space,
    Singing I saw, with others who sat round.

V.

Of his last sight of Fiammetta.

Round her red garland and her golden hair
  I saw a fire about Fiammetta's head ;
  Thence to a little cloud I watched it fade,
Than silver or than gold more brightly fair ;
And like a pearl that a gold ring doth bear,
  Even so an angel sat therein, who sped
  Alone and glorious throughout heaven, array'd

In sapphires and in gold that lit the air.
Then I rejoiced as hoping happy things,
    Who rather should have then discerned how God
    Had haste to make my lady all His own,
Even as it came to pass.   And with these stings
    Of sorrow, and with life's most weary load
    I dwell, who fain would be where she is gone.

VI.

Of three Girls and of their Talk.

By a clear well, within a little field
    Full of green grass and flowers of every hue,
    Sat three young girls, relating (as I knew)
Their loves.   And each had twined a bough to shield
Her lovely face ; and the green leaves did yield
    The golden hair their shadow ; while the two
    Sweet colours mingled, both blown lightly through
With a soft wind for ever stirred and still'd.
After a little while one of them said,
    (I heard her,) " Think ! If, ere the next hour struck,
    Each of our lovers should come here to-day,
Think you that we should fly or feel afraid ? "
    To whom the others answered, " From such luck
    A girl would be a fool to run away."

END OF PART I.

PART II.

POETS CHIEFLY BEFORE DANTE.

TABLE OF POETS IN PART II.

I. CIULLO D'ALCAMO, 1172—78.

Ciullo is a popular form of the name Vincenzo, and Alcamo an Arab fortress some miles from Palermo. The Dialogue, which is the only known production of this poet, holds here the place generally accorded to it as the earliest Italian poem (exclusive of one or two dubious inscriptions) which has been preserved to our day. Arguments have sometimes been brought to prove that it must be assigned to a later date than the poem by Folcachiero, which follows it in this volume ; thus ascribing the first honours of Italian poetry to Tuscany, and not to Sicily, as is commonly supposed. Trucchi, however, (in the preface to his valuable collection,) states his belief that the two poems are about contemporaneous, fixing the date of that by Ciullo between 1172 and 1178,— chiefly from the fact that the fame of Saladin, to whom this poet alludes, was most in men's mouths during that interval. At first sight, any casual reader of the original would suppose that this poem must be unquestionably the earliest of all, as its language is far the most unformed and difficult ; but much of this might, of course, be dependent on the inferior dialect of Sicily, mixed however in this instance (as far as I can judge) with mere nondescript *patois*.

II. FOLCACHIERO DE' FOLCACHIERI, KNIGHT OF SIENA, 1177.

The above date has been assigned with probability to

Folcachiero's Canzone, on account of its first line, where the whole world is said to be " living without war"; an assertion which seems to refer its production to the period of the celebrated peace concluded at Venice between Frederick Barbarossa and Pope Alexander III.

III. LODOVICO DELLA VERNACCIA, 1200.

IV. SAINT FRANCIS OF ASSISI; BORN, 1182; DIED, 1226.

His baptismal name was Giovanni, and his father was Bernardone Moriconi, whose mercantile pursuits he shared till the age of twenty-five; after which his life underwent the extraordinary change which resulted in his canonisation, by Gregory IX., three years after his death, and in the formation of the Religious Order called Franciscans.

V. FREDERICK II., EMPEROR; BORN, 1194; DIED, 1250.

The life of Frederick II., and his excommunication and deposition from the Empire by Innocent IV., to whom, however, he did not succumb, are matters of history which need no repetition. Intellectually, he was in all ways a highly-gifted and accomplished prince; and lovingly cultivated the Italian language, in preference to the many others with which he was familiar. The poem of his which I give has great passionate beauty; yet I believe that an allegorical interpretation may here probably be admissible; and that the lady of the poem may be the Empire, or perhaps the Church herself, held in bondage by the Pope.

VI. ENZO, KING OF SARDINIA; BORN, 1225; DIED, 1272.

The unfortunate Enzo was a natural son of Frederick II., and was born at Palermo. By his own warlike enterprise, at an early age (it is said at fifteen!) he subjugated the Island of Sardinia, and was made King of it by his father. Afterwards he joined Frederick in his war against the Church, and displayed the highest promise as a leader; but at the age of twenty-five was taken prisoner by the Bolognese, whom no threats or promises from the Emperor could induce to set him at liberty. He died in prison at Bologna, after a confinement of nearly twenty-three years. A hard fate indeed for one who, while moving among men, excited their hopes and homage, still on record, by his great military genius and brilliant gifts of mind and person.

VII. GUIDO GUINICELLI, 1220.

This poet, certainly the greatest of his time, belonged to a noble and even princely Bolognese family. Nothing seems known of his life, except that he was married to a lady named Beatrice, and that in 1274, having adhered to the Imperial cause, he was sent into exile, but whither cannot be learned. He died two years afterwards. The highest praise has been bestowed by Dante on Guinicelli, in the *Commedia* (Purg. C. xxvi.), in the *Convito*, and in the *De Vulgari Eloquio;* and many instances might be cited in which the works of the great Florentine contain reminiscences of his Bolognese predecessor; especially the third canzone of Dante's *Convito* may be compared with Guido's most famous one "On the Gentle Heart."

VIII. GUERZO DI MONTECANTI, 1220.

IX. INGHILFREDI, SICILIANO, 1220.

X. RINALDO D'AQUINO, 1250.

I have placed this poet, belonging to a Neapolitan family, under the date usually assigned to him; but Trucchi states his belief that he flourished much earlier, and was a contemporary of Folcachiero; partly on account of two lines in one of his poems which say,—

> " Lo Imperadore con pace
> Tutto il mondo mantene."

If so, the mistake would be easily accounted for, as there seem to have been various members of the family named Rinaldo, at different dates.

XI. Jacopo da Lentino, 1250.

This Sicilian poet is generally called "the Notary of Lentino." The low estimate expressed of him, as well as of Bonaggiunta and Guittone, by Dante (Purg. C. xxiv.), must be understood as referring in great measure to their want of grammatical purity and nobility of style, as we may judge when the passage is taken in conjunction with the principles of the *De Vulgari Eloquio.* However, Dante also attributes his own superiority to the fact of his writing only when love (or natural impulse) really prompted him,—the highest certainly of all laws relating to art :—

> " Io mi son un che quando
> Amor mi spira, noto, ed in quel modo
> Ch' ei detta dentro, vo significando."

A translation does not suffer from such offences of dialect as may exist in its original ; and I think my readers will agree that, chargeable as he is with some conventionality of sentiment, the Notary of Lentino is often not without his claims to beauty and feeling. There is a peculiar charm in the sonnet which stands first among my specimens.

XII. Mazzeo di Ricco, Da Messina, 1250.

XIII. Pannuccio dal Bagno, Pisano, 1250.

XIV. Giacomino Pugliesi, Knight of Prato, 1250.

Of this poet there seems nothing to be learnt ; but he deserves special notice as possessing rather more poetic individuality than usual, and also as furnishing the only instance, among Dante's predecessors, of a poem (and a very beautiful one) written on a lady's death.

XV. Fra Guittone d'Arezzo, 1250.

Guittone was not a monk, but derived the prefix to his name from the fact of his belonging to the religious and military order of *Cavalieri di Santa Maria.* He seems to have enjoyed a greater literary reputation than almost any writer of his day ; but certainly his poems, of which many have been preserved, cannot be said to possess merit of a prominent kind ; and Dante shows l y various allusions that he considered them much over-rated.   The sonnet I have given is somewhat remarkable, from Petrarch's having transplanted its last line into his *Trionfi d'Amore* (cap. III.).   Guittone is the author of a series of Italian letters to various eminent persons, which are the earliest known epistolary writings in the language.

XVI. BARTOLOMEO DI SANT' ANGELO, 1250.

XVII. SALADINO DA PAVIA, 1250.

XVIII. BONAGGIUNTA URBICIANI, DA LUCCA, 1250.

XIX. MEO ABBRACCIAVACCA, DA PISTOIA, 1250.

XX. UBALDO DI MARCO, 1250.

XXI. SIMBUONO GIUDICE, 1250.

XXII. MASOLINO DA TODI, 1250.

XXIII. ONESTO DI BONCIMA, BOLOGNESE, 1250.

Onesto was a doctor of laws, and an early friend of Cino da Pistoia.   He was living as late as 1301, though his career as a poet may be fixed somewhat further back.

XXIV. TERINO DA CASTEL FIORENTINO, 1250.

XXV. MAESTRO MIGLIORE, DA FIORENZA, 1250.

XXVI. DELLO DA SIGNA, 1250.

XXVII. FOLGORE DA SAN GEMINIANO, 1250.

XXVIII. GUIDO DELLE COLONNE, 1250.

This Sicilian poet has few equals among his contemporaries, and is ranked high by Dante in his treatise *De Vulgari Eloquio.*   He visited England, and wrote in Latin a *Historia de regibus et rebus Angliæ*, as well as a *Historia destructionis Trojæ.*

XXIX. PIER MORONELLI, DI FIORENZA, 1250.

XXX. CIUNCIO FIORENTINO, 1250.

XXXI. RUGGIERI DI AMICI, SICILIANO, 1250.

XXXII. CARNINO GHIBERTI, DA FIORENZA, 1250.

XXXIII. PRINZIVALLE DORIA, 1250.

Prinzivalle commenced by writing Italian poetry, but afterwards composed verses entirely in Provençal, for the love of Beatrice, Countess of Provence. He wrote also, in Provençal prose, a treatise " On the dainty Madness of Love," and another " On the War of Charles, King of Naples, against the tyrant Manfredi." He held various high offices, and died at Naples in 1276.

XXXIV. RUSTICO DI FILIPPO; BORN ABOUT 1200; DIED, 1270.

The writings of this Tuscan poet (called also Rustico Barbuto) show signs of more vigour and versatility than was common in his day, and he probably began writing in Italian verse even before many of those already mentioned. In his old age, he, though a Ghibelline, received the dedication of the *Tesoretto* from the Guelf Brunetto Latini, who there pays him unqualified homage for surpassing worth in peace and war. It is strange that more should not be known regarding this doubtless remarkable man. His compositions have sometimes much humour, and on the whole convey the impression of an active and energetic nature. Moreover, Trucchi pronounces some of them to be as pure in language as the poems of Dante or Guido Cavalcanti, though written thirty or forty years earlier.

XXXV. PUCCIARELLO DI FIORENZA, 1260.

XXXVI. ALBERTUCCIO DELLA VIOLA, 1260.

XXXVII. TOMMASO BUZZUOLA, DA FAENZA, 1280.

XXXVIII. NOFFO BONAGUIDA, 1280.

XXXIX. Lippo Paschi de' Bardi, 1280.

XL. Ser Pace, Notaio da Fiorenza, 1280.

XLI. Niccolò degli Albizzi, 1300.

The noble Florentine family of Albizzi produced writers of poetry in more than one generation. The vivid and admirable sonnet which I have translated is the only one I have met with by Niccolò. I must confess my inability to trace the circumstances which gave rise to it.

XLII. Francesco da Barberino ; born, 1264 ; died, 1348.

With the exception of Brunetto Latini, (whose poems are neither very poetical nor well adapted for extract,) Francesco da Barberino shows by far the most sustained productiveness among the poets who preceded Dante, or were contemporaries of his youth. Though born only one year in advance of Dante, Barberino seems to have undertaken, if not completed, his two long poetic treatises, some years before the commencement of the *Commedia*.

This poet was born at Barberino di Valdelsa, of a noble family, his father being Neri di Rinuccio da Barberino. Up to the year of his father's death, 1296, he pursued the study of law chiefly in Bologna and Padua ; but afterwards removed to Florence for the same purpose, and seems to have been there, even earlier, one of the many distinguished disciples of Brunetto Latini, who probably had more influence than any other one man in forming the youth of his time to the great things they accomplished. After this he travelled in France and elsewhere ; and on his return to Italy in 1313, was the first who, by special favour of Pope Clement V., received the grade of Doctor of Laws in Florence. Both as lawyer and as citizen, he held great trusts and discharged them honourably. He was twice married, the name of his second wife being Barna di Tano, and had several chil-

dren.   At the age of eighty-four he died in the great
Plague of Florence.   Of the two works which Barberino
has left, one bears the title of *Documenti d'Amore*, lite-
rally "Documents of Love," but perhaps more properly
rendered as "Laws of Courtesy"; while the other is
called *Del Reggimento e dei Costumi delle Donne*,—"Of
the Government and Conduct of Women."   They may
be described, in the main, as manuals of good breeding,
or social chivalry, the one for men and the other for
women.   Mixed with vagueness, tediousness, and not
seldom with artless absurdity, they contain much simple
wisdom, much curious record of manners, and (as my
specimens show) occasional poetic sweetness or power,
though these last are far from being their most promi-
nent merits.   The first-named treatise, however, has
much more of such qualities than the second; and con-
tains, moreover, passages of homely humour which startle
by their truth as if written yesterday.   At the same
time, the second book is quite as well worth reading, for
the sake of its authoritative minuteness in matters which
ladies, now-a-days, would probably consider their own
undisputed region; and also for the quaint gravity of
certain surprising prose anecdotes of real life, with which
it is interspersed.   Both these works remained long un-
printed, the first edition of the *Documenti d'Amore* being
that edited by Ubaldini in 1640, at which time he reports
the *Reggimento, etc.*, to be only possessed by his age
"in name and in desire."   This treatise was afterwards
brought to light, but never printed till 1815.   I should
not forget to state that Barberino attained some know-
ledge of drawing, and that Ubaldini had seen his original
MS. of the *Documenti*, containing, as he says, skilful
miniatures by the author.

Barberino never appears to have taken a very active
part in politics, but he inclined to the Imperial and Ghibel-
line party.   This contributes with other things to render
it rather singular that we find no poetic correspond-
ence or apparent communication of any kind between

him and his many great countrymen, contemporaries of
his long life, and with whom he had more than one
bond of sympathy.   His career stretched from Dante,
Guido Cavalcanti, and Cino da Pistoia, to Petrarca and
Boccaccio ; yet only in one respectful but not enthusiastic
notice of him by the last-named writer *(Genealogia degli
Dei)*, do we ever meet with an allusion to him by any of
the greatest men of his time.   Nor in his own writings,
as far as I remember, are they ever referred to.   His
epitaph is said to have been written by Boccaccio, but
this is doubtful.

For some interesting notices of, and translations from,
Barberino, I may refer the reader to the tract on " Italian
Courtesy Books," by my brother W. M. Rossetti, issued
by the Early English Text Society.

XLIII. FAZIO DEGLI UBERTI, 1326—60.

The dates of this poet's birth and death are not ascer-
tainable, but I have set against his name two dates which
result from his writings as belonging to his lifetime.   He
was a member of that great house of the Uberti which
was driven from Florence on the expulsion of the Ghibel-
lines in 1267, and which was ever afterwards specially
excluded by name from the various amnesties offered
from time to time to the exiled Florentines.   His grand-
father was Farinata degli Uberti, whose stern nature,
unyielding even amid penal fires, has been recorded by
Dante in the tenth canto of the *Inferno*.   Farinata's son
Lapo, himself a poet, was the father of Fazio (*i.e.* Boni-
fazio), who was no doubt born in the lifetime of Dante,
and in some place of exile, but where is not known.   In
his youth he was enamoured of a certain Veronese lady
named Angiola, and was afterwards married, but whether
to her or not is again among the uncertainties.   Certain
it is that he had a son named Leopardo, who, after his
father's death at Verona, settled in Venice, where his de-
scendants maintained an honourable rank for the space
of two succeeding centuries.   Though Fazio appears to

16

have suffered sometimes from poverty, he enjoyed high reputation as a poet, and is even said, on the authority of various early writers, to have publicly received the laurel crown; but in what city of Italy this took place we do not learn.

There is much beauty in several of Fazio's lyrical poems, of which, however, no great number have been preserved. The finest of all is the Canzone which I have translated; whose excellence is such as to have procured it the high honour of being attributed to Dante, so that it is to be found in most editions of the *Canzoniere;* and as far as poetic beauty is concerned, it must be allowed to hold even there an eminent place. Its style, however, (as Monti was the first to point out in our own day, though Ubaldini, in his Glossary to Barberino, had already quoted it as the work of Fazio,) is more particularizing than accords with the practice of Dante; while, though certainly more perfect than any other poem by Fazio, its manner is quite his; bearing especially a strong resemblance throughout in structure to one canzone, where he speaks of his love with minute reference to the seasons of the year. Moreover, Fraticelli tells us that it is not attributed to Dante in any one of the many ancient MSS. he had seen, but has been fathered on him solely on the authority of a printed collection of 1518. This contested Canzone is well worth fighting for; and the victor would deserve to receive his prize at the hands of a peerless Queen of Beauty, for never was beauty better described. I believe we may decide that the triumph belongs by right to Fazio.

An exile by inheritance, Fazio seems to have acquired restless tastes; and in the latter years of his life (which was prolonged to old age), he travelled over a great part of Europe, and composed his long poem entitled *Il Dittamondo,*—"The Song of the World." This work, though by no means contemptible in point of execution, certainly falls far short of its conception, which is a grand one; the topics of which it treats in great measure,—geography and natural history,—rendering it in those days the native home of all credulities and monstrosities. In scheme it was intended as an earthly parallel to Dante's Sacred Poem, doing for this world what he did for the other. At Fazio's death it remained unfinished, but I should think by very little; the plan of the work seeming in the main accomplished. The whole earth (or rather all that was then known of it) is traversed,—its surface and its history,—ending with the Holy Land, and thus bringing Man's world as near as may be to God's; that is, to the point at which Dante's office begins. No conception could well be nobler, or worthier even now of being dealt with by a great master. To the work of such a man, Fazio's work might afford such first materials as have usually been furnished beforehand to the greatest poets by some unconscious steward.

XLIV. FRANCO SACCHETTI; BORN, 1335; DIED, SHORTLY AFTER 1400.

This excellent writer is the only member of my gathering who was born after the death of Dante, which event (in 1321) preceded Franco's birth by some fourteen years. I have introduced a few specimens of his poetry, partly because their attraction was irresistible, but also because he is the earliest Italian poet with whom playfulness is the chief characteristic; for even with Boccaccio, in his poetry, this is hardly the case, and we can but ill accept as playfulness the cynical humour of Cecco Angiolieri: perhaps Rustico di Filippo alone might put in claims to priority in this respect. However, Franco Sacchetti wrote poems also on political subjects; and had he belonged more strictly to the period of which I treat, there is no one who would better have deserved abundant selection. Besides his poetry, he is the author of a well-known series of three hundred stories; and Trucchi gives a list of prose works by him which are still in MS., and whose subjects are genealogical, historical, natural-historical, and even theological. He was a prolific writer, and one who well merits complete and careful publication. The pieces which I have translated, like many others of his, are written for music.

Franco Sacchetti was a Florentine noble by birth, and was the son of Benci di Uguccione Sacchetti. Between this family and the Alighieri there had been a *vendetta* of long standing (spoken of here in the *Appendix* to *Part I.*), but which was probably set at rest before Franco's time, by the deaths of at least one Alighieri and two Sacchetti. After some years passed in study, Franco devoted himself to commerce, like many nobles of the republic, and for that purpose spent some time in Sclavonia, whose uncongenial influences he has recorded in an amusing poem. As his literary fame increased, he was called to many important offices; was one of the *Priori* in 1383, and for some time was deputed to the government of Faenza, in the absence of its lord, Astorre Manfredi. He was three times married; to Felice degli Strozzi, to Ghita Gherardini, and to Nannina di Santi Bruni.

XLV. Anonymous Poems.

CIULLO D' ALCAMO.

DIALOGUE.

Lover and Lady.

HE.

THOU sweetly-smelling fresh red rose
   That near thy summer art,
Of whom each damsel and each dame
   Would fain be counterpart ;
Oh ! from this fire to draw me forth
   Be it in thy good heart :
For night or day there is no rest with me,
Thinking of none, my lady, but of thee.

SHE.

If thou hast set thy thoughts on me,
   Thou hast done a foolish thing.
Yea, all the pine-wood of this world
   Together might'st thou bring,
And make thee ships, and plough the sea
   Therewith for corn-sowing,
Ere any way to win me could be found :
For I am going to shear my locks all round.

HE.

Lady, before thou shear thy locks
   I hope I may be dead :
For I should lose such joy thereby
   And gain such grief instead.

Merely to pass and look at thee,
    Rose of the garden-bed,
Has comforted me much, once and again.
Oh ! if thou wouldst but love, what were it then !

SHE.

Nay, though my heart were prone to love,
    I would not grant it leave.
Hark ! should my father or his kin
    But find thee here this eve,
Thy loving body and lost breath
    Our moat may well receive.
Whatever path to come here thou dost know,
By the same path I counsel thee to go.

HE.

And if thy kinsfolk find me here,
    Shall I be drowned then ?   Marry,
I'll set, for price against my head,
    Two thousand agostari.
I think thy father would not do't
    For all his lands in Bari.
Long life to the Emperor !   Be God's the praise !
Thou hear'st, my beauty, what thy servant says.

SHE.

And am I then to have no peace
    Morning or evening ?
I have strong coffers of my own
    And much good gold therein ;
So that if thou couldst offer me
    The wealth of Saladin,
And add to that the Soldan's money-hoard,
Thy suit would not be anything toward.

HE.

I have known many women, love,
   Whose thoughts were high and proud,
And yet have been made gentle by
   Man's speech not over-loud.
If we but press ye long enough,
   At length ye will be bow'd ;
For still a woman's weaker than a man.
When the end comes, recall how this began.

SHE.

God grant that I may die before
   Any such end do come,—
Before the sight of a chaste maid
   Seem to me troublesome !
I marked thee here all yestereve
   Lurking about my home,
And now I say, Leave climbing, lest thou fall,
For these thy words delight me not at all.

HE.

How many are the cunning chains
   Thou hast wound round my heart !
Only to think upon thy voice
   Sometimes I groan apart.
For I did never love a maid
   Of this world, as thou art,
So much as I love thee, thou crimson rose.
Thou wilt be mine at last : this my soul knows.

SHE.

If I could think it would be so,
   Small pride it were of mine
That all my beauty should be meant
   But to make thee to shine.

Sooner than stoop to that, I'd shear
 These golden tresses fine,
And make one of some holy sisterhood ;
Escaping so thy love, which is not good.

HE.

If thou unto the cloister fly,
 Thou cruel lady and cold,
Unto the cloister I will come
 And by the cloister hold ;
For such a conquest liketh me
 Much better than much gold ;
At matins and at vespers I shall be
Still where thou art. Have I not conquered thee ?

SHE.

Out and alack ! wherefore am I
 Tormented in suchwise ?
Lord Jesus Christ the Saviour,
 In whom my best hope lies,
O give me strength that I may hush
 This vain man's blasphemies !
Let him seek through the earth ; 'tis long and broad
He will find fairer damsels, O my God !

HE.

I have sought through Calabria,
 Lombardy, and Tuscany,
Rome, Pisa, Lucca, Genoa,
 All between sea and sea :
Yea, even to Babylon I went
 And distant Barbary :
But not a woman found I anywhere
Equal to thee, who art indeed most fair.

SHE.

If thou have all this love for me,
    Thou canst no better do
Than ask me of my father dear
    And my dear mother too :
They willing, to the abbey-church
    We will together go,
And, before Advent, thou and I will wed ;
After the which, I'll do as thou hast said.

HE.

These thy conditions, lady mine,
    Are altogether nought :
Despite of them, I'll make a net
    Wherein thou shalt be caught.
What, wilt thou put on wings to fly ?
    Nay, but of wax they're wrought,—
They'll let thee fall to earth, not rise with thee :
So, if thou canst, then keep thyself from me.

SHE.

Think not to fright me with thy nets
    And suchlike childish gear ;
I am safe pent within the walls
    Of this strong castle here ;
A boy before he is a man
    Could give me as much fear.
If suddenly thou get not hence again,
It is my prayer thou mayst be found and slain.

HE.

Wouldst thou in very truth that I
    Were slain, and for thy sake ?
Then let them hew me to such mince
    As a man's limbs may make !

But meanwhile I shall not stir hence
    Till of that fruit I take
Which thou hast in thy garden, ripe enough :
All day and night I thirst to think thereof.

SHE.

None have partaken of that fruit,
    Not Counts nor Cavaliers :
Though many have reached up for it,
    Barons and great Seigneurs,
They all went hence in wrath because
    They could not make it theirs.
Then how canst *thou* think to succeed alone
Who hast not a thousand ounces of thine own ?

HE.

How many nosegays I have sent
    Unto thy house, sweet soul !
At least till I am put to proof,
    This scorn of thine control.
For if the wind, so fair for thee,
    Turn ever and wax foul,
Be sure that thou shalt say when all is done,
" Now is my heart heavy for him that's gone."

SHE.

If by my grief thou couldst be grieved,
    God send me a grief soon !
I tell thee that though all my friends
    Prayed me as for a boon,
Saying, " Even for the love of us,
    Love thou this worthless loon,"
Thou shouldst not have the thing that thou dost hope
No, verily ; not for the realm o' the Pope.

HE.

Now could I wish that I in truth
 Were dead here in thy house :
My soul would get its vengeance then ;
 Once known, the thing would rouse
A rabble, and they'd point and say,—
 "Lo ! she that breaks her vows,
And, in her dainty chamber, stabs !" Love, see :
One strikes just thus : it is soon done, pardie !

SHE.

If now thou do not hasten hence,
 (My curse companioning,)
That my stout friends will find thee here
 Is a most certain thing :
After the which, my gallant sir,
 Thy points of reasoning
May chance, I think, to stand thee in small stead,
Thou hast no friend, sweet friend, to bring thee aid.

HE.

Thou sayest truly, saying that
 I have not any friend :
A landless stranger, lady mine,
 None but his sword defend.
One year ago, my love began,
 And now, is this the end ?
Oh ! the rich dress thou worest on that day
Since when thou art walking at my side alway !

SHE.

So 'twas my dress enamoured thee !
 What marvel ? I did wear
A cloth of samite silver-flowered,
 And gems within my hair.

But one more word ; if on Christ's Book
  To wed me thou didst swear,
There's nothing now could win me to be thine :
I had rather make my bed in the sea-brine.

HE.

And if thou make thy bed therein,
  Most courteous lady and bland,
I'll follow all among the waves,
  Paddling with foot and hand ;
Then, when the sea hath done with thee,
  I'll seek thee on the sand.
For I will not be conquered in this strife :
I'll wait, but win ; or losing, lose my life.

SHE.

For Father, Son, and Holy Ghost,
  Three times I cross myself.
Thou art no godless heretic,
  Nor Jew, whose God's his pelf :
Even as I know it then, meseems,
  Thou needs must know thyself
That woman, when the breath in her doth cease,
Loseth all savour and all loveliness.

HE.

Woe's me !   Perforce it must be said
  No craft could then avail :
So that if thou be thus resolved,
  I know my suit must fail.
Then have some pity, of thy grace !
  Thou mayst, love, very well ;
For though thou love not me, my love is such
That 'tis enough for both—yea overmuch.

SHE.

Is it even so ?   Learn then that I
    Do love thee from my heart.
To-morrow, early in the day,
    Come here, but now depart.
By thine obedience in this thing
    I shall know what thou art,
And if thy love be real or nothing worth ;
Do but go now, and I am thine henceforth.

HE.

Nay, for such promise, my own life,
    I will not stir a foot.
I've said, if thou wouldst tear away
    My love even from its root,
I have a dagger at my side
    Which thou mayst take to do't :
But as for going hence, it will not be.
O hate me not ! my heart is burning me.

SHE.

Think'st thou I know not that thy heart
    Is hot and burns to death ?
Of all that thou or I can say,
    But one word succoureth.
Till thou upon the Holy Book
    Give me thy bounden faith,
God is my witness that I will not yield :
For with thy sword 'twere better to be kill'd.

HE.

Then on Christ's Book, borne with me still
    To read from and to pray,
(I took it, fairest, in a church,
    The priest being gone away,)

I swear that my whole self shall be
    Thine always from this day.
And now at once give joy for all my grief,
Lest my soul fly, that's thinner than a leaf.

SHE.

Now that this oath is sworn, sweet lord,
    There is no need to speak :
My heart, that was so strong before,
    Now feels itself grow weak.
If any of my words were harsh,
    Thy pardon : I am meek
Now, and will give thee entrance presently.
It is best so, sith so it was to be.

FOLCACHIERO DE' FOLCACHIERI, KNIGHT OF SIENA.

CANZONE.

He speaks of his condition through Love.

ALL the whole world is living without war,
　And yet I cannot find out any peace.
　　O God! that this should be!
O God! what does the earth sustain me for?
　My life seems made for other lives' ill-ease:
　　All men look strange to me;
　　Nor are the wood-flowers now
　　As once, when up above
　　The happy birds in love
Made such sweet verses, going from bough to bough.

And if I come where other gentlemen
　Bear arms, or say of love some joyful thing—
　　Then is my grief most sore,
And all my·soul turns round upon me then:
　Folk also gaze upon me, whispering,
　　Because I am not what I was before.
　　I know not what I am.
　　I know how wearisome
　　My life is now become,
And that the days I pass seem all the same.

I think that I shall die ; yea, death begins ;
   Though 'tis no set-down sickness that I have,
      Nor are my pains set down.
But to wear raiment seems a burden since
   This came, nor ever any food I crave ;
      Not any cure is known
      To me, nor unto whom
      I might commend my case :
      This evil therefore stays
Still where it is, and hope can find no room.

I know that it must certainly be Love :
   No other Lord, being thus set over me,
      Had judged me to this curse ;
With such high hand he rules, sitting above
   That of myself he takes two parts in fee,
      Only the third being hers.
      Yet if through service I
      Be justified with God,
      He shall remove this load,
Because my heart with inmost love doth sigh.

Gentle my lady, after I am gone,
   There will not come another, it may be,
      To show thee love like mine :
For nothing can I do, neither have done,
   Except what proves that I belong to thee
      And am a thing of thine.
      Be it not said that I
      Despaired and perished, then ;
      But pour thy grace, like rain,
On him who is burned up, yea, visibly.

LODOVICO DELLA VERNACCIA.

SONNET.

He exhorts the State to vigilance.

THINK a brief while on the most marvellous arts
  Of our high-purposed labour, citizens;
  And having thought, draw clear conclusion thence;
And say, do not ours seem but childish parts?
Also on these intestine sores and smarts
  Ponder advisedly; and the deep sense
  Thereof shall bow your heads in penitence,
And like a thorn shall grow into your hearts.
If, of our foreign foes, some prince or lord
  Is now, perchance, some whit less troublesome,
    Shall the sword therefore drop into the sheath?
    Nay, grasp it as the friend that warranteth:
  For unto this vile rout, our foes at home,
Nothing is high or awful save the sword.

SAINT FRANCIS OF ASSISI.

CANTICA.

*Our Lord Christ: of Order.**

SET LOVE in order, thou that lovest Me.
   Never was virtue out of order found ;
And though I fill thy heart desirously,
   By thine own virtue I must keep My ground :
When to My love thou dost bring charity,
   Even she must come with order girt and gown'd.
      Look how the trees are bound
      To order, bearing fruit ;
      And by one thing compute,
In all things earthly, order's grace or gain.

All earthly things I had the making of
   Were numbered and were measured then by Me;
And each was ordered to its end by Love,
   Each kept, through order, clean for ministry.
Charity most of all, when known enough,
   Is of her very nature orderly.
      Lo, now ! what heat in thee,
      Soul, can have bred this rout ?
      Thou putt'st all order out.
Even this love's heat must be its curb and rein.

---

* This speech occurs in a long poem on Divine Love, half
ecstatic, half scholastic, and hardly appreciable now. The passage
stands well by itself, and is the only one spoken by our Lord.

FREDERICK II. EMPEROR.

CANZONE.

Of his Lady in bondage.

For grief I am about to sing,
  Even as another would for joy ;
  Mine eyes which the hot tears destroy
Are scarce enough for sorrowing :
  To speak of such a grievous thing
  Also my tongue I must employ,
Saying : Woe's me, who am full of woes !
  Not while I live shall my sighs cease
  For her in whom my heart found peace :
I am become like unto those
  That cannot sleep for weariness,
Now I have lost my crimson rose.

And yet I will not call her lost ;
  She is not gone out of the earth ;
  She is but girded with a girth
Of hate, that clips her in like frost.
Thus says she every hour almost :—
  " When I was born, 'twas an ill birth !
O that I never had been born.
  If I am still to fall asleep
  Weeping, and when I wake to weep ;

If he whom I most loathe and scorn
    Is still to have me his, and keep
Smiling about me night and morn !

" O that I never had been born
    A woman ! a poor, helpless fool,
    Who can but stoop beneath the rule
Of him she needs must loathe and scorn !
If ever I feel less forlorn,
    I stand all day in fear and dule,
Lest he discern it, and with rough
    Speech mock at me, or with his smile
    So hard you scarce could call it guile :
No man is there to say, ' Enough.'
    O, but if God waits a long while,
Death cannot always stand aloof !

" Thou, God the Lord, dost know all this :
    Give me a little comfort then,
    Him who is worst among bad men
Smite thou for me.   Those limbs of his
Once hidden where the sharp worm is,
    Perhaps I might see hope again.
Yet for a certain period
    Would I seem like as one that saith
    Strange things for grief, and murmureth
With smitten palms and hair abroad :
    Still whispering under my held breath,
' Shall I not praise Thy name, O God ? '

" Thou, God the Lord, dost know all this :
    It is a very weary thing
    Thus to be always trembling : .
And till the breath of his life cease,
The hate in him will but increase,
    And with his hate my suffering.
Each morn I hear his voice bid them

That watch me, to be faithful spies
   Lest I go forth and see the skies;
Each night, to each, he saith the same :—
   And in my soul and in mine eyes
There is a burning heat like flame."

Thus grieves she now : but she shall wear
   This love of mine, whereof I spoke,
   About her body for a cloak,
And for a garland in her hair,
Even yet : because I mean to prove,
Not to speak only, this my love.

ENZO, KING OF SARDINIA.

SONNET.

On the Fitness of Seasons.

THERE is a time to mount ; to humble thee
 A time ; a time to talk, and hold thy peace ;
 A time to labour, and a time to cease ;
A time to take thy measures patiently ;
A time to watch what Time's next step may be ;
 A time to make light count of menaces,
 And to think over them a time there is ;
There is a time when to seem not to see.
Wherefore I hold him well-advised and sage
 Who evermore keeps prudence facing him,
  And lets his life slide with occasion ;
And so comports himself, through youth to age,
 That never any man at any time
  Can say, Not thus, but thus thou shouldst have done.

GUIDO GUINICELLI.

I.

SONNET.

Concerning Lucy.

WHEN Lucy draws her mantle round her face,
  So sweeter than all else she is to see,
  That hence unto the hills there lives not he
Whose whole soul would not love her for her grace.
Then seems she like a daughter of some race
  That holds high rule in France or Germany :
  And a snake's head stricken off suddenly
Throbs never as then throbs my heart to embrace
Her body in these arms, even were she loth ;—
  To kiss her lips, to kiss her cheeks, to kiss
    The lids of her two eyes which are two flames.
    Yet what my heart so longs for, my heart blames :
  For surely sorrow might be bred from this
Where some man's patient love abides its growth.

II.

CANZONE.

Of the Gentle Heart.

WITHIN the gentle heart Love shelters him
   As birds within the green shade of the grove.
Before the gentle heart, in nature's scheme,
    Love was not, nor the gentle heart ere Love.
       For with the sun, at once,
So sprang the light immediately ; nor was
       Its birth before the sun's.
And Love hath his effect in gentleness
       Of very self; even as
Within the middle fire the heat's excess.

The fire of Love comes to the gentle heart
   Like as its virtue to a precious stone ;
To which no star its influence can impart
    Till it is made a pure thing by the sun :
       For when the sun hath smit
From out its essence that which there was vile,
       The star endoweth it.
And so the heart created by God's breath
       Pure, true, and clean from guile,
A woman, like a star, enamoureth.

In gentle heart Love for like reason is
   For which the lamp's high flame is fanned and bow'd :
Clear, piercing bright, it shines for its own bliss ;
    Nor would it burn there else, it is so proud.
       For evil natures meet
With Love as it were water met with fire,

As cold abhorring heat.
Through gentle heart Love doth a track divine,—
    Like knowing like; the same
As diamond runs through iron in the mine.

The sun strikes full upon the mud all day :
    It remains vile, nor the sun's worth is less.
" By race I am gentle," the proud man doth say :
    He is the mud, the sun is gentleness.
        Let no man predicate
That aught the name of gentleness should have,
        Even in a king's estate,
Except the heart there be a gentle man's.
        The star-beam lights the wave,—
Heaven holds the star and the star's radiance.

God, in the understanding of high Heaven,
    Burns more than in our sight the living sun :
There to behold His Face unveiled is given ;
    And Heaven, whose will is homage paid to One
        Fulfils the things which live
In God, from the beginning excellent.
        So should my lady give
That truth which in her eyes is glorified,
        On which her heart is bent,
To me whose service waiteth at her side.

My lady, God shall ask, "What daredst thou ?
    (When my soul stands with all her acts review'd ;)
" Thou passedst Heaven, into My sight, as now,
    To make Me of vain love similitude.
        To me doth praise belong,
And to the Queen of all the realm of grace
        Who slayeth fraud and wrong."
Then may I plead : "As though from Thee he came,
        Love wore an angel's face :
Lord, if I loved her, count it not my shame."

III.

SONNET.

He will praise his Lady.

YEA, let me praise my lady whom I love :
   Likening her unto the lily and rose :
 Brighter than morning star her visage glows ;
She is beneath even as her Saint above ;
She is as the air in summer which God wove
   Of purple and of vermilion glorious ;
   As gold and jewels richer than man knows.
Love's self, being love for her, must holier prove.
Ever as she walks she hath a sober grace,
   Making bold men abashed and good men glad ;
   If she delight thee not, thy heart must err.
No man dare look on her, his thoughts being base :
   Nay, let me say even more than I have said ;—
   No man could think base thoughts who looked on her.

IV.

CANZONE.

He perceives his Rashness in Love, but has no choice.

I HOLD him, verily, of mean emprise,
  Whose rashness tempts a strength too great to bear;
As I have done, alas! who turned mine eyes
  Upon those perilous eyes of the most fair.
      Unto her eyes I bow'd;
No need her other beauties in that hour
      Should aid them, cold and proud:
As when the vassals of a mighty lord,
      What time he needs his power,
Are all girt round him to make strong his sword.

With such exceeding force the stroke was dealt
  That by mine eyes its path might not be stay'd;
But deep into the heart it pierced, which felt
  The pang of the sharp wound, and waxed afraid;
      Then rested in strange wise,
As when some creature utterly outworn
      Sinks into bed and lies.
And she the while doth in no manner care,
      But goes her way in scorn,
Beholding herself alway proud and fair.

And she may be as proud as she shall please,
   For she is still the fairest woman found :
A sun she seems among the rest ; and these
   Have all their beauties in her splendour drown'd..
      In her is every grace,—
Simplicity of wisdom, noble speech,
      Accomplished loveliness ;
All earthly beauty is her diadem,
      This truth my song would teach,—
My lady is of ladies chosen gem.

Love to my lady's service yieldeth me,—
   Will I, or will I not, the thing is so,—
Nor other reason can I say or see,
   Except that where it lists the wind doth blow.
      He rules and gives no sign ;
Nor once from her did show of love upbuoy
      This passion which is mine.
It is because her virtue's strength and stir
      So fill her full of joy
That I am glad to die for love of her.

V.

SONNET.

Of Moderation and Tolerance.

HE that has grown to wisdom hurries not,
  But thinks and weighs what Reason bids him do
And after thinking he retains his thought
  Until as he conceived the fact ensue.
Let no man to o'erweening pride be wrought,
  But count his state as Fortune's gift and due.
He is a fool who deems that none has sought
  The truth, save he alone, or knows it true.
Many strange birds are on the air abroad,
  Nor all are of one flight or of one force,
    But each after his kind dissimilar :
To each was portioned of the breath of God,
  Who gave them divers instincts from one source.
    Then judge not thou thy fellows what they are.

VI.

SONNET.

Of Human Presumption.

AMONG my thoughts I count it wonderful,
    How foolishness in man should be so rife
    That masterly he takes the world to wife
As though no end were set unto his rule :
In labour alway that his ease be full,
    As though there never were another life ;
    Till Death throws all his order into strife,
And round his head his purposes doth pull.
And evermore one sees the other die,
    And sees how all conditions turn to change,
        Yet in no wise may the blind wretch be heal'd.
    I therefore say, that sin can even estrange
Man's very sight, and his heart satisfy
        To live as lives a sheep upon the field.

GUERZO DI MONTECANTI.

SONNET.

He is out of heart with his Time.

IF any man would know the very cause
  Which makes me to forget my speech in rhyme,
  All the sweet songs I sang in other time,—
I'll tell it in a sonnet's simple clause.
I hourly have beheld how good withdraws
  To nothing, and how evil mounts the while:
  Until my heart is gnawed as with a file,
Nor aught of this world's worth is what it was.
At last there is no other remedy
  But to behold the universal end;
    And so upon this hope my thoughts are urged:
To whom, since truth is sunk and dead at sea,
  There has no other part or prayer remain'd,
    Except of seeing the world's self submerged.

INGHILFREDI, SICILIANO.

CANZONE.

He rebukes the Evil of that Time.

HARD is it for a man to please all men :
   I therefore speak in doubt,
     And as one may that looketh to be chid.
But who can hold his peace in these days ?—when
   Guilt cunningly slips out,
     And Innocence atones for what he did ;
     When worth is crushed, even if it be not hid ;
When on crushed worth, guile sets his foot to rise ;
And when the things wise men have counted wise
     Make fools to smile and stare and lift the lid.

Let none who have not wisdom govern you :
   For he that was a fool
     At first shall scarce grow wise under the sun.
And as it is, my whole heart bleeds anew
   To think how hard a school
     Young hope grows old at, as these seasons run.
     Behold, sirs, we have reached this thing for one :—
The lord before his servant bends the knee,
And service puts on lordship suddenly.
     Ye speak o' the end ? Ye have not yet begun.

I would not have ye without counsel ta'en
   Follow my words ; nor meant,
     If one should talk and act not, to praise him
But who, being much opposed, speaks not again,

Confesseth himself shent
   And put to silence,—by some loud-mouthed mime,
   Perchance, for whom I speak not in this rhyme.
Strive what ye can ; and if ye cannot all,
Yet should not your hearts fall :
   The fruit commends the flower in God's good time.

(For without fruit, the flower delights not God :)
   Wherefore let him whom Hope
   Puts off, remember time is not gone by.
Let him say calmly : " Thus far on this road
   A foolish trust buoyed up
   My soul, and made it like the summer fly
   Burned in the flame it seeks : even so was I :
But now I'll aid myself : for still this trust,
I find, falleth to dust :
   The fish gapes for the bait-hook, and doth die."

And yet myself, who bid ye do this thing,—
   Am I not also spurn'd
   By the proud feet of Hope continually ;
Till that which gave me such good comforting
   Is altogether turn'd
   Unto a fire whose heat consumeth me ?
   I am so girt with grief that my thoughts be
Tired of themselves, and from my soul I loathe
Silence and converse both ;
   And my own face is what I hate to see.

Because no act is meet now nor unmeet.
   He that does evil, men applaud his name,
   And the well-doer must put up with shame :
Yea, and the worst man sits in the best seat.

RINALDO D'AQUINO.

I.

CANZONE.

He is resolved to be joyful in Love.

A THING is in my mind,—
    To have my joy again,
Which I had almost put away from me.
    It were in foolish kind
    For ever to refrain
From song, and renounce gladness utterly.
Seeing that I am given into the rule
    Of Love, whom only pleasure makes alive,
        Whom pleasure nourishes and brings to growth :
            The wherefore sullen sloth
        Will he not suffer in those serving him ;
            But pleasant they must seem,
    That good folk love them and their service thrive ;
Nor even their pain must make them sorrowful.

    So bear he him that thence
        The praise of men be gain'd,—
He that would put his hope in noble Love ;
    For by great excellence
        Alone can be attain'd
That amorous joy which wisdom may approve.
The way of Love is this, righteous and just ;

Then whoso would be held of good account,
   To seek the way of Love must him befit,—
      Pleasure, to wit.
   Through pleasure, man attains his worthiness :
      For he must please
All men, so bearing him that Love may mount
In their esteem ; Love's self being in his trust.

   Trustful in servitude
      I have been and will be,
And loyal unto Love my whole life through
   A hundred-fold of good
      Hath he not guerdoned me
For what I have endured of grief and woe ?
Since he hath given me unto one of whom
   Thus much he said,—thou mightest seek for aye
   Another of such worth so beauteous.
      Joy therefore may keep house
   In this my heart, that it hath loved so well.
      Meseems I scarce could dwell
Ever in weary life or in dismay
If to true service still my heart gave room

   Serving at her pleasaùnce
      Whose service pleasureth,
I am enriched with all the wealth of Love.
   Song hath no utterance
      For my life's joyful breath
Since in this lady's grace my homage throve.
   Yea, for I think it would be difficult
   One should conceive my former abject case :—
      Therefore have knowledge of me from this rhyme.
      My penance-time
      Is all accomplished now, and all forgot,
         So that no jot
Do I remember of mine evil days.
It is my lady's will that I exult.

Exulting let me take
My joyful comfort, then,
Seeing myself in so much blessedness.
Mine ease even as mine ache
Accepting, let me gain
No pride towards Love ; but with all humbleness,
Even still, my pleasurable service pay.
For a good servant ne'er was left to pine :
Great shall his guerdon be who greatly bears.
But, because he that fears
To speak too much, by his own silence shent,
Hath sometimes made lament,—
I am thus boastful, lady ; being thine
For homage and obedience night and day.

II.

CANZONE.

A Lady, in Spring, repents of her Coldness.

Now, when it flowereth,
  And when the banks and fields
    Are greener every day,
And sweet is each bird's breath,
  In the tree where he builds
    Singing after his way,—
Spring comes to us with hasty step and brief,
    Everywhere in leaf,
And everywhere makes people laugh and play.

Love is brought unto me
  In the scent of the flower
    And in the bird's blithe noise.
When day begins to be,
  I hear in every bower
    New verses finding voice :
From every branch around me and above,
    A minstrels' court of love,
The birds contend in song about love's joys.

What time I hear the lark
  And nightingale keep Spring,
    My heart will pant and yearn
For love. (Ye all may mark

The unkindly comforting
    Of fire that will not burn.)
And, being in the shadow of the fresh wood,
    How excellently good
A thing love is, I cannot choose but learn.

    Let me ask grace ; for I,
        Being loved, loved not again.
            Now springtime makes me love,
    And bids me satisfy
        The lover whose fierce pain
        I thought too lightly of :
For that the pain is fierce I do feel now.
        And yet this pride is slow
To free my heart, which pity would fain move.

    Wherefore I pray thee, Love,
        That thy breath turn me o'er,
            Even as the wind a leaf ;
    And I will set thee above
        This heart of mine, that's sore
        Perplexed, to be its chief.
Let also the dear youth, whose passion must
        Henceforward have good trust,
Be happy without words ; for words bring grief.

JACOPO DA LENTINO.

I.

SONNET.

Of his Lady in Heaven.

I HAVE it in my heart to serve God so
   That into Paradise I shall repair,—
   The holy place through the which everywhere
I have heard say that joy and solace flow.
Without my lady I were loth to go,—
   She who has the bright face and the bright hair
   Because if she were absent, I being there,
My pleasure would be less than nought, I know.
Look you, I say not this to such intent
   As that I there would deal in any sin :
   I only would behold her gracious mien,
   And beautiful soft eyes, and lovely face,
That so it should be my complete content
   To see my lady joyful in her place.

II.

CANZONETTA.

Of his Lady, and of her Portrait.

MARVELLOUSLY elate,
　　Love makes my spirit warm
　　　With noble sympathies:
As one whose mind is set
　　Upon some glorious form,
　　　To paint it as it is;—
I verily who bear
Thy face at heart, most fair,
　　　Am like to him in this.

Not outwardly declared,
　　Within me dwells enclosed
　　　Thine image as thou art.
Ah! strangely hath it fared!
　　I know not if thou know'st
　　　The love within my heart.
Exceedingly afraid,
My hope I have not said,
　　　But gazed on thee apart.

Because desire was strong,
　　I made a portraiture
　　　In thine own likeness, love;

When absence has grown long,
  I gaze, till I am sure
    That I behold thee move ;
As one who purposeth
To save himself by faith,
    Yet sees not, nor can prove.

Then comes the burning pain :
  As with the man that hath
    A fire within his breast,—
When most he struggles, then
  Most boils the flame in wrath,
    And will not let him rest.
So still I burned and shook,
To pass, and not to look
    In thy face, loveliest.

For where thou art I pass,
  And do not lift mine eyes,
    Lady, to look on thee :
But, as I go, alas !
  With bitterness of sighs
    I mourn exceedingly.
Alas ! the constant woe !
Myself I do not know,
    So sore it troubles me.

And I have sung thy praise,
  Lady, and many times
    Have told thy beauties o'er.
Hast heard in anyways,
  Perchance, that these my rhymes
    Are song-craft and no more ?
Nay, rather deem, when thou
Shalt see me pass and bow,
    These words I sicken for.

Delicate song of mine,
 Go sing thou a new strain:
Seek, with the first sunshine,
Our lady, mine and thine,—
 The rose of Love's domain,
Than red gold comelier.
 " Lady, in Love's name hark
 To Jacopo the clerk,
Born in Lentino here."

III.

SONNET.

No Jewel is worth his Lady.

SAPPHIRE, nor diamond, nor emerald,
  Nor other precious stones past reckoning,
  Topaz, nor pearl, nor ruby like a king,
Nor that most virtuous jewel, jasper call'd,
Nor amethyst, nor onyx, nor basalt,
  Each counted for a very marvellous thing,
  Is half so excellently gladdening
As is my lady's head uncoronall'd.
All beauty by her beauty is made dim ;
  Like to the stars she is for loftiness ;
    And with her voice she taketh away grief.
    She is fairer than a bud, or than a leaf.
  Christ have her well in keeping, of His grace,
And make her holy and beloved, like Him !

IV.

CANZONETTA.

He will neither boast nor lament to his Lady.

LOVE will not have me cry
   For grace, as others do ;
Nor as they vaunt, that I
   Should vaunt my love to you.
For service, such as all
Can pay, is counted small ;
Nor is it much to praise
   The thing which all must know ;—
   Such pittance to bestow
On you my love gainsays.

Love lets me not turn shape
   As chance or use may strike ;
As one may see an ape
   Counterfeit all alike
Then, lady, unto you
Be it not mine to sue,
For grace or pitying.
   Many the lovers be
   That of such suit are free,—
It is a common thing.

A gem, the more 'tis rare,
  The more its cost will mount :
And, be it not so fair,
  It is of more account.
So, coming from the East,
The sapphire is increased
In worth, though scarce so bright ;
  I therefore seek thy face
  Not to solicit grace,
Being cheapened and made slight.

So is the colosmine
  Now cheapened, which in fame
Was once so brave and fine,
  But now is a mean gem.
So be such prayers for grace
Not heard in any place ;
Would they indeed hold fast
  Their worth, be they not said,
  Nor by true lovers made
Before nine years be past.

Lady, sans sigh or groan,
  My longing thou canst see ;
Much better am I known
  Than to myself, to thee.
And is there nothing else
That in my heart avails
For love but groan and sigh ?
  And wilt thou have it thus,
  This love betwixen us ?—
Much rather let me die.

V.

CANZONETTA.

Of his Lady, and of his making her Likeness.

My Lady mine,* I send
  These sighs in joy to thee
Though, loving till the end,
  There were no hope for me
That I should speak my love ;
  And I have loved indeed,
  Though, having fearful heed,
It was not spoken of.

Thou art so high and great
  That whom I love I fear ;
Which thing to circumstate
  I have no messenger : .
Wherefore to Love I pray,
  On whom each lover cries,
  That these my tears and sighs
Find unto thee a way.

Well have I wished, when I
  At heart with sighs have ach'd,
That there were in each sigh
  Spirit and intellect,
The which, where thou dost sit,
  Should kneel and sue for aid,
  Since I am thus afraid
And have no strength for it.

---

* Madonna mia.

Thou, lady, killest me,
   Yet keepest me in pain,
For thou must surely see
   How, fearing, I am fain.
Ah! why not send me still
   Some solace, small and slight,
   So that I should not quite
Despair of thy good will?

Thy grace, all else above,
   Even now while I implore,
Enamoureth my love
   To love thee still the more.
Yet scarce should I know well—
   A greater love to gain,
   Even if a greater pain,
Lady, were possible.

Joy did that day relax
   My griefs continual stress,
When I essayed in wax
   Thy beauty's life-likeness.
Ah! much more beautiful
   Than golden-haired Yseult,—
   Who mak'st all men exult,
Who bring'st all women dule.

And certes without blame
   Thy love might fall to me,
Though it should chance my name
   Were never heard of thee.
Yea, for thy love, in fine,
   Lentino gave me birth,
   Who am not nothing worth
If worthy to be thine.

VI.

SONNET.

Of his Lady's face.

HER face has made my life most proud and glad;
　Her face has made my life quite wearisome;
　It comforts me when other troubles come,
And amid other joys it strikes me sad.
Truly I think her face can drive me mad;
　For now I am too loud, and anon dumb.　.
　There is no second face in Christendom
Has a like power, nor shall have, nor has had.
What man in living face has seen such eyes,
　Or such a lovely bending of the head,
　　Or mouth that opens to so sweet a smile?
In speech, my heart before her faints and dies,
　And into Heaven seems to be spirited;
　　So that I count me blest a certain while.

VII.

CANZONE.

At the end of his Hope.

REMEMBERING this—how Love
    Mocks me, and bids me hoard
Mine ill reward that keeps me nigh to death,—
    How it doth still behove
    I suffer the keen sword,
Whenee undeplor'd I may not draw my breath
    In memory of this thing
    Sighing and sorrowing,
    I am languid at the heart
      For her to whom I bow,
      Craving her pity now,
    And who still turns apart.

    I am dying, and through her—
    This flower, from paradise
Sent in some wise, that I might have no rest.
    Truly she did not err
    To come before his eyes
Who fails and dies, by her sweet smile possess'd ;
    For, through her countenance
    (Fair brows and lofty glance !)
    I live in constant dule.
      Of lovers' hearts the chief
      For sorrow and much grief,
    My heart is sorrowful.

For Love has made me weep
    With sighs that do him wrong,
Since, when most strong my joy, he gave this woe.
    I am broken, as a ship
      Perishing of the song,
Sweet, sweet and long, the songs the sirens know.
    The mariner forgets,
    Voyaging in those straits,
    And dies assuredly.
      Yea, from her pride perverse,
      Who hath my heart as hers,
    Even such my death must be.

I deemed her not so fell
    And hard but she would greet,
From her high seat, at length, the love I bring ;
    For I have loved her well ;—
      Nor that her face so sweet
In so much heat would keep me languishing ;
    Seeing that she I serve
    All honour doth deserve
    For worth unparallel'd.
      Yet what availeth moan
      But for more grief alone ?
    O God ! that it avail'd !

Thou, my new song, shalt pray
    To her, who for no end
Each day doth tend her virtues that they grow,—
    Since she to love saith nay ;—
      (More charms she had attain'd
Than sea hath sand, and wisdom even so) ;—
    Pray thou to her that she
    For my love pity me,
    Since with my love I burn,—
      That of the fruit of love,
      While help may come thereof,
    She give to me in turn.

MAZZEO DI RICCO, DA MESSINA.

I.

CANZONE.

He solicits his Lady's Pity.

THE lofty worth and lovely excellence,
    Dear lady, that thou hast,
Hold me consuming in the fire of love :
That I am much afeared and wildered thence,
    As who, being meanly plac'd,
Would win unto some height he dreameth of
    Yet, if it be decreed,
After the multiplying of vain thought,
By Fortune's favour he at last is brought
To his far hope, the mighty bliss indeed.

Thus, in considering thy loveliness,
    Love maketh me afear'd,—
So high art thou, joyful, and full of good ;—
And all the more, thy scorn being never less.
    Yet is this comfort heard,—
That underneath the water fire doth brood,
    Which thing would seem unfit
By law of nature.   So may thy scorn prove
Changed at the last, through pity into love
If favourable Fortune should permit.

Lady, though I do love past utterance,
      Let it not seem amiss,
Neither rebuke thou the enamoured eyes.
Look thou thyself on thine own countenance,
      From that charm unto this,
    All thy perfections of sufficiencies.
      So shalt thou rest assured
    That thine exceeding beauty lures me on
    Perforce, as by the passive magnet-stone
The needle, of its nature's self, is lured.

Certes, it was of Love's dispiteousness
      That I must set my life
On thee, proud lady, who accept'st it not.
And how should I attain unto thy grace,
      That falter, thus at strife
    To speak to thee the thing which is my thought ?
      Thou, lovely as thou art,
    I pray for God, when thou dost pass me by,
    Look upon me : so shalt thou certify,
By my cheek's ailing, that which ails my heart.

So thoroughly my love doth tend toward
      Thy love its lofty scope,
    That I may never think to ease my pain ;
Because the ice, when it is frozen hard
      May have no further hope
    That it should ever become snow again.
      But, since Love bids me bend
      Unto thy seigniory,
      Have pity thou on me,
That so upon thyself all grace descend.

II.

CANZONE.

After Six Years' service he renounces his Lady.

I LABOURED these six years
　　For thee, thou bitter sweet ;
　　Yea, more than it is meet
That speech should now rehearse
　　Or song should rhyme to thee ;
But love gains never aught
　　From thee, by depth or length ;
　　Unto thine eyes such strength
And calmness thou hast taught,
　　That I say wearily :—
"The child is most like me,
Who thinks in the clear stream
To catch the round flat moon
And draw it all a-dripping unto him,—
Who fancies he can take into his hand
　　The flame o' the lamp, but soon
　　Screams and is nigh to swoon
At the sharp heat his flesh may not withstand."

Though it be late to learn
　　How sore I was possest,
　　Yet do I count me blest,
Because I still can spurn
　　This thrall which is so mean.

For when a man, once sick,
   Has got his health anew,
   The fever which boiled through
His veins, and made him weak,
   Is as it had not been.
   For all that I had seen,
Thy spirit, like thy face,
   More excellently shone
Than precious crystals in an untrod place.
Go to : thy worth is but as glass, the cheat,
   Which, to gaze thereupon,
   Seems crystal, even as one,
But only is a cunning counterfeit.

Foiled hope has made me mad,
   As one who, playing high,
   Thought to grow rich thereby,
And loses what he had.
   Yet I can now perceive
How true the saying is
   That says : "If one turn back
   Out of an evil track
Through loss which has been his,
   He gains, and need not grieve."
   To me now, by your leave,
It chances as to him
   Who of his purse is free
To one whose memory for such debts is dim.
Long time he speaks no word thereof, being loth :
   But having asked, when he
   Is answered slightingly,
Then shall he lose his patience and be wroth.

III.

SONNET.

Of Self-seeing.

IF any his own foolishness might see
  As he can see his fellow's foolishness,
  His evil speakings could not but prove less,
For his own fault would vex him inwardly.
But, by old custom, each man deems that he
  Has to himself all this world's worthiness ;
  And thou, perchance, in blind contentedness,
Scorn'st *him*, yet know'st not what *I* think of *thee*.
Wherefore I wish it were so ordered
  That each of us might know the good that's his,
    And also the ill,—his honour and his shame.
For oft a man has on his proper head
  Such weight of sins, that, did he know but this,
    He could not for his life give others blame.

PANNUCCIO DAL BAGNO, PISANO.

CANZONE.

Of his Change through Love.

My lady, thy delightful high command,
 Thy wisdom's great intent,
 The worth which ever rules thee in thy sway,
(Whose righteousness of strength hath ta'en in hand
 Such full accomplishment
 As height makes worthy of more height alway,)
Have granted to thy servant some poor due
 Of thy perfection; who
From them has gained a proper will so fix'd,
 With other thought unmix'd,
That nothing save thy service now impels
His life, and his heart longs for nothing else.

Beneath thy pleasure, lady mine, I am:
 The circuit of my will,
 The force of all my life, to serve thee so:
Never but only this I think or name,
 Nor ever can I fill
 My heart with other joy that man may know.
And hence a sovereign blessedness I draw,
 Who soon most clearly saw
That not alone my perfect pleasure is
 In this my life-service :

But Love has made my soul with thine to touch
Till my heart feels unworthy of so much.

For all that I could strive, it were not worth
    That I should be uplift
  Into thy love, as certainly I know :
Since one to thy deserving should stretch forth
    His love for a free gift,
  And be full fain to serve and sit below.
And forasmuch as this is verity,
    It came to pass with thee
That seeing how my love was not loud-tongued
    Yet for thy service long'd—
As only thy pure wisdom brought to pass,—
Thou knew'st my heart for only what it was.

Also because thou thus at once didst learn
    This heart of mine and thine,
  With all its love for thee, which was and is ;
Thy lofty sense that could so well discern
    Wrought even in me some sign
  Of thee, and of itself some emphasis,
Which evermore might hold my purpose fast.
    For lo ! thy law is pass'd
That this my love should manifestly be
    To serve and honour thee :
And so I do : and my delight is full,
Accepted for the servant of thy rule.

Without almost, I am all rapturous,
    Since thus my will was set
  To serve, thou flower of joy, thine excellence :
Nor ever seems it anything could rouse
    A pain or a regret,
  But on thee dwells mine every thought and sense ;
Considering that from thee all virtues spread
    As from a fountain-head,—

That in thy gift is wisdom's best avail
  And honour without fail ;
With whom each sovereign good dwells separate,
Fulfilling the perfection of thy state.

  Lady, since I conceived
Thy pleasurable aspect in my heart,
  My life has been apart
In shining brightness and the place of truth ;
  Which till that time, good sooth,
Groped among shadows in a darken'd place
  Where many hours and days
It hardly ever had remembered good.
  But now my servitude
Is thine, and I am full of joy and rest.
  A man from a wild beast
Thou madest me, since for thy love I lived.

GIACOMINO PUGLIESI, KNIGHT OF PRATO.

I.

CANZONETTA.

Of his Lady in Absence.

THE sweetly-favoured face
  She has, and her good cheer,
Have filled me full of grace
  When I have walked with her.
They did upon that day:
  And everything that pass'd
  Comes back from first to last
Now that I am away.

There went from her meek mouth
  A poor low sigh which made
My heart sink down for drouth.
  She stooped, and sobbed, and said,
" Sir, I entreat of you
  Make little tarrying:
  It is not a good thing
To leave one's love and go."

But when I turned about
  Saying, "God keep you well!"
As she look'd up, I thought
  Her lips that were quite pale

Strove much to speak, but she
   Had not half strength enough :
   My own dear graceful love
Would not let go of me.

I am not so far, sweet maid,
   That now the old love's unfelt :
1 believe Tristram had
   No such love for Yseult :
And when I see your eyes
   And feel your breath again,
   I shall forget this pain
And my whole heart will rise.

II.

CANZONETTA.

To his Lady, in Spring.

To see the green returning
  To stream-side, garden, and meadow,—
To hear the birds give warning,
  (The laughter of sun and shadow
Awaking them full of revel,)
  It puts me in strength to carol
A music measured and level,
  This grief in joy to apparel ;
For the deaths of lovers are evil.

Love is a foolish riot,
  And to be loved is a burden ;
Who loves and is loved in quiet
  Has all the world for his guerdon.
Ladies on him take pity
  Who for their sake hath trouble :
Yet, if any heart be a city
  From love embarrèd double,
Thereof is a joyful ditty.

That heart shall be always joyful ;—
  But I in the heart, my lady,
Have jealous doubts unlawful,
  And stubborn pride stands ready.
Yet love is not with a measure,

But still is willing to suffer
Service at his good pleasure :
  · The whole Love hath to offer
Tends to his perfect treasure.

Thine be this prelude-music
    That was of thy commanding ;
Thy gaze was not delusive,—
Of my heart thou hadst understanding.
Lady, by thine attemp'rance
    Thou heldst my life from pining :
This tress thou gav'st, in semblance
    Like gold of the third refining,
Which I do keep for remembrance.

III.

CANZÒNE.

Of his dead Lady.

DEATH, why hast thou madé life so hard to bear,
  Taking my lady hence?   Hast thou no whit
Of shame?   The youngest flower and the most fair
  Thou hast plucked away, and the world wanteth it.
O leaden Death, hast thou no pitying?
Our warm love's very spring
  Thou stopp'st, and endest what was holy and meet;
And of my gladdening
Mak'st a most woful thing,
And in my heart dost bid the bird not sing
    That sang so sweet.

Once the great joy and solace that I had
  Was more than is with other gentlemen :—
Now is my love gone hence, who made me glad.
  With her that hope I lived in she hath ta'en
And left me nothing but these sighs and tears,—
Nothing of the old years
  That come not back again,
Wherein I was so happy, being hers.
Now to mine eyes her face no more appears,
Nor doth her voice make music in mine ears,
    As it did then.

O God, why hast thou made my grief so deep?
　Why set me in the dark to grope and pine?
Why parted me from her companionship,
　And crushed the hope which was a gift of thine?
To think, dear, that I never any more
Can see thee as before!
　Who is it shuts thee in?
Who hides that smile for which my heart is sore,
And drowns those words that I am longing for,
　　Lady of mine?

Where is my lady, and the lovely face
　She had, and the sweet motion when she walk'd?—
Her chaste, mild favour—her so delicate grace—
　Her eyes, her mouth, and the dear way she talk'd?—
Her courteous bending—her most noble air—
The soft fall of her hair? . . . .
My lady—she to whom my soul
　A gladness brought!
Now I do never see her anywhere,
And may not, looking in her eyes, gain there
　The blessing which I sought.

So if I had the realm of Hungary,
　With Greece, and all the Almayn even to France,
Or Saint Sophia's treasure-hoard, you see
　All could not give me back her countenance.
For since the day when my dear lady died
From us, (with God being born and glorified,)
　　No more pleasaunce
Her image bringeth, seated at my side,
But only tears. Ay me! the strength and pride
　　Which it brought once.

Had I my will, beloved, I would say
　To God, unto whose bidding all things bow,

That we were still together night and day :
   Yet be it done as His behests allow.
   do remember that while she remain'd
With me, she often called me her sweet friend ;
    But does not now,
Because God drew her towards Him, in the end.
Lady, that peace which none but He can send
    Be thine.   Even so.

FRA GUITTONE D'AREZZO.

Sonnet.

To the Blessed Virgin Mary.

Lady of Heaven, the mother glorified
   Of glory, which is Jesus,—He whose death
   Us from the gates of Hell delivereth
And our first parents' error sets aside :—
Behold this earthly Love, how his darts glide—
   How sharpened—to what fate—throughout this earth !
   Pitiful Mother, partner of our birth,
Win these from following where his flight doth guide.
And O, inspire in me that holy love
   Which leads the soul back to its origin,
    Till of all other love the link do fail.
This water only can this fire reprove,—
   Only such cure suffice for suchlike sin ;
    As nail from out a plank is struck by nail.

BARTOLOMEO DI SANT' ANGELO.

SONNET.

He jests concerning his Poverty.

I AM so passing rich in poverty
    That I could furnish forth Paris and Rome,
    Pisa and Padua and Byzantium,
Venice and Lucca, Florence and Forlì;
For I possess in actual specie,
    Of nihil and of nothing a great sum;
    And unto this my hoard whole shiploads come,
What between nought and zero, annually.
In gold and precious jewels I have got
    A hundred ciphers' worth, all roundly writ;
      And therewithal am free to feast my friend.
      Because I need not be afraid to spend,
    Nor doubt the safety of my wealth a whit:—
No thief will ever steal thereof, God wot.

SALADINO DA PAVIA.

DIALOGUE.

Lover and Lady.

SHE.

FAIR sir, this love of ours,
In joy begun so well,
I see at length to fail upon thy part :
Wherefore my heart sinks very heavily.
Fair sir, this love of ours
Began with amorous longing, well I ween :
Yea, of one mind, yea, of one heart and will
This love of ours hath been.
Now these are sad and still ;
For on thy part at length it fails, I see.
And now thou art gone from me,
Quite lost to me thou art ;
Wherefore my heart in this pain languisheth,
Which sinks it unto death thus heavily.

HE.

Lady, for will of mine
Our love had never changed in anywise,
Had not the choice been thine
With so much scorn my homage to despise.
I swore not to yield sign
Of holding 'gainst all hope my heart-service.

Nay, let thus much suffice :—
From thee whom I have serv'd,
All undeserved contempt is my reward,—
Rich prize prepar'd to guerdon fealty !

SHE.

Fair sir, it oft is found
That ladies who would try their lovers so,
Have for a season frown'd,
Not from their heart but in mere outward show.
Then chide not on such ground,
Since ladies oft have tried their lovers so.
Alas, but I will go,
If now it be thy will.
Yet turn thee still, alas ! for I do fear
Thou lov'st elsewhere, and therefore fly'st from me.

HE.

Lady, there needs no doubt
Of my good faith, nor any nice suspense
Lest love be elsewhere sought.
For thine did yield me no such recompense,—
Rest thou assured in thought,—
That now, within my life's circumference,
I should not quite dispense
My heart from woman's laws,
Which for no cause give pain and sore annoy,
And for one joy a world of misery.

BONAGGIUNTA URBICIANI, DA LUCCA.

CANZONE.

Of the true End of Love ; with a Prayer to his Lady.

NEVER was joy or good that did not soothe
    And beget glorying,
  Neither a glorying without perfect love.
Wherefore, if one would compass of a truth
    The flight of his soul's wing,
  To bear a loving heart must him behove.
Since from the flower man still expects the fruit,
  And, out of love, that he desireth ;
    Seeing that by good faith
  Alone hath love its comfort and its joy ;
For, suffering falsehood, love were at the root
Dead of all worth, which living must aspire ;
    Nor could it breed desire
  If its reward were less than its annoy.

Even such the joy, the triumph, and pleasaunce,
    Whose issue honour is,
  And grace, and the most delicate teaching sent
To amorous knowledge, its inheritance ;
    Because Love's properties
  Alter not by a true accomplishment ;

But it were scarcely well if one should gain,
 Without much pain so great a blessedness;
  He errs, when all things bless,
 Whose heart had else been humbled to implore.
He gets not joy who gives no joy again;
Nor can win love whose love hath little scope;
  Nor fully can know hope
 Who leaves not of the thing most languished for.

Wherefore his choice must err immeasurably
  Who seeks the image when
 He might behold the thing substantial.
I at the noon have seen dark night to be,
  Against earth's natural plan,
 And what was good to worst abasement fall.
Then be thus much sufficient, lady mine;
 If of thy mildness pity may be born,
  Count thou my grief outworn,
 And turn into sweet joy this bitter ill;
Lest I might change, if left too long to pine:
As one who, journeying, in mid path should stay,
  And not pursue his way,
 But should go back against his proper will.

Natheless I hope, yea trust, to make an end
  Of the beginning made,
 Even by this sign—that yet I triumph not.
And if in truth, against my will constrain'd,
  To turn my steps essay'd,
 No courage have I, neither strength, God wot.
Such is Love's rule, who thus subdueth me
 By thy sweet face, lovely and delicate;
  Through which I live elate,
 But in such longing that I die for love.
Ah! and these words as nothing seem to be:
For love to such a constant fear has chid
  My heart that I keep hid
 Much more than I have dared to tell thee of

II.

Canzonetta.

How he dreams of his Lady.

Lady, my wedded thought,
When to thy shape 'tis wrought,
Can think of nothing else
   But only of thy grace,
   And of those gentle ways
Wherein thy life excels.
For ever, sweet one, dwells
Thine image on my sight,
   (Even as it were the gem
   Whose name is as thy name)*
And fills the sense with light.

Continual ponderings
That brood upon these things
Yield constant agony :
   Yea, the same thoughts have crept
   About me as I slept.
My spirit looks at me,
And asks, " Is sleep for thee ?
Nay, mourner, do not sleep,
   But fix thine eyes, for lo !
   Love's fulness thou shalt know
By steadfast gaze and deep."

* The lady was probably called Diamante, Margherita, or some similar name. (Note to Flor. Ed. 1816).

Then, burning, I awake,
Sore tempted to partake
Of dreams that seek thy sight:
   Until, being greatly stirr'd,
   I turn to where I heard
That whisper in the night;
And there a breath of light
Shines like a silver star.
   The same is mine own soul,
   Which lures me to the goal
Of dreams that gaze afar.

But now my sleep is lost;
And through this uttermost
Sharp longing for thine eyes
   At length it may be said
   That I indeed am mad
With love's extremities.
Yet when in such sweet wise
Thou passest and dost smile,
   My heart so fondly burns,
   That unto sweetness turns
Its bitter pang the while.

Even so Love rends apart
My spirit and my heart,
Lady, in loving thee;
   Till when I see thee now,
   Life beats within my brow
And would be gone from me.
So hear I ceaselessly,
Love's whisper well fulfill'd—
   Even I am he, even so,
   Whose flame thy heart doth know:
And while I strive I yield.

III.

Sonnet.

Of Wisdom and Foresight.

Such wisdom as a little child displays
   Were not amiss in certain lords of fame :
For where he fell, thenceforth he shuns the place,
   And having suffered blows, he feareth them.
Who knows not this may forfeit all he sways
   At length, and find his friends go as they came.
O therefore on the past time turn thy face,
   And, if thy will do err, forget the same.
Because repentance brings not back the past :
   Better thy will should bend than thy life break :
     Who owns not this, by him shall it appear.
And, because even from fools the wise may make
Wisdom, the first should count himself the last,
   Since a dog scourged can bid the lion fear.

IV.

SONNET.

Of Continence in Speech.

WHOSO abandons peace for war-seeking,
   'Tis of all reason he should bear the smart.
Whoso hath evil speech, his medicine
   Is silence, lest it seem a hateful art.
To vex the wasps' nest is not a wise thing ;
   Yet who rebukes his neighbour in good part,
A hundred years shall show his right therein.
   Too prone to fear, one wrongs another's heart.
If ye but knew what may be known to me,
   Ye would fall sorry sick, nor be thus bold
     To cry among your fellows your ill thought.
Wherefore I would that every one of ye
   Who thinketh ill, his ill thought should withhold :
     If that ye would not hear it, speak it not.

MEO ABBRACCIAVACCA, DA PISTOIA.

I.

CANZONE.

He will be silent and watchful in his Love.

YOUR joyful understanding, lady mine,
    Those honours of fair life
  Which all in you agree to pleasantness,
Long since to service did my heart assign ;
    That never it has strife,
  Nor once remembers other means of grace ;
But this desire alone gives light to it.
  Behold, my pleasure, by your favour, drew
     Me, lady, unto you,
All beauty's and all joy's reflection here :
  From whom good women also have thought fit
    To take their life's example every day ;
     Whom also to obey
My wish and will have wrought, with love and fear.

With love and fear to yield obedience, I
    Might never half deserve :
  Yet you must know, merely to look on me,
How my heart holds its love and lives thereby ;
    Though, well intent to serve,
  It can accept Love's arrow silently.

'Twere late to wait, ere I would render plain
  My heart, (thus much I tell you, as I should,)
    Which, to be understood,
Craves therefore the fine quickness of your glance.
So shall you know my love of such high strain
  As never yet was shown by its own will;
    Whose proffer is so still,
That love in heart hates love in countenance.

In countenance oft the heart is evident
    Full clad in mirth's attire,
      Wherein at times it overweens to waste:
Which yet of selfish joy or foul intent
    Doth hide the deep desire,
      And is, of heavy surety, double-faced;
Upon things double therefore look ye twice.
    O ye that love! not what is fair alone
      Desire to make your own,
But a wise woman, fair in purity;
  Nor think that any, without sacrifice
    Of his own nature, suffers service still;
      But out of high free-will;
In honour propped, though bowed in dignity.

In dignity as best I may, must I
    The guerdon very grand,
      The whole of it, secured in purpose, sing?
Lady, whom all my heart doth magnify,
    You took me in your hand,
      Ah! not ungraced with other guerdoning:
For you of your sweet reason gave me rest
    From yearning, from desire, from potent pain;
      Till, now, if Death should gain
Me to his kingdom, it would pleasure me,
  Having obeyed the whole of your behest.
    Since you have drawn, and I am yours by lot,
      I pray you doubt me not
Lest my faith swerve, for this could never be.

Could never be ; because the natural heart
     Will absolutely build
    Her dwelling-place within the gates of truth ;
And, if it be no grief to bear her part,
     Why, then by change were fill'd
    The measure of her shame beyond all truth.
And therefore no delay shall once disturb
    My bounden service, nor bring grief to it ;
     Nor unto you deceit.
True virtue her provision first affords,
Ere she yield grace, lest afterward some curb
    Or check should come, and evil enter in :
     For alway shame and sin
Stand covered, ready, full of faithful words.

II.

BALLATA.

His Life is by Contraries.

By the long sojourning
   That I have made with grief,
      I am quite changed, you see ;—
      If I weep, 'tis for glee ;
I smile at a sad thing ;
   Despair is my relief.

Good hap makes me afraid ;
Ruin seems rest and shade ;
   In May the year is old ;
With friends I am ill at ease ;
Among foes I find peace ;
   At noonday I feel cold.

The thing that strengthens others, frightens me.
   If I am grieved, I sing ;
   I chafe at comforting ;
Ill fortune makes me smile exultingly.

And yet, though all my days are thus,—despite
   A shaken mind, and eyes
   Which see by contraries,—
I know that without wings is an ill flight.

UBALDO DI MARCO.

SONNET.

Of a Lady's Love for him.

My body resting in a haunt of mine,
 I ranged among alternate memories;
 What while an unseen noble lady's eyes
Were fixed upon me, yet she gave no sign;
To stay and go she sweetly did incline,
 Always afraid lest there were any spies;
 Then reached to me,—and smelt it in sweet wise,
And reached to me—some sprig of bloom or bine.
Conscious of perfume, on my side I leant,
 And rose upon my feet, and gazed around
  To see the plant whose flower could so beguile.
Finding it not, I sought it by the scent;
 And by the scent, in truth, the plant I found,
  And rested in its shadow a great while.

SIMBUONO GIUDICE.

CANZONE.

He finds that Love has beguiled him, but will trust in his Lady.

OFTEN the day had a most joyful morn
　　That bringeth grief at last
Unto the human heart which deemed all well :
Of a sweet seed the fruit was often born
　　That hath a bitter taste :
Of mine own knowledge, oft it thus befell.
I say it for myself, who, foolishly
　　Expectant of all joy,
　　　Triumphing undertook
To love a lady proud and beautiful,
For one poor glance vouchsafed in mirth to me :
　　Wherefrom sprang all annoy :
　　　For, since the day Love shook
My heart, she ever hath been cold and cruel.

Well thought I to possess my joy complete
　　When that sweet look of hers
I felt upon me, amorous and kind :
Now is my hope even underneath my feet.
　　And still the arrow stirs
　　Within my heart—(oh hurt no skill can bind !)—
Which through mine eyes found entrance cunningly !

In manner as through glass
Light pierces from the sun,
And breaks it not, but wins its way beyond,—
As into an unaltered mirror, free
And still, some shape may pass
Yet has my heart begun
To break, methinks, for I on death grow fond.

But, even though death were longed for, the sharp wound
I have might yet be heal'd,
And I not altogether sink to death.
In mine own foolishness the curse I found,
Who foolish faith did yield
Unto mine eyes, in hope that sickeneth.
Yet might love still exult and not be sad—
(For some such utterance
Is at my secret heart)—
If from herself the cure it could obtain,—
Who hath indeed the power Achilles had,
To wit, that of his lance
The wound could by no art
Be closed till it were touched therewith again.

So must I needs appeal for pity now
From her on her own fault,
And in my prayer put meek humility :
For certes her much worth will not allow
That anything be call'd
Treacherousness in such an one as she,
In whom is judgment and true excellence.
Wherefore I cry for grace ;
Not doubting that all good,
Joy, wisdom, pity, must from her be shed ;
For scarcely should it deal in death's offence,
The so-belovèd face
So watched for ; rather should
All death and ill be thereby subjected.

And since, in hope of mercy, I have bent
      Unto her ordinance
Humbly my heart, my body, and my life,
Giving her perfect power acknowledgment,—
      I think some kinder glance
She'll deign, and, in mere pity, pause from strife.
She surely shall enact the good lord's part:
      When one whom force compels
        Doth yield, he is pacified,
Forgiving him therein where he did err.
Ah! well I know she hath the noble heart
      Which in the lion quells
        Obduracy of pride;
Whose nobleness is for a crown on her.

MASOLINO DA TODI.

SONNET.

Of Work and Wealth.

A MAN should hold in very dear esteem
   The first possession that his labours gain'd ;
   For, though great riches be at length attain'd,
From that first mite they were increased to him.
Who followeth after his own wilful whim
   Shall see himself outwitted in the end ;
   Wherefore I still would have him apprehend
His fall, who toils not being once supreme.
Thou seldom shalt find folly, of the worst,
   Holding companionship with poverty,
     Because it is distracted of much care.
Howbeit, if one that hath been poor at first
   Is brought at last to wealth and dignity,
     Still the worst folly thou shalt find it there.

ONESTO DI BONCIMA, BOLOGNESE.

I.

SONNET.

Of the Last Judgment.

UPON that cruel season when our Lord
  Shall come to judge the world eternally;
When to no man shall anything afford
  Peace in the heart, how pure soe'er it be;
When heaven shall break asunder at His word,
  With a great trembling of the earth and sea;
When even the just shall fear the dreadful sword,—
  The wicked crying, "Where shall I cover me?"—
When no one angel in His presence stands
  That shall not be affrighted of that wrath,
    Except the Virgin Lady, she our guide;—
How shall I then escape, whom sin commands?
  Out and alas on me! There is no path,
    If in her prayers I be not justified.

II.

SONNET.

He wishes that he could meet his Lady alone.

WHETHER all grace have failed I scarce may scan,
  Be it of mere mischance, or art's ill sway,
  That this-wise, Monday, Tuesday, every day,
Afflicts me, through her means, with bale and ban.
Now are my days but as a painful span ;
  Nor once " Take heed of dying " did she say.
  I thank thee for my life thus cast away,
Thou who hast wearied out a living man.
Yet, oh ! my Lord, if I were blest no more
  Than thus much,—clothed with thy humility,
  To find her for a single hour alone,—
Such perfectness of joy would triumph o'er
  This grief wherein I waste, that I should be
  As a new image of Love to look upon.

TERINO DA CASTEL FIORENTINO.

SONNET.

To Onesto di Boncima, in Answer to the foregoing.

IF, as thou say'st, thy love tormenteth thee,
  That thou thereby wast in the fear of death,
Messer Onesto, couldst thou bear to be
  Far from Love's self, and breathing other breath ?
Nay, thou wouldst pass beyond the greater sea
  (I do not speak of the Alps, an easy path),
For thy life's gladdening ; if so to see
  That light which for *my* life no comfort hath,
But rather makes my grief the bitterer :
  For I have neither ford nor bridge—no course
To reach my lady, or send word to her.
And there is not a greater pain, I think,
  Than to see waters at the limpid source,
And to be much athirst, and not to drink.

MAESTRO MIGLIORE, DA FIORENZA.

SONNET.

He declares all Love to be Grief.

LOVE taking leave, my heart then leaveth me,
 And is enamour'd even while it would shun ;
 For I have looked so long upon the sun
That the sun's glory is now in all I see.
To its first will unwilling may not be
 This heart (though by its will its death be won),
 Having remembrance of the joy forerun :
Yea, all life else seems dying constantly.
Ay and alas ! in love is no relief,
 For any man who loveth in full heart,
  That is not rather grief than gratefulness.
Whoso desires it, the beginning is grief ;
 Also the end is grief, most grievous smart ;
  And grief is in the middle, and is call'd grace.

DELLO DA SIGNA.

BALLATA.

His Creed of Ideal Love.

PROHIBITING all hope
Of the fulfilment of the joy of love,
　My lady chose me for her lover still.

　So am I lifted up
To trust her heart which piteous pulses move,
　Her face which is her joy made visible.

　Nor have I any fear
Lest love and service should be met with scorn,
　Nor doubt that thus I shall rejoice the more.

　For ruth is born of prayer ;
Also, of ruth delicious love is born ;
　And service wrought makes glad the servitor.

Behold, I, serving more than others, love
　One lovely more than all :
　And, singing and exulting, look for joy
There where my homage is for ever paid.

And, for I know she does not disapprove
　If on her grace I call,
　My soul's good trust I will not yet destroy,
Though Love's fulfilment stand prohibited.

FOLGORE DA SAN GEMINIANO.

I.

SONNET.

To the Guelf Faction.

BECAUSE ye made your backs your shields, it came
  To pass, ye Guelfs, that these your enemies
  From hares grew lions : and because your eyes
Turned homeward, and your spurs e'en did the same,
Full many an one who still might win the game
  In fevered tracts of exile pines and dies.
  Ye blew your bubbles as the falcon flies,
And the wind broke them up and scattered them.
This counsel, therefore.   Shape your high resolves
  In good King Robert's humour,* and afresh
    Accept your shames, forgive, and go your way.
    And so her peace is made with Pisa !   Yea,
  What cares she for the miserable flesh
That in the wilderness has fed the wolves?

---

  * See what is said in allusion to his government of Florence by
Dante (*Parad.* C. VIII.).

II.

SONNET.

To the Same.

WERE ye but constant, Guelfs, in war or peace,
  As in divisions ye are constant still !
  There is no wisdom in your stubborn will,
Wherein all good things wane, all harms increase.
But each upon his fellow looks, and sees
  And looks again, and likes his favour ill ;
  And traitors rule ye ; and on his own sill
Each stirs the fire of household enmities.
What, Guelfs ! and is Monte Catini * quite
  Forgot,—where still the mothers and sad wives
    Keep widowhood, and curse the Ghibellins ?
    O fathers, brothers, yea, all dearest kins !
  Those men of ye that cherish kindred lives
Even once again must set their teeth and fight.

---

* The battle of Monte Catini was fought and won by the Ghibelline leader, Uguccione della Faggiola, against the Florentines, August 29, 1315. This would seem to date Folgore's career further on than the period usually assigned to him (about 1260), and the question arises whether the above sonnet be really his.

III.

SONNET.

Of Virtue.

THE flower of Virtue is the heart's content ;
   And fame is Virtue's fruit that she doth bear ;
   And Virtue's vase is fair without and fair
Within ; and Virtue's mirror brooks no taint ;
And Virtue by her names is sage and saint ;
   And Virtue hath a steadfast front and clear ;
   And Love is Virtue's constant minister ;
And Virtue's gift of gifts is pure descent.
And Virtue dwells with knowledge, and therein
   Her cherished home of rest is real love ;
     And Virtue's strength is in a suffering will ;
And Virtue's work is life exempt from sin,
   With arms that aid ; and in the sum hereof,
   All Virtue is to render good for ill.

OF THE MONTHS.

Twelve Sonnets.

Addressed to a Fellowship of Sienese Nobles. *

DEDICATION.

Unto the blithe and lordly Fellowship,
  (I know not where, but wheresoe'er, I know,
  Lordly and blithe,) be greeting ; and thereto,
Dogs, hawks, and a full purse wherein to dip ;
Quails struck i' the flight ; nags mettled to the whip ;
  Hart-hounds, hare-hounds, and blood-hounds even so ;
  And o'er that realm, a crown for Niccolò,
Whose praise in Siena springs from lip to lip.

---

* This fellowship or club (*Brigata*), so highly approved and encouraged by our Folgore, is the same to which, and to some of its members by name, scornful allusion is made by Dante (*Inferno*, C. xxix. l. 130), where he speaks of the hare-brained character of the Sienese. Mr. Cayley, in his valuable notes on Dante, says of it : "A dozen extravagant youths of Siena had put together by equal contributions 216,000 florins to spend in pleasuring ; they were reduced in about a twelvemonth to the extremes of poverty. It was their practice to give mutual entertainments twice a-month ; at each of which, three tables having been sumptuously covered they would feast at one, wash their hands on another, and throw the last out of window."

There exists a second curious series of sonnets for the months, addressed also to this club, by Cene della Chitarra d'Arezzo. Here, however, all sorts of disasters and discomforts, in the same

Tingoccio, Atuin di Togno, and Ancaiàn,
   Bartolo and Mugaro and Faènot,
Who well might pass for children of King Ban,
   Courteous and valiant more than Lancelot,—
To each, God speed ! how worthy every man
   To hold high tournament in Camelot.

---

pursuits of which Folgore treats, are imagined for the prodigals ; each sonnet, too, being composed with the same terminations in its rhymes as the corresponding one among his. They would seem to have been written after the ruin of the club, as a satirical prophecy of the year to succeed the golden one. But this second series, though sometimes laughable, not having the poetical merit of the first, I have not included it.

JANUARY.

FOR January I give you vests of skins,
　And mighty fires in hall, and torches lit ;
　Chambers and happy beds with all things fit ;
Smooth silken sheets, rough furry counterpanes ;
And sweetmeats baked ; and one that deftly spins
　Warm arras ; and Douay cloth, and store of it ;
　And on this merry manner still to twit
The wind, when most his mastery the wind wins.
Or issuing forth at seasons in the day,
　Ye'll fling soft handfuls of the fair white snow
Among the damsels standing round, in play :
　And when you all are tired and all aglow,
Indoors again the court shall hold its sway,
　And the free Fellowship continue so.

FEBRUARY.

IN February I give you gallant sport
　Of harts and hinds and great wild boars ; and all
　Your company good foresters and tall,
With buskins strong, with jerkins close and short ;
And in your leashes, hounds of brave report ;
　And from your purses, plenteous money-fall,
　In very spleen of misers' starveling gall,
Who at your generous customs snarl and snort.
At dusk wend homeward, ye and all your folk,
　All laden from the wilds, to your carouse,
　With merriment and songs accompanied :
And so draw wine and let the kitchen smoke ;
　And so be till the first watch glorious ;
　　Then sound sleep to you till the day be wide.

MARCH.

In March I give you plenteous fisheries
  Of lamprey and of salmon, eel and trout,
  Dental and dolphin, sturgeon, all the rout
Of fish in all the streams that fill the seas.
With fishermen and fishing-boats at ease,
  Sail-barques and arrow-barques, and galleons stout,
  To bear you, while the season lasts, far out,
And back, through spring, to any port you please.
But with fair mansions see that it be fill'd,
  With everything exactly to your mind,
  And every sort of comfortable folk.
No convent suffer there, nor priestly guild :
  Leave the mad monks to preach after their kind
  Their scanty truth, their lies beyond a joke.

APRIL.

I give you meadow-lands in April, fair
  With over-growth of beautiful green grass ;
  There among fountains the glad hours shall pass,
And pleasant ladies bring you solace there.
With steeds of Spain and ambling palfreys rare ;
  Provençal songs and dances that surpass ;
  And quaint French mummings ; and through hollow
      brass
A sound of German music on the air.
And gardens ye shall have, that every one
  May lie at ease about the fragrant place ;
    And each with fitting reverence shall bow down
    Unto that youth to whom I gave a crown
  Of precious jewels like to those that grace
The Babylonian Kaiser, Prester John.

MAY.

I give you horses for your games in May,
   And all of them well trained unto the course,—
   Each docile, swift, erect, a goodly horse ;
With armour on their chests, and bells at play
Between their brows, and pennons fair and gay ;
   Fine nets, and housings meet for warriors,
   Emblazoned with the shields ye claim for yours ;
Gules, argent, or, all dizzy at noonday.
And spears shall split, and fruit go flying up
In merry counterchange for wreaths that drop
   From balconies and casements far above ;
And tender damsels with young men and youths
Shall kiss together on the cheeks and mouths ;
   And every day be glad with joyful love.

JUNE.

In June I give you a close-wooded fell,
   With crowns of thicket coiled about its head,
   With thirty villas twelve times turreted,
All girdling round a little citadel ;
And in the midst a springhead and fair well
   With thousand conduits branched and shining speed,
   Wounding the garden and the tender mead,
Yet to the freshened grass acceptable.
And lemons, citrons, dates, and oranges,
   And all the fruits whose savour is most rare,
Shall shine within the shadow of your trees ;
   And every one shall be a lover there ;
Until your life, so filled with courtesies,
   Throughout the world be counted debonair.

22

JULY.

For July, in Siena, by the willow-tree,
   I give you barrels of white Tuscan wine
   In ice far down your cellars stored supine;
And morn and eve to eat in company
Of those vast jellies dear to you and me;
   Of partridges and youngling pheasants sweet,
   Boiled capons, sovereign kids : and let their treat
Be veal and garlic, with whom these agree.
Let time slip by, till by-and-by, all day;
   And never swelter through the heat at all,
But move at ease at home, sound, cool, and gay;
   And wear sweet-coloured robes that lightly fall;
And keep your tables set in fresh array,
   Not coaxing spleen to be your seneschal.

AUGUST.

For August, be your dwelling thirty towers
   Within an Alpine valley mountainous,
   Where never the sea-wind may vex your house,
But clear life separate, like a star, be yours.
There horses shall wait saddled at all hours,
   That ye may mount at morning or at eve :
   On each hand either ridge ye shall perceive,
A mile apart, which soon a good beast scours.
So alway, drawing homewards, ye shall tread
   Your valley parted by a rivulet
     Which day and night shall flow sedate and smooth.
There all through noon ye may possess the shade,
   And there your open purses shall entreat
     The best of Tuscan cheer to feed your youth.

SEPTEMBER.

AND in September, O what keen delight !
  Falcons and astors, merlins, sparrowhawks ;
  Decoy-birds that shall lure your game in flocks ;
And hounds with bells : and gauntlets stout and tight ;
Wide pouches ; crossbows shooting out of sight ;
  Arblasts and javelins ; balls and ball-cases ;
  All birds the best to fly at ; moulting these,
Those reared by hand ; with finches mean and slight ;
And for their chase, all birds the best to fly ;
  And each to each of you be lavish still
    In gifts ; and robbery find no gainsaying ;
And if you meet with travellers going by,
  Their purses from your purse's flow shall fill ;
    And avarice be the only outcast thing.

OCTOBER.

NEXT, for October, to some sheltered coign
  Flouting the winds, I'll hope to find you slunk ;
  Though in bird-shooting (lest all sport be sunk),
Your foot still press the turf, the horse your groin.
At night with sweethearts in the dance you'll join,
  And drink the blessed must, and get quite drunk,
  There's no such life for any human trunk ;
And that's a truth that rings like golden coin !
Then, out of bed again when morning's come,
  Let your hands drench your face refreshingly,
    And take your physic roast, with flask and knife.
Sounder and snugger you shall feel at home
  Than lake-fish, river-fish, or fish at sea,
    Inheriting the cream of Christian life.

NOVEMBER.

LET baths and wine-butts be November's due,
  With thirty mule-loads of broad gold-pieces ;
  And canopy with silk the streets that freeze ;
And keep your drink-horns steadily in view.
Let every trader have his gain of you :
  Clareta shall your lamps and torches send,—
  Caëta, citron-candies without end ;
And each shall drink, and help his neighbour to.
And let the cold be great, and the fire grand :
  And still for fowls, and pastries sweetly wrought,
  For hares and kids, for roast and boiled, be sure
You always have your appetites at hand ;
  And then let night howl and heaven fall, so nought
  Be missed that makes a man's bed-furniture.

DECEMBER.

LAST, for December, houses on the plain,
  Ground-floors to live in, logs heaped mountain-high,
  And carpets stretched, and newest games to try,
And torches lit, and gifts from man to man :
(Your host, a drunkard and a Catalan ;)
  And whole dead pigs, and cunning cooks to ply
  Each throat with tit-bits that shall satisfy ;
And wine-butts of Saint Galganus' brave span.
And be your coats well-lined and tightly bound,
  And wrap yourselves in cloaks of strength and weight,
  With gallant hoods to put your faces through.
And make your game of abject vagabond
  Abandoned miserable reprobate
    Misers ; don't let them have a chance with you.

CONCLUSION.

AND now take thought, my sonnet, who is he
  That most is full of every gentleness;
  And say to him (for thou shalt quickly guess
His name) that all his 'hests are law to me.
For if I held fair Paris town in fee,
  And were not called his friend, 'twere surely less.
  Ah ! had he but the emperor's wealth, my place
Were fitted in his love more steadily
Than is Saint Francis at Assisi.   Alway
  Commend him unto me and his,—not least
    To Caian, held so dear in the blithe band.
"Folgore da San Geminiano" (say,)
  "Has sent me, charging me to travel fast,
    Because his heart went with you in your hand

OF THE WEEK.

Seven Sonnets.

DEDICATION.

There is among my thoughts the joyous plan
    To fashion a bright-jewelled carcanet,
    Which I upon such worthy brows would set,
To say, it suits them fairly as it can.
And now I have newly found a gentleman,
    Of courtesies and birth commensurate,
    Who better would become the imperial state
Than fits the gem within the signet's span. '
Carlo di Messer Guerra Cavicciuoli,*
    Of him I speak,—brave, wise, of just award
    And generous service, let who list command :
    And lithelier limbed than ounce or leopard.
He holds not money-bags, as children, holy ;
    For Lombard Esté hath no freer hand.

---

* That is, according to early Tuscan nomenclature, Carlo, *the son of* Messer Guerra Cavicciuoli.

MONDAY.

The Day of Songs and Love.

Now with the moon the day-star Lucifer
   Departs, and night is gone at last, and day
   Brings, making all men's spirits strong and gay,
A gentle wind to gladden the new air.
Lo ! this is Monday, the week's harbinger ;
   Let music breathe her softest matin-lay,
   And let the loving damsels sing to-day,
And the sun wound with heat at noontide here.
And thou, young lord, arise and do not sleep,
   For now the amorous day inviteth thee
The harvest of thy lady's youth to reap.
   Let coursers round the door, and palfreys, be,
   With squires and pages clad delightfully ;
And Love's commandments have thou heed to keep.

TUESDAY.

The Day of Battles.

To a new world on Tuesday shifts my song,
   Where beat of drum is heard, and trumpet-blast ;
   Where footmen armed and horsemen armed go past,
And bells say ding to bells that answer dong ;
Where he the first and after him the throng,
   Armed all of them with coats and hoods of steel,
   Shall see their foes and make their foes to feel,
And so in wrack and rout drive them along.
Then hither, thither, dragging on the field
   His master, empty-seated goes the horse,
'Mid entrails strown abroad of soldiers kill'd ;
   Till blow to camp those trumpeters of yours
Who noise awhile your triumph and are still'd,
   And to your tents you come back conquerors.

WEDNESDAY.

The Day of Feasts.

AND every Wednesday, as the swift days move,
  Pheasant and peacock-shooting out of doors
  You'll have, and multitude of hares to course,
And after you come home, good cheer enough ;
And sweetest ladies at the board above,
  Children of kings and counts and senators ;
  And comely-favoured youthful bachelors
To serve them, bearing garlands, for true love.
  And still let cups of gold and silver ware,
Runlets of vernage-wine and wine of Greece,
  Comfits and cakes be found at bidding there ;
And let your gifts of birds and game increase :
  And let all those who in your banquet share
Sit with bright faces perfectly at ease.

THURSDAY.

The Day of Jousts and Tournaments.

FOR Thursday be the tournament prepar'd,
  And gentlemen in lordly jousts compete :
  First man with man, together let them meet,—
By fifties and by hundreds afterward.
Let arms with housings each be fitly pair'd,
  And fitly hold your battle to its heat
  From the third hour to vespers, after meat ;
Till the best-winded be at last declared.
Then back unto your beauties, as ye came :
  Where upon sovereign beds, with wise control
    Of leaches, shall your hurts be swathed in bands.
  The ladies shall assist with their own hands,
And each be so well paid in seeing them
  That on the morrow he be sound and whole.

FRIDAY.

The Day of Hunting.

LET Friday be your highest hunting-tide,—
    No hound nor brach nor mastiff absent thence,—
    Through a low wood, by many miles of dens,
All covert, where the cunning beasts abide :
Which now driven forth, at first you scatter wide,—
    Then close on them, and rip out blood and breath :
    Till all your huntsmen's horns wind at the death,
And you count up how many beasts have died.
Then, men and dogs together brought, you'll say :
    Go fairly greet from us this friend and that,
        Bid each make haste to blithest wassailings.
        Might not one vow that the whole pack had wings ?
    What ! hither, Beauty, Dian, Dragon, what !
I think we held a royal hunt to-day.

SATURDAY.

The Day of Hawking.

I'VE jolliest merriment for Saturday :—
    The very choicest of all hawks to fly
    That crane or heron could be stricken by,
As up and down you course the steep highway.
So shall the wild geese, in your deadly play,
    Lose at each stroke a wing, a tail, a thigh ;
    And man with man and horse with horse shall vie,
Till you all shout for glory and holiday.
Then, going home, you'll closely charge the cook :
    " All this is for to-morrow's roast and stew.
Skin, lop, and truss : hang pots on every hook.
    And we must have fine wine and white bread too,
Because this time we mean to feast : so look
    We do not think your kitchens lost on you."

SUNDAY.

The Day of Balls and Deeds of Arms in Florence.

AND on the morrow, at first peep o' the day
  Which follows, and which men as Sunday spell,—
  Whom most him liketh, dame or damozel,
Your chief shall choose out of the sweet array.
So in the palace painted and made gay
  Shall he converse with her whom he loves best ;
  And what he wishes, his desire express'd
Shall bring to presence there, without gainsay.
And youths shall dance, and men do feats of arms,
  And Florence be sought out on every side
From orchards and from vineyards and from farms :
  That they who fill her streets from far and wide
In your fine temper may discern such charms
  As shall from day to day be magnified.

GUIDO DELLE COLONNE.

Canzone.

To Love and to his Lady.

O Love, who all this while hast urged me on,
   Shaking the reins, with never any rest,—
   Slacken for pity somewhat of thy haste ;
I am oppress'd with languor and foredone,—
Having outrun the power of sufferance,—
   Having much more endured than who, through faith
   That his heart holds, makes no account of death.
Love is assuredly a fair mischance,
And well may it be called a happy ill :
   Yet thou, my lady, on this constant sting,
So sharp a thing, have thou some pity still,—
Howbeit a sweet thing too, unless it kill.

O comely-favoured, whose soft eyes prevail,
   More fair than is another on this ground,—
   Lift now my mournful heart out of its stound,
Which thus is bound for thee in great travail :
For a high gale a little rain may end.
   Also, my lady, be not angered thou
   That Love should thee enforce, to whom all bow.
There is but little shame to apprehend
If to a higher strength the conquest be ;
   And all the more to Love who conquers all.
Why then appal my heart with doubts of thee ?
Courage and patience triumph certainly.

I do not say that with such loveliness
  Such pride may not beseem; it suits thee well,
  For in a lovely lady pride may dwell,
Lest homage fail and high esteem grow less:
Yet pride's excess is not a thing to praise.
  Therefore, my lady, let thy harshness gain
  Some touch of pity which may still restrain
Thy hand, ere Death cut short these hours and days.
The sun is very high and full of light,
  And the more bright the higher he doth ride:
So let thy pride, my lady, and thy height,
Stand me in stead and turn to my delight.

Still inmostly I love thee, labouring still
  That others may not know my secret smart
  Oh! what a pain it is for the grieved heart
To hold apart and not to show its ill!
Yet by no will the face can hide the soul;
  And ever with the eyes the heart has need
  To be in all things willingly agreed.
It were a mighty strength that should control
The heart's fierce beat, and never speak a word:
  It were a mighty strength, I say again,
To hide such pain, and to be sovran lord
Of any heart that had such love to hoard.

For Love can make the wisest turn astray;
  Love, at its most, of measure still has least;
  He is the maddest man who loves the best;
It is Love's jest, to make men's hearts alway
So hot that they by coldness cannot cool.
  The eyes unto the heart bear messages
  Of the beginnings of all pain and ease:
And thou, my lady, in thy hand dost rule
Mine eyes and heart which thou hast made thine own
  Love rocks my life with tempests on the deep,
Even as a ship round which the winds are blown:
Thou art my pennon that will not go down.

PIER MORONELLI, DI FIORENZA.

CANZONETTA.

A bitter Song to his Lady.

O LADY amorous,
Merciless lady,
Full blithely play'd ye
These your beguilings.
So with an urchin
A man makes merry,—
In mirth grows clamorous,
Laughs and rejoices,—
But when his choice is
To fall aweary,
Cheats him with silence.
This is Love's portion :—
In much wayfaring
With many burdens
He loads his servants,
But at the sharing,
The underservice
And overservice
Are alike barren.

As my disaster
Your jest I cherish,
And well may perish,
Even so a falcon

Is sometimes taken
And scantly cautell'd;
Till when his master
At length to loose him,
To train and use him,
Is after all gone,—
The creature's throttled
And will not waken.
Wherefore, my lady,
If you will own me,
O look upon me!
If I'm not thought on,
At least perceive me!
O do not leave me
So much forgotten!

If, lady, truly
You wish my profit,
What follows of it
Though still you say so?—
For all your well-wishes
I still am waiting.
I grow unruly,
And deem at last I'm
Only your pastime.
A child will play so,
Who greatly relishes
Sporting and petting
With a little wild bird:
Unaware he kills it,—
Then turns it, feels it,
Calls it with a mild word,
Is angry after,—
Then again in laughter
Loud is the child heard.

O my delightful
My own my lady,

Upon the Mayday
Which brought me to you
Was all my haste then
But a fool's venture ?
To have my sight full
Of you propitious
Truly my wish was,
And to pursue you
And let love chasten
My heart to the centre.
But warming, lady,
May end in burning.
Of all this yearning
What comes, I beg you ?
In all your glances
What is't a man sees ?—
Fever and ague.

CIUNCIO FIORENTINO.

CANZONE.

*Of his Love; with the Figures of a Stag, of Water, and
of an Eagle.*

LADY, with all the pains that I can take,
  I'll sing my love renewed, if I may, well,
    And only in your praise.
The stag in his old age seeks out a snake
  And eats it, and then drinks, (I have heard tell,)
    Fearing the hidden ways
Of the snake's poison, and renews his youth.
    Even such a draught, in truth,
Was your sweet welcome, which cast out of me,
    With whole cure instantly,
Whatever pain I felt, for my own good,
When first we met that I might be renew'd.

A thing that has its proper essence changed
  By virtue of some powerful influence,
    As water has by fire,
Returns to be itself, no more estranged,
  So soon as that has ceased which gave offence :
    Yea, now will more aspire
Than ever, as the thing it first was made.
    Thine advent long delay'd
Even thus had almost worn me out of love,
    Biding so far above :
But now that thou hast brought love back for me,
It mounts too much,—O lady, up to thee.

I have heard tell, and can esteem it true,
How that an eagle looking on the sun,
Rejoicing for his part
And bringing oft his young to look there too,—
If one gaze longer than another one,
On him will set his heart.
So I am made aware that Love doth lead
All lovers, by their need,
To gaze upon the brightness of their loves;
And whosoever moves
His eyes the least from gazing upon her,
The same shall be Love's inward minister.

RUGGIERI DI AMICI, SICILIANO.

CANZONETTA.

For a Renewal of Favours.

I PLAY this sweet prelude
 For the best heart, and queen
Of gentle womanhood,
 From here unto Messene;
Of flowers the fairest one;
The star that's next the sun;
 The brightest star of all.
What time I look at her,
My thoughts do crowd and stir
 And are made musical.

Sweetest my lady, then
 Wilt thou not just permit,
As once I spoke, again
 That I should speak of it?
My heart is burning me
Within, though outwardly
 I seem so brave and gay.
Ah! dost thou not sometimes
Remember the sweet rhymes
 Our lips made on that day?--

When I her heart did move
 By kisses and by vows,
Whom I then called my love,
 Fair-haired, with silver brows:

She sang there as we sat ;
Nor then withheld she aught
  Which it were right to give ;
But said, " Indeed I will
Be thine through good and ill
  As long as I may live."

And while I live, dear love,
  In gladness and in need
Myself I will approve
  To be thine own indeed.
 If any man dare blame
Our loves,—bring him to shame,
  O God ! and of this year
Let him not see the May.
Is't not a vile thing, say,
  To freeze at Midsummer ?

CARNINO GHIBERTI, DA FIORENZA.

CANZONE.

Being absent from his Lady, he fears Death.

I AM afar, but near thee is my heart;
    Only soliciting
  That this long absence seem not ill to thee :
For, if thou knew'st what pain and evil smart
    The lack of thy sweet countenance can bring,
  Thou wouldst remember me compassionately.
  Even as my case, the stag's is wont to be,
    Which, thinking to escape
His death, escaping whence the pack gives cry,
    Is wounded and doth die.
So, in my spirit imagining thy shape,
  I would fly Death, and Death o'ermasters me.

I am o'erpower'd of Death when, telling o'er
    Thy beauties in my thought,
  I seem to have that which I have not : then
I am as he who in each meteor,
Dazzled and wildered, sees the thing he sought.
    In suchwise Love deals with me among men :—
    Thee whom I have not, yet who dost sustain
My life, he bringeth in his arms to me
Full oft,—yet I approach not unto thee.
Ah! if we be not joined i' the very flesh,
    It cannot last but I indeed shall die
      By burden of this love that weigheth so.

As an o'erladen bough, while yet 'tis fresh,
  Breaks, and itself and fruit are lost thereby,—
    So shall I, love, be lost, alas for woe !
And, if this slay indeed that thus doth rive
  My heart, how then shall I be comforted ?
        Thou, as a lioness
        Her cub, in sore distress
Might'st toil to bring me out of death alive :
  But couldst thou raise me up, if I were dead ?

Oh ! but an' if thou wouldst, I were more glad
      Of death than life,—thus kept
  From thee and the true life thy face can bring.
So in nowise could death be harsh or bad ;
  But it should seem to me that I had slept
  And was awakened with thy summoning.
  Yet, sith the hope thereof is a vain thing,
        I, in fast fealty,
        Can like the Assassin * be,
Who, to be subject to his lord in all,
  Goes and accepts his death and has no heed :
  Even as he doth so could I do indeed.
Nevertheless, this one memorial—
The last—I send thee, for Love orders it.
He, this last once, wills that thus much be writ
  In prayer that it may fall 'twixt thee and me
        After the manner of
        Two birds that feast their love
Even unto anguish, till, if neither quit
  The other, one must perish utterly.

---

* Alluding to the Syrian tribe of Assassins, whose chief was
the Old Man of the Mountain.

PRINZIVALLE DORIA.

CANZONE.

Of his Love, with the Figure of a sudden Storm.

EVEN as the day when it is yet at dawning
   Seems mild and kind, being fair to look upon,
While the birds carol underneath their awning
   Of leaves, as if they never would have done ;
   Which on a sudden changes, just at noon,
And the broad light is broken into rain
   That stops and comes again ;
Even as the traveller, who had held his way
   Hopeful and glad because of the bright weather,
   Forgetteth then his gladness altogether ;
Even so am I, through Love, alas the day !

It plainly is through Love that I am so.
   At first, he let me still grow happier
Each day, and made her kindness seem to grow ;
   But now he has quite changed her heart in her.
   And I, whose hopes throbbed and were all astir
For times when I should call her mine aloud,
   And in her pride be proud
Who is more fair than gems are, ye may say,
   Having that fairness which holds hearts in rule ;—
   I have learnt now to count him but a fool
Who before evening says, A goodly day.

It had been better not to have begun,
  Since, having known my error, 'tis too late.
This thing from which I suffer, thou hast done,
    Lady : canst thou restore me my first state ?
    The wound thou gavest canst thou medicate ?
Not thou, forsooth : thou hast not any art
    To keep death from my heart.
O lady ! where is now my life's full meed
    Of peace,—mine once, and which thou took'st away ?
    Surely it cannot now be far from day :
Night is already very long indeed.

The sea is much more beautiful at rest
    Than when the storm is trampling over it.
Wherefore, to see the smile which has so bless'd
    This heart of mine, deem'st thou these eyes unfit ?
    There is no maid so lovely, it is writ,
That by such stern unwomanly regard
    Her face may not be marr'd.
I therefore pray of thee, my own soul's wife,
    That thou remember me who am forgot.
    How shall I stand without thee ?   Art thou not
The pillar of the building of my life ?

RUSTICO DI FILIPPO

I.

SONNET.

Of the making of Master Messerin.

WHEN God had finished Master Messerin,
    He really thought it something to have done:
    Bird, man, and beast had got a chance in one,
And each felt flattered, it was hoped, therein.
For he is like a goose i' the windpipe thin,
    And like a cameleopard high i' the loins ;
    To which, for manhood, you'll be told, he joins
Some kinds of flesh-hues and a callow chin.
As to his singing, he affects the crow ;
    As to his learning, beasts in general ;
    And sets all square by dressing like a man.
God made him, having nothing else to do ;
    And proved there is not anything at all
        He cannot make, if that's a thing He can.

II.

SONNET.

*Of the Safety of Messer Fazio.**

MASTER BERTUCCIO, you are called to account
  That you guard Fazio's life from poison ill :
  And every man in Florence tells me still
He has no horse that he can safely mount.
A mighty war-horse worth a thousand pound
  Stands in Cremona stabled at his will ;
  Which for his honoured person should fulfil
Its use.   Nay, sir, I pray you be not found
So poor a steward.   For all fame of yours
  Is cared for best, believe me, when I say :—
    Our Florence gives Bertuccio charge of one
Who rides her own proud spirit like a horse ;
  Whom Cocciolo himself must needs obey ;
    And whom she loves best, being her strongest
      son.

---

* I have not been able to trace the Fazio to whom this sonnet
refers.

III.

SONNET.

Of Messer Ugolino. *

IF any one had anything to say
   To the Lord Ugolino, because he's
   Not staunch, and never minds his promises,
'Twere hardly courteous, for it is his way.
Courteous it were to say such sayings nay:
   As thus: He's true, sir, only takes his ease
   And don't care merely if it plague or please,
And has good thoughts, no doubt, if they would stay.
Now I know he's so loyal every whit
   And altogether worth such a good word
As worst would best and best would worst befit.
   He'd love his party with a dear accord
If only he could once quite care for it,
   But can't run post for any Law or Lord.

---

* The character here drawn certainly suggests Count Ugolino
de' Gherardeschi, though it would seem that Rustico died nearly
twenty years before the tragedy of the Tower of Famine.

PUCCIARELLO DI FIORENZA.

SONNET.

Of Expediency.

PASS and let pass,—this counsel I would give,—
  And wrap thy cloak what way the wind may blow ;
  Who cannot raise himself were wise to know
How best, by dint of stooping, he may thrive.
Take for ensample this : when the winds drive
  Against it, how the sapling tree bends low,
  And, once being prone, abideth even so
Till the hard harsh wind cease to rend and rive.
Wherefore, when thou behold'st thyself abased,
  Be blind, deaf, dumb ; yet therewith none the less
    Note thou in peace what thou shalt hear and see,
Till from such state by Fortune thou be raised.
  Then hack, lop, buffet, thrust, and so redress
    Thine ill that it may not return on thee.

ALBERTUCCIO DELLA VIOLA.

CANZONE.

Of his Lady dancing.

AMONG the dancers I beheld her dance,
Her who alone is my heart's sustenance.

So, as she danced, I took this wound of her;
  Alas! the flower of flowers, she did not fail.
Woe's me! I will be Jew and blasphemer
  If the good god of Love do not prevail
To bring me to thy grace, oh! thou most fair.
  My lady and my lord! alas for wail!
How many days and how much sufferance?

Oh! would to God that I had never seen
  Her face, nor had beheld her dancing so!
Then had I missed this wound which is so keen—
  Yea, mortal—for I think not to win through
Unless her love be my sweet medicine;
  Whereof I am in doubt, alas for woe!
Fearing therein but such a little chance.

She was apparelled in a Syrian cloth,
  My lady :—oh! but she did grace the same,
Gladdening all folk, that they were nowise loth
  At sight of her to put their ills from them.

But upon me her power hath had such growth
    That nought of joy thenceforth, but a live flame,
Stirs at my heart,—which is her countenance.

Sweet-smelling rose, sweet, sweet to smell and see,
    Great solace had she in her eyes for all ;
But heavy woe is mine ; for upon me
    Her eyes, as they were wont, did never fall.
Which thing if it were done advisedly,
    I would choose death, that could no more appal,
Not caring for my life's continuance.

TOMMASO BUZZUOLA, DA FAENZA.

SONNET.

He is in awe of his Lady.

EVEN as the moon amid the stars doth shed
　　Her lovelier splendour of exceeding light,—
Even so my lady seems the queen and head
　　Among all other ladies in my sight.
Her human visage, like an angel's made,
　　Is glorious even to beauty's perfect height;
And with her simple bearing soft and staid
　　All secret modesties of soul unite.
I therefore feel a dread in loving her;
　　Because of thinking on her excellence,
　　　The wisdom and the beauty which she has.
　　I pray her for the sake of God,—whereas
　　I am her servant, yet in sore suspense
Have held my peace,—to have me in her care.

NOFFO BONAGUIDA.

SONNET.

He is enjoined to pure Love.

A SPIRIT of Love, with Love's intelligence,
  Maketh his sojourn alway in my breast,
  Maintaining me in perfect joy and rest;
Nor could I live an hour, were he gone thence:
Through whom my love hath such full permanence
  That thereby other loves seem. dispossess'd.
  I have no pain, nor am with sighs oppress'd,
So calm is the benignant influence.
Because this spirit of Love, who speaks to me
  Of my dear lady's tenderness and worth,
    Says: "More than thus to love her seek thou not,
    Even as she loves thee in her wedded thought;
But honour her in thy heart delicately:
  For this is the most blessed joy on earth."

LIPPO PASCHI DE' BARDI.

SONNET.

He solicits a Lady's Favours.

WERT thou as prone to yield unto my prayer
    The thing, sweet virgin, which I ask of thee,
    As to repeat, with all humility,
" Pray you go hence, and of your speech forbear ; "—
Then unto joy might I my heart prepare,
    Having my fellows in subserviency ;
    But, for that thou contemn'st and mockest me,
Whether of life or death I take no care.
Because my heart may not assuage its drouth
    Nor ever may again rejoice at all
        Till the sweet face bend to be felt of man,—
Till tenderly the beautiful soft mouth
    I kiss by thy good leave ; thenceforth to call
        Blessing and triumph Love's extremest ban.

SER PACE, NOTAIO DA FIORENZA.

SONNET.

A Return to Love.

A FRESH content of fresh enamouring
   Yields me afresh, at length, the sense of song,
   Who had well-nigh forgotten Love so long :
But now my homage he will have me bring.
So that my life is now a joyful thing,
   Having new-found desire, elate and strong,
   In her to whom all grace and worth belong,
On whom I now attend for ministering.
The countenance remembering, with the limbs,
   She was all imaged on my heart at once
     Suddenly by a single look at her :
Whom when I now behold, a heat there seems
   Within, as of a subtle fire that runs
     Unto my heart, and remains burning there.

NICCOLÒ DEGLI ALBIZZI.

PROLONGED SONNET.

When the Troops were returning from Milan.

IF you could see, fair brother, how dead beat
  The fellows look who come through Rome to-day,—
  Black yellow smoke-dried visages,—you'd say
They thought their haste at going all too fleet.
Their empty victual-waggons up the street
  Over the bridge dreadfully sound and sway ;
  Their eyes, as hanged men's, turning the wrong way ;
And nothing on their backs, or heads, or feet.
One sees the ribs and all the skeletons
  Of their gaunt horses ; and a sorry sight
Are the torn saddles, crammed with straw and stones.
  They are ashamed, and march throughout the night ;
Stumbling, for hunger, on their marrowbones ;
  Like barrels rolling, jolting, in this plight.
Their arms all gone, not even their swords are saved ;
And each as silent as a man being shaved.

FRANCESCO DA BARBERINO.

I.

·BLANK VERSE.*

A Virgin declares her Beauties.

Do not conceive that I shall here recount
All my own beauty : yet I promise you
That you, by what I tell, shall understand
All that befits and that is well to know.

My bosom, which is very softly made,
Of a white even colour without stain,
Bears two fair apples, fragrant, sweetly-savoured,
Gathered together from the Tree of Life
The which is in the midst of Paradise.
And these no person ever yet has touched ;
For out of nurse's and of mother's hands
I was, when God in secret gave them me.
These ere I yield I must know well to whom ;
And for that I would not be robbed of them,
I speak not all the virtue that they have ;
Yet thus far speaking :—blessed were the man
Who once should touch them, were it but a little ;—
See them I say not, for that might not be.

---

* Extracted from his long treatise, in unrhymed verse and in
prose, " Of the Government and Conduct of Women ", (*Del Reggi-
mento e dei Costumi delle Donne.*)

My girdle, clipping pleasure round about,
Over my clear dress even unto my knees
Hangs down with sweet precision tenderly;
And under it Virginity abides.
Faithful and simple and of plain belief
She is, with her fair garland bright like gold;
And very fearful if she overhears
Speech of herself; the wherefore ye perceive
That I speak soft lest she be made ashamed.

Lo! this is she who hath for company
The Son of God and Mother of the Son;
Lo! this is she who sits with many in heaven;
Lo! this is she with whom are few on earth.

II.

Sentenze.*

Of Sloth against Sin.

There is a vice which oft
  I've heard men praise ; and divers forms it has ;
  And it is this.   Whereas
Some, by their wisdom, lordship, or repute,

When tumults are afoot,
  Might stifle them, or at the least allay,—
  These certain ones will say,
" The wise man bids thee fly the noise of men."

One says, "Wouldst thou maintain
  Worship,—avoid where thou mayst not avail ;
  And do not breed worse ail
By adding one more voice to strife begun."

Another, with this one,
  Avers, "I could but bear a small expense,
  Or yield a slight defence."
A third says this, " I could but offer words."

---

* This and the three following pieces are extracted from his
" Documents of Love " (*Documenti d Amore*).

Or one, whose tongue records
    Unwillingly his own base heart, will say,
    "I'll not be led astray
To bear a hand in others' life or death."

They have it in their teeth!
    For unto this each man is pledged and bound;
    And this thing shall be found
Entered against him at the Judgment Day.

III.

Of Sins in Speech.

Now these four things, if thou
   Consider, are so bad that none are worse.
   First,—among counsellors
To thrust thyself, when not called absolutely.

And in the other three
   Many offend by their own evil wit.
   When men in council sit,
One talks because he loves not to be still ;

And one to have his will ;
   And one for nothing else but only show.
   These rules were well to know,
First for the first, for the others afterward.

Where many are repair'd
   And met together, never go with them
   Unless thou'rt called by name.
This for the first : now for the other three.

What truly thou dost see
   Turn in thy mind, and faithfully report;
   And in the plainest sort
Thy wisdom may, proffer thy counselling.

There is another thing
 Belongs hereto, the which is on this wise.
 If one should ask advice
Of thine for his own need whate'er it be,—

This is my word to thee :—
 Deny it if it be not clearly of use :
 Or turn to some excuse
That may avail, and thou shalt have done well.

IV.

SENTENZE.

Of Importunities and Troublesome Persons.

THERE is a vice prevails
  Concerning which I'll set you on your guard ;
  And other four, which hard
It were (as may be thought) that I should blame.

Some think that still of *them*—
  Whate'er is said—some ill speech lies beneath;
  And this to them is death :
Whereby we plainly may perceive their sins.

And now let others wince.
  One sort there is, who, thinking that they please,
  (Because no wit's in these,)
Where'er you go, will stick to you all day,

And answer, (when you say,
  " Don't let me tire you out!") "Oh never mind—
  Say nothing of the kind,—
It's quite a pleasure to be where you are !"

A second,—when, as far
  As he could follow you, the whole day long
  He's sung you his dull song,
And you for courtesy have borne with it,—

Will think you've had a treat.
    A third will take his special snug delight,—
    Some day you've come in sight
Of some great thought and got it well in view,—

Just then to drop on you.
    A fourth, for any insult you've received
    Will say he *is so* grieved,
And daily bring the subject up again.

So now I would be fain
    To show you your best course at all such times;
    And counsel you in rhymes
That you yourself offend not in likewise.

In these four cases lies
    This help :—to think upon your own affair,
    Just showing here and there
By just a word that you are listening ;

And still to the last thing
    That's said to you attend in your reply,
    And let the rest go by,—
It's quite a chance if he remembers them.

Yet do not, all the same,
    Deny your ear to any speech of weight.
    But if importunate
The speaker is, and will not be denied,

Just turn the speech aside
    When you can find some plausible pretence ;
    For if you have the sense,
By a quick question or a sudden doubt

You may so put him out
    That he shall not remember where he was,
    And by such means you'll pass
Upon your way and be well rid of him.

And now it may beseem
   I give you the advice I promised you.
   Before you have to do
With men whom you must meet continually,

Take notice what they be;
   And so you shall find readily enough
   If you can win their love,
And give yourself for answer Yes or No.

And finding Yes, do so
   That still the love between you may increase.
   Yet if they be of these
Whom sometimes it is hard to understand,

Let some slight cause be plann'd,
   And seem to go,—so you shall learn their will:
   And if but one sit still
As 'twere in thought,—then go, unless he call.

Lastly, if insult gall
   Your friend, this is the course that you should take.
   At first 'tis well you make
As much lament thereof as you think fit,—

Then speak no more of it,
   Unless himself should bring it up again;
   And then no more refrain
From full discourse, but say his grief is yours.

,

V.

SENTENZE.

Of Caution.

SAY, wouldst thou guard thy son,
That sorrow he may shun ?
Begin at the beginning
And let him keep from sinning.
Wouldst guard thy house ?   One door
Make to it, and no more.
Wouldst guard thine orchard-wall ?
Be free of fruit to all,

FAZIO DEGLI UBERTI.

I.

CANZONE.

His Portrait of his Lady, Angiola of Verona.

I LOOK at the crisp golden-threaded hair
    Whereof, to thrall my heart, Love twists a net :
    Using at times a string of pearls for bait,
      And sometimes with a single rose therein.
I look into her eyes which unaware
    Through mine own eyes to my heart penetrate ;
    Their splendour, that is excellently great,
      To the sun's radiance seeming near akin,
      Yet from herself a sweeter light to win.
So that I, gazing on that lovely one,
    Discourse in this wise with my secret thought :—
    " Woe's me ! why am I not,
Even as my wish, alone with her alone,—
    That hair of hers, so heavily uplaid,
    To shed down braid by braid,
And make myself two mirrors of her eyes
Within whose light all other glory dies ? "

I look at the amorous beautiful mouth,
    The spacious forehead which her locks enclose,
    The small white teeth, the straight and shapely nose,
      And the clear brows of a sweet pencilling.

And then the thought within me gains full growth,
  Saying, " Be careful that thy glance now goes
  Between her lips, red as an open rose,
    Quite full of every dear and precious thing ;
    And listen to her gracious answering,
Born of the gentle mind that in her dwells,
  Which from all things can glean the nobler half.
  Look thou when she doth laugh
How much her laugh is sweeter than aught else."
  Thus evermore my spirit makes avow
  Touching her mouth ; till now
I would give anything that I possess,
Only to hear her mouth say frankly, "Yes."

I look at her white easy neck, so well
  From shoulders and from bosom lifted out ;
  And at her round cleft chin, which beyond doubt
    No fancy in the world could have design'd.
And then, with longing grown more voluble,
  "Were it not pleasant now," pursues my thought,
  "To have that neck within thy two arms caught
    And kiss it till the mark were left behind ?"
    Then, urgently : " The eyelids of thy mind
Open thou : if such loveliness be given
  To sight here,—what of that which she doth hide ?
  Only the wondrous ride
Of sun and planets through the visible heaven
  Tells us that there beyond is Paradise.
  Thus, if thou fix thine eyes,
Of a truth certainly thou must infer
That every earthly joy abides in her."

I look at the large arms, so lithe and round,—
  At the hands, which are white and rosy too,—
  At the long fingers, clasped and woven through,
    Bright with the ring which one of them doth wear.
Then my thought whispers : " Were thy body wound
  Within those arms, as loving women's do,

In all thy veins were born a life made new
   Which thou couldst find no language to declare.
   Behold if any picture can compare
With her just limbs, each fit in shape and size,
   Or match her angel's colour like a pearl.
   She is a gentle girl
To see ; yet when it needs, her scorn can rise.
   Meek, bashful, and in all things temperate,
   Her virtue holds its state ;
In whose least act there is that gift express'd
Which of all reverence makes her worthiest."

Soft as a peacock steps she, or as a stork
   Straight on herself, taller and statelier :
   'Tis a good sight how every limb doth stir
   For ever in a womanly sweet way.
"Open thy soul to see God's perfect work,"
   (My thought begins afresh,) "and look at her
   When with some lady-friend exceeding fair
   She bends and mingles arms and locks in play.
   Even as all lesser lights vanish away,
When the sun moves, before his dazzling face,
   So is this lady brighter than all these.
   How should she fail to please,—
Love's self being no more than her loveliness ?
   In all her ways some beauty springs to view ;
   All that she loves to do
Tends alway to her honour's single scope ;
And only from good deeds she draws her hope."

Song, thou canst surely say, without pretence,
   That since the first fair woman ever made,
   Not one can have display'd
   More power upon all hearts than this one doth ;
   Because in her are both
Loveliness and the soul's true excellence :—
And yet (woe's me !) is pity absent thence ?

II.

EXTRACT FROM THE "DITTAMONDO." *

(LIB. IV. CAP. 23.)

Of England, and of its Marvels.

Now to Great Britain we must make our way,
Unto which kingdom Brutus gave its name
What time he won it from the giants' rule.
'Tis thought at first its name was Albion,
And Anglia, from a damsel, afterwards.
The island is so great and rich and fair,
It conquers others that in Europe be,
Even as the sun surpasses other stars.

---

* I am quite sorry (after the foregoing love-song, the original
of which is not perhaps surpassed by any poem of its class in
existence) to endanger the English reader's respect for Fazio by
these extracts from the *Dittamondo*, or "Song of the World," in
which he will find his own country endowed with some astounding
properties. However, there are a few fine characteristic sentences,
and the rest is no more absurd than other travellers' tales of that
day ; while the table of our Norman line of kings is not without
some historical interest. It must be remembered that the love-
song was the work of Fazio's youth, and the *Dittamondo* that of
his old age, when we may suppose his powers to have been no
longer at their best. Besides what I have given relating to Great
Britain, there is a table of the Saxon dynasty, and some surprising
facts about Scotland and Ireland; as well as a curious passage
written in French, and purporting to be an account, given by a
royal courier, of Edward the Third's invasion of France. I felt

Many and great sheep-pastures bountifully
Nature has set there, and herein more bless'd,
That they can hold themselves secure from wolves.
Jet also doth the hollow land enrich,
(Whose properties my guide Solinus here
Told me, and how its colour comes to it;)
And pearls are found in great abundance too.
The people are as white and comely-faced
As they of Ethiop land are black and foul.
Many hot springs and limpid fountain-heads
We found about this land, and spacious plains,
And divers beasts that dwell within thick woods.
Plentiful orchards too and fertile fields
It has, and castle-forts, and cities fair
With palaces and girth of lofty walls.
And proud wide rivers without any fords
We saw, and flesh, and fish, and crops enough.
Justice is strong throughout those provinces.

Now this I saw not; but so strange a thing
It was to hear, and by all men confirm'd,
That it is fit to note it as I heard ;—
To wit, there is a certain islet here
Among the rest, where folk are born with tails,
Short, as are found in stags and such-like beasts.*

---

half disposed to include these, but was afraid of overloading with
such matter a selection made chiefly for the sake of poetic beauty.
I should mention that the *Dittamondo*, like Dante's great poem, is
written in *terza rima;* but as perfect literality was of primary
importance in the above extracts, I have departed for once from
my rule of fidelity to the original metre.

* Mediæval Britons would seem really to have been credited
with this slight peculiarity. At the siege of Damietta, Cœur-de-
Lion's bastard brother is said to have pointed out the prudence of
deferring the assault, and to have received for rejoinder from the
French crusaders, "See now these faint-hearted English with the
tails!" To which the Englishman replied, "You will need stout
hearts to keep near our tails when the assault is made."

For this I vouch,—that when a child is freed
From swaddling bands, the mother without stay
Passes elsewhere, and 'scapes the care of it.

I put no faith herein; but it is said
Among them, how such marvellous trees are there
That they grow birds, and this is their sole fruit.*

Forty times eighty is the circuit ta'en,
With ten times fifteen, if I do not err,
By our miles reckoning its circumference.
Here every metal may be dug; and here
I found the people to be given to God,
Steadfast, and strong, and restive to constraint.
Nor is this strange, when one considereth;
For courage, beauty, and large-heartedness,
Were there, as it is said, in ancient days.

North Wales, and Orkney, and the banks of Thames,
Strangoure and Listenois and Northumberland,
I chose with my companion to behold.†
We went to London, and I saw the Tower

---

* This is the Barnacle-tree, often described in old books of travels and natural history, and which Sir Thomas Browne classes gravely among his "Vulgar Errors."

† What follows relates to the Romances of the Round Table. The only allusion here which I cannot trace to the *Mort d'Arthur* is one where "Rech" and "Nida" are spoken of: it seems however that, by a perversion hardly too corrupt for Fazio, these might be the Geraint and Enid whose story occurs in the *Mabinogion*, and has been used by Tennyson in his *Idylls of the King*. Why Fazio should have "joyed to see" Merlin's stone "for another's love" seems inscrutable; unless indeed the words "*per amor altrui*" are a mere idiom, and Merlin himself is meant; and even then Merlin, in his compulsory niche under the stone, may hardly have been grateful for such friendly interest.

I should not omit, in this second edition, to acknowledge several obligations, as regards the above extract from the *Dittamondo*, to the unknown author of an acute and kindly article in the *Spectator* for January 18th, 1862.

Where Guenevere her honour did defend,
With the Thames river which runs close to it.
I saw the castle which by force was ta'en
With the three shields by gallant Lancelot,
The second year that he did deeds of arms.
I beheld Camelot despoiled and waste ;
And was where one and the other had her birth,
The maids of Corbonek and Astolat.
Also I saw the castle where Geraint
Lay with his Enid ; likewise Merlin's stone,
Which for another's love I joyed to see.
I found the tract where is the pine-tree well,
And where of old the knight of the black shield
With weeping and with laughter kept the pass,
What time the pitiless and bitter dwarf
Before Sir Gawaine's eyes discourteously
With many heavy stripes led him away.
I saw the valley which Sir Tristram won
When having slain the giant hand to hand
He set the stranger knights from prison free.
And last I viewed the field, at Salisbury,
Of that great martyrdom which left the world
Empty of honour, valour, and delight.

So, compassing that Island round and round,
I saw and hearkened many things and more
Which might be fair to tell but which I hide.

III.

EXTRACT FROM THE "DITTAMONDO."

(LIB. IV. CAP. 25.)

Of the Dukes of Normandy, and thence of the Kings of England, from William the First to Edward the Third.

THOU well hast heard that Rollo had two sons,
One William Longsword, and the other Richard,
Whom thou now know'st to the marrow, as I do.*
Daring and watchful, as a leopard is,
Was William, fair in body and in face,
Ready at all times, never slow to act.
He fought great battles, but at last was slain
By the earl of Flanders ; so that in his place
Richard his son was o'er the people set.
And next in order, lit with blessed flame
Of the Holy Spirit, his son followed him,
Who justly lived 'twixt more and less midway,—
His father's likeness, as in shape in name.
So unto him succeeded as his heir
Robert the Frank, high-counselled and august :
And thereon following, I proceed to tell
How William, who was Robert's son, did make
The realm of England his co-heritage.

---

* The speaker here is the poet's guide Solinus (a historical and geographical writer of the third century,) who bears the same relation to him which Virgil bears to Dante in the *Commedia.*

The same was brave and courteous certainly,
Generous and gracious, humble before God,
Master in war and versed in counsel too.
He with great following came from Normandy
And fought with Harold, and so left him slain,
And took the realm, and held it at his will.
Thus did this kingdom change its signiory;
And know that all the kings it since has had
Only from this man take their origin.
Therefore, that thou mayst quite forget its past,
I say this happened when, since our Lord's Love,
Some thousand years and sixty were gone by.

While the fourth Henry ruled as emperor,
This king of England fought in many wars,
And waxed through all in honour and account,
And William Rufus next succeeded him;
Tall, strong, and comely-limbed, but therewith proud
And grasping, and a killer of his kind.
In body he was like his father much,
But was in nature more his contrary
Than fire and water when they come together;
Yet so far good that he won fame in arms,
And by himself risked many an enterprise,
All which he brought with honour to an end,
Also if he were bad, he gat great ill;
For, chasing once the deer within a wood,
And having wandered from his company,
Him by mischance a servant of his own
Hit with an arrow, that he fell and died.
And after him Henry the First was king,
His brother, but therewith the father's like,
Being well with God and just in peace and war.
Next Stephen, on his death, the kingdom seized,
But with sore strife; of whom thus much be said,
That he was frank and good is told of him.
And after him another Henry reigned,
Who, when the war in France was waged and done.

Passed beyond seas with the first Frederick.
Then Richard came, who, after heavy toil
At sea, was captive made in Germany,
Leaving the Sepulchre to join his host.
Who being dead, full heavy was the wrath
Of John his brother ; and so well he took
Revenge, that still a moan is made of it.
This John in kingly largesse and in war
Delighted, when the kingdom fell to him ;
Hunting and riding ever in hot haste.

Handsome in body and most poor in heart,
Henry his son and heir succeeded him,
Of whom to speak I count it wretchedness.
Yet there's some good to say of him, I grant ;
Because of him was the good Edward born,
Whose valour still is famous in the world.
The same was he who, being without dread
Of the Old Man's Assassins, captured them,
And who repaid the jester if he lied.*
The same was he who over seas wrought scathe
So many times to Malekdar, and bent
Unto the Christian rule whole provinces.
He was a giant of his body, and great
And proud to view, and of such strength of soul
As never saddens with adversity.

His reign was long; and when his death befell,
The second Edward mounted to the throne,
Who was of one kind with his grandfather.
I say from what report still says of him,
That he was evil, of base intellect,
And would not be advised by any man·
Conceive, good heart ! that how to thatch a roof
With straw,—conceive !—he held himself expert,

---

* This may either refer to some special incident or merely mean
generally that he would not suffer lying even in a jester.

And therein constantly would take delight !
By fraud he seized the Earl of Lancaster,
And what he did with him I say not here,
But that he left him neither town nor tower.
And thiswise,.step by step, thou mayst perceive
That I to the third Edward have advanced,
Who now lives strong and full of enterprise,
And who already has grown manifest
For the best Christian known of in the world.
Thus I have told, as thou wouldst have me tell,
The race of William even unto the end.

FRANCO SACCHETTI.

I.

BALLATA.

His Talk with certain Peasant-girls.

" YE graceful peasant-girls and mountain-maids,
Whence come ye homeward through these evening
    shades ?"

" We come from where the forest skirts the hill;
    A very little cottage is our home,
Where with our father and our mother still
    We live, and love our life, nor wish to roam.
    Back every evening from the field we come
And bring with us our sheep from pasturing there."

" Where, tell me, is the hamlet of your birth,
    Whose fruitage is the sweetest by so much ?
Ye seem to me as creatures worship-worth,
    The shining of your countenance is such.
    No gold about your clothes, coarse to the touch,
Nor silver; yet with such an angel's air !

" I think your beauties might make great complaint
    Of being thus shown over mount and dell ;
Because no city is so excellent
    But that your stay therein were honourable.
    In very truth, now, does it like ye well
To live so poorly on the hill-side here ?"

" Better it liketh one of us, pardie,
   Behind her flock to seek the pasture-stance,
Far better than it liketh one of ye
   To ride unto your curtained rooms and dance.
   We seek no riches, neither golden chance
Save wealth of flowers to weave into our hair."

Ballad, if I were now as once I was,
   I'd make myself a shepherd on some hill,
And, without telling any one, would pass
   Where these girls went, and follow at their will;
   And " Mary " and " Martin " we would murmur still,
And I would be for ever where they were.

II.

CATCH.

On a Fine Day.

"Be stirring, girls! we ought to have a run :
   Look, did you ever see so fine a day ?
   Fling spindles right away,
      And rocks and reels and wools :
      Now don't be fools,—
To-day your spinning's done.
Up with you, up with you !"   So, one by one,
   They caught hands, catch who can,
   Then singing, singing, to the river they ran,
   They ran, they ran
To the river, the river ;
   And the merry-go-round
   Carries them at a bound
To the mill o'er the river.
"Miller, miller, miller,
      Weigh me this lady
      And this other.   Now, steady !"
"You weigh a hundred, you,
And this one weighs two."
"Why, dear, you do get stout !"
"You think so, dear, no doubt :
Are you in a decline ?"
"Keep your temper, and I'll keep mine.

Come, girls," ("O thank you, miller!")
"We'll go home when you will."
So, as we crossed the hill,
A clown came in great grief
Crying, "Stop thief! stop thief!
O what a wretch I am!"
"Well, fellow, here's a clatter!
Well, what's the matter?"
"O Lord, O Lord, the wolf has got my lamb!"
Now at that word of woe,
The beauties came and clung about me so
    That if wolf had but shown himself, maybe
    I too had caught a lamb that fled to me.

III.

CATCH.

On a Wet Day.

As I walked thinking through a little grove,
  Some girls that gathered flowers came passing me,
  Saying, "Look here! look there!" delightedly.
"O here it is!" "What's that?" "A lily, love."
"And there are violets!"
"Further for roses! Oh the lovely pets—
The darling beauties! Oh the nasty thorn!
Look here, my hand's all torn!"
"What's that that jumps?" "Oh don't! it's a grass-
    hopper!"
"Come run, come run,
Here's bluebells!" "Oh what fun!"
"Not that way! Stop her!"
"Yes, this way!" "Pluck them, then!"
"Oh, I've found mushrooms! Oh look here!" "Oh, I'm
Quite sure that further on we'll get wild thyme."

"Oh we shall stay too long, it's going to rain!
There's lightning, oh there's thunder!"
"Oh shan't we hear the vesper-bell, I wonder?"
"Why, it's not nones, you silly little thing;
And don't you hear the nightingales that sing
Fly away O die away?"
"O I hear something! Hush!"

"Why, where? what is it then?" "Ah! in that bush!"
So every girl here knocks it, shakes and shocks it,
Till with the stir they make
Out skurries a great snake.
"O Lord! O me! Alack! Ah me! alack!"
They scream, and then all run and scream again,
And then in heavy drops down comes the rain.

Each running at the other in a fright,
Each trying to get before the other, and crying,
And flying, stumbling, tumbling, wrong or right;
One sets her knee
There where her foot should be;
One has her hands and dress
All smothered up with mud in a fine mess;
And one gets trampled on by two or three.
What's gathered is let fall
About the wood and not picked up at all.
The wreaths of flowers are scattered on the ground;
And still as screaming hustling without rest
They run this way and that and round and round,
She thinks herself in luck who runs the best.

I stook quite still to have a perfect view,
And never noticed till I got wet through.

ANONYMOUS POEMS.

I.

SONNET.

A Lady laments for her lost Lover, by similitude of a Falcon.

ALAS for me, who loved a falcon well !
   So well I loved him, I was nearly dead :
   Ever at my low call he bent his head,
And ate of mine, not much, but all that fell.
Now he has fled, how high I cannot tell,
   Much higher now than ever he has fled,
   And is in a fair garden housed and fed ;
Another lady, alas ! shall love him well.
O my own falcon whom I taught and rear'd !
   Sweet bells of shining gold I gave to thee
That in the chase thou shouldst not be afeard.
   Now thou hast risen like the risen sea,
Broken thy jesses loose, and disappear'd,
   As soon as thou wast skilled in falconry.

II.

BALLATA.

One speaks of the Beginning of his Love.

This fairest one of all the stars, whose flame,
For ever lit, my inner spirit fills,
Came to me first one day between the hills.
I wondered very much ; but God the Lord
Said, " From Our Virtue, lo ! this light is pour'd."
So in a dream it seemed that I was led
By a great Master to a garden spread
With lilies underfoot and overhead.

III.

BALLATA.

One speaks of his False Lady.

When the last greyness dwells throughout the air,
    And the first star appears,
Appeared to me a lady very fair.
I seemed to know her well by her sweet air ;
    And, gazing, I was hers.
To honour her, I followed her : and then . . . .
Ah ! what thou givest, God give thee again,
Whenever thou remain'st as I remain.

IV.

BALLATA.

One speaks of his Feigned and Real Love.

FOR no love borne by me,
Neither because I care
To find that thou art fair,—
To give another pain I gaze on thee.

And now, lest such as thought that thou couldst move
My heart, should read this verse,
I will say here, another has my love.
An angel of the spheres
She seems, and I am hers;
Who has more gentleness
And owns a fairer face
Than any woman else,—at least, to me.

Sweeter than any, more in all at ease,
Lighter and lovelier.
Not to disparage thee; for whoso sees
May like thee more than her.
This vest will one prefer
And one another vest.
To me she seems the best,
And I am hers, and let what will be, be.

For no love borne by me,
Neither because I care
To find that thou art fair,—
To give another pain, I gaze on thee.

V.

BALLATA.

Of True and False Singing.

A LITTLE wild bird sometimes at my ear
   Sings his own verses very clear :
Others sing louder that I do not hear.
For singing loudly is not singing well ;
   But ever by the song that's soft and low
The master-singer's voice is plain to tell.
   Few have it and yet all are masters now,
And each of them can trill out what he calls
His ballads, canzonets, and madrigals.
The world with masters is so covered o'er,
There is no room for pupils any more.

NOTES BY W. M. ROSSETTI.

Page 29.

" An awkward *intermezzo* to the volume." The term " intermezzo " was correct when my brother wrote it ; because his introduction, regarding Dante and his friends, appeared in the *middle* of the original volume entitled *The Early Italian Poets*, 1861. On republishing the book in 1874, my brother inverted the order of his translations, and made those taken from Dante and his friends to appear in the opening pages of the volume. The word " intermezzo " ought then to have disappeared ; it must have been left through inadvertence.

Page 34.

" This sonnet is divided," etc. It may be as well to mention that the expositions (of which this is the first) appended to the various poems of the *Vita Nuova* were translated by me, not by my brother. Several foot-notes are also mine. The translation of the *Vita Nuova* had been done by my brother at a very early date, probably 1847-8 ; when he was more inclined to consult his own preferences in the way of translating than to be at the rigid beck of his original. When he had to prepare the work, 1860, for publication, he felt that he had taken too great a liberty, and asked me to supply what was wanted in relation to these expositions, etc.

Page 121.

OF A CONSECRATED IMAGE RESEMBLING HIS LADY.—It is no part of my business to revise the translations and interpretations of my brother : yet I may be excused for observing that there is not in this Italian sonnet anything to indicate that Cavalcanti considered the Image to resemble "his Lady"—*i.e.*, the woman he was in love with. He speaks of "la Donna mia," which comes to the same thing as "la Madonna," the Virgin Mary. That the Image did really represent the Virgin Mary is apparent from the reply which Guido Orlandi returned to this sonnet.

Page 224.

"Aguglino would be eaglet," etc. Here again my brother is at fault. Aguglino does indeed mean eaglet: it is the name of a coin stamped (I presume) with the imperial eagle. There can be no real doubt that Aguglino is the correct reading; and that the whole of my brother's surmise about "Avolino" is gratuitous. I pointed this out to him when the book was in course of reprinting. He then admitted the fact; but (with perhaps pardonable weakness for what he had many years before thought out with ingenuity, and argued with plausibility) he ultimately decided not to interfere with the text as printed.

THE END

www.ingramcontent.com/pod-product-compliance
Lightning Source LLC
Chambersburg PA
CBHW030941110726
47900CB00004B/1082